Food Television and Otherness in the Age of Globalization

Food Television and Otherness in the Age of Globalization

Casey Ryan Kelly

LEXINGTON BOOKS
Lanham • Boulder • New York • London

Published by Lexington Books
An imprint of The Rowman & Littlefield Publishing Group, Inc.
4501 Forbes Boulevard, Suite 200, Lanham, Maryland 20706
www.rowman.com

Unit A, Whitacre Mews, 26-34 Stannary Street, London SE11 4AB

British Library Cataloguing in Publication Information Available

Library of Congress Cataloging-in-Publication Data
The hardback edition of this book was previously catalogued by the Library of Congress as follows:

Names: Kelly, Casey Ryan, 1979- author.
Title: Food television and otherness in the age of globalization / Casey Ryan Kelly.
Description: Lanham : Lexington Books, 2017. | Includes bibliographical references and index.
Identifiers: LCCN 2016054739 (print) | LCCN 2017015559 (ebook)
Subjects: LCSH: Television cooking shows—History and criticism. | Food on television. | Television and globalization. | Food—Social aspects. | Other (Philosophy) in mass media.
Classification: LCC PN1992.8F66 (ebook) | LCC PN1992.8F66 K45 2017 (print) | DDC 791.45/6564—dc23 LC record available at http://lccn.loc.gov/2016054739

ISBN 978-1-4985-4444-3 (cloth : alk. paper)
ISBN 978-1-4985-4446-7 (pbk. : alk. paper)
ISBN 978-1-4985-4445-0 (electronic)

Printed in the United States of America

Contents

Acknowledgments   vii

Introduction: Eating the Empire   1

1   The Neocolonial Plate: *Bizarre Foods with Andrew Zimmern*   23

2   Exoticizing Poverty: *Bizarre Foods America*   47

3   From the Plantation to the Prairie: *The Pioneer Woman*   65

4   America, the Abundant: *Man v. Food* and *Diners, Drive-Ins
    and Dives*   89

5   Going Native: Anthony Bourdain and *No Reservations*   113

Conclusion   139

Selected Bibliography   145

Index   149

About the Author   153

Acknowledgments

As someone who writes extensively about the subject, I watch a lot of television. Often, my research demands that I commandeer my home television, testing the patience of my very supportive spouse. But as she also writes about film and television—some of which is better than others—I suppose turnabout is fair play. At any rate, I would be remiss if I did not start by thanking Kristen E. Hoerl for not only tolerating the background noise of hundreds of episodes of food and travel programs but also for reading drafts of this book and helping me work through the conceptual and critical challenges of this project. Of course, there are many people who contributed to this project who are worth mentioning even as I am aware that I will inevitably leave someone out. First, I would like to thank the Butler University Institute for Research and Scholarship for providing generous financial support for the completion of this project. I would also like to thank my college and department colleagues for supporting my research, including Kristin Swenson, Ann Savage, Allison Harthcock, Mark Rademacher, Kevin Wang, Rose Campbell, Kristen Hoerl, and surely many others. Throughout this process, Lexington Books was incredibly supportive of this project from its most nascent stages through review and production. Nicolette Amstutz and Jimmy Hamill were champions of this book project and made the process more pleasant than I could have anticipated. Without Nicolette's outreach and encouragement, this book would likely never have come together.

There are many other people outside of my institution who have been supportive of my work and deserve acknowledgment. I would like to thank a collaborative group of food scholars in communication studies with whom I regularly write, present, and discuss my work, including Amy Young, Justin Eckstein, Donovan Conely, Jamie Wright, Jeff Rice, and Anjali Vats. I hope this book contributes to our ongoing pursuit to make foodways an important object of study in our discipline. There are many more people who, while they did not necessarily contribute to this project, have supported my career throughout everything I have done, including but not limited to Cate Palczewski, Randy Lake, Jason Edward Black, Kent Ono, Danielle Endres, Claire Sisco King, Dana Cloud, Chuck Morris, Dan Brouwer, Rob Asen, Angela Aguayo, and Michael Lee. There are countless others, to be sure. I would also like to acknowledge the emotional and professional support of my colleague and close friend

Matthew May, to whom I can always turn for advice and camaraderie. Finally, I have to thank my parents Marvin Kelly and Diane Kelly for everything.

Introduction

Eating the Empire

Once contained within the glossy-coated pages of elite culinary magazines, taste is a concept that has become democratized and made accessible to mass audiences through the proliferation of food media.[1] Since its launch in 1993, the Scripps-owned Food Network has transformed culinary television from the instructional demonstrations of PBS's *The French Chef* with Julia Child to interactive programming about the relationship between food and culture, featuring international travel, adventure, Americana, consumer kitsch, food ecologies, homemaking, entertainment, games, and competition.[2] The notion that cooking is hip and that an active interest in food is a signifier of cosmopolitan values are the byproduct of contemporary media culture. In large measure, the Food Network, along with other Scripps subsidiaries such as the Travel Channel (1987–) and the Cooking Channel (2010–), created the celebrity chef phenomenon, launching the careers of culinary moguls and restaurateurs such as Mario Batali, Bobby Flay, Andrew Zimmern, Rachel Ray, Guy Fieri, and Paula Deen. As of 2013, Scripps-owned food programming reached an estimated 99 million US households and remains popular with young affluent consumers who have an interest in arts and leisure, but most importantly, access to disposable income.[3]

Today, nearly every major network features some kind of program about the food industry, ranging from Fox's *Hells Kitchen*, Bravo's *Top Chef*, Spike's *Bar Rescue*, to Netflix's *Chef's Table*. Food programming has even infiltrated daytime network television in the place of popular soap operas and talk shows. Programs such as ABC's *The Chew* (2011–) and CBS's *Rachel Ray Show* (2006–) are weekday cooking-themed talk shows hosted by food personalities, modeled after the format of successful programs such as *The View* and *Ellen*.[4] Meanwhile, bestselling books such as Michael Pollan's *The Botany of Desire* (2001) and Hollywood documentaries such as *Food Inc.* (2008), *Supersize Me* (2004), and *Food Matters* (2008) attempt to keep pace with the public's fascination with food culture and politics. And despite the overall decline in revenues in magazine publishing, food magazines (*Bon Apetit*, *Food Network Magazine*, *Food and Wine*, and *Saveur*) still remain the fastest growing and most lucrative in the industry, even independent magazines such as David Chang and Peter

Meehan's *Lucky Peach*.[5] In 2014, cookbooks authored by popular food personalities generated almost a quarter of a billion dollars in revenue.[6]

With so much enthusiasm for culinary culture, it is remarkable that the amount of time Americans spend cooking has declined over the past fifty years.[7] Yet, the amount of time Americans spend watching food media continues to grow.[8] Anthony Bourdain (*No Reservations, Parts Unknown*) humorously called food programming the new pornography: "watching people make things on TV that they're not going to be doing themselves any time soon, just like porn."[9] In the commodity realm of popular culture, food preparation and consumption are transformed into a distant spectacle made present to audiences through choreographed screen action on sets constructed to resemble professional dojos of culinary sport or idyllic home kitchens that conjure nostalgia for the shared family meal. For instance, the set for Ree Drummond's *The Pioneer Woman* (Food Network) is elaborately constructed to convey a sense of warmth and the folksy simplicity of living on the America frontier.[10] At the Drummond ranch—where children play, men work, and women tend to the hearth—the spectator is a welcomed guest who vicariously partakes in a simulacra of wholesome American country life. With recipes structured around the rhythms of a working cattle ranch, Drummond's on-screen performances appear to be the authentic and spontaneous habits of, in her words, "an accidental country girl."[11] Surrounded by the iconography of Americana, shots of happy children and a satisfied husband testify—by way of shared meals—to the tenability and desirability of mythic American values.

If Americans are less likely to spend time actually replicating Drummond's recipes at home, then what are they actually consuming when they watch her program? Ostensibly, Americans consume a vision of social life, embodied in how different cultural groups produce, consume, and relate to food. Indeed, the profitability and popularity of food media as a form of entertainment suggests a significant transformation in the public meaning of cooking, food, and taste. Food television has evolved from a site of pragmatic domestic advice and cooking instruction to one in which culture is refracted and constituted through encounters with food. In other words, in food television the symbolic value of cooking often far surpasses its instrumental function. Television is increasingly concerned with *foodways*, or the cultural, social, and economic practices that accompany food production and consumption. Note, for instance, how food media tours American audiences through the iconic roadside diners of Route 66, the Juke Joints of the Mississippi Delta, the food stalls of the Jemaa El Fnaa in Marrakech, the tuna auction blocks of the Tsukiji Fish Market in Tokyo, and the squirrel cook-offs of rural West Virginia. Audiences accompany hosts to traditional home-cooked meals in the family kitchens of anointed community ambassadors to local cuisine.

Home or abroad, each site serves as a commonsense marker of distinct cultural practices.

Even the meticulously constructed sets of modern cooking instruction programs situate food preparation in social context: the bourgeois leisure culture of the Hampton Islands (*Barefoot Contessa*), the frontier nostalgia of the family ranch (*The Pioneer Woman*), the slow-paced life of southern tradition (*Paula Deen's Kitchen*), the comfort and modern convenience of the suburb (*Semi-Homemade*). At home or on the road, representations of foodways become a point of access to the rituals and patterns that predicate different cultural identities. Linda Keller Brown and Kay Mussell explain that while food provides nourishment, food*ways* "bind individuals together, define the limits of the group's outreach and identity, distinguish in-group from out-group, serve as a medium of inter-group communication, celebrate cultural cohesion, and provide a context for performance of group rituals."[12] Hence, on television, foodways are a material practice used to signify not only cultural belonging but also the differences that often fracture along lines of region, class, race, gender, and nationality. For instance, *Bizarre Foods with Andrew Zimmern* (Travel Channel) distinguishes the mundane food rituals of everyday suburban America from the exotic yet challenging food cultures of Africa, Latin America, and Asia. Western audiences are situated as universal subjects from whom all other eaters are marked as "mysterious" or "exotic." Meanwhile, a program such as Guy Fieri's *Diners, Drive-Ins and Dives* treats the culture and cuisine of any-town America as a sign of working-class tenacity and success. The program normalizes and romanticizes the indulgent high-calorie foodways of American mass culture, folding them into a narrative of American prosperity and upward mobility. The contrast here reflects how food television treats American foodways with familiarity and reverence and foreign foodways as uncanny and abnormal.

Food television no longer simply tells audiences how to cook recipes but instead how food production and consumption constitute the building blocks of culture. Food preparation and consumption become epistemic practices that produce knowledge about space, place, and identity.[13] Thus, Sarah Murray argues that food programming can be conceived of as a "race, classed, and gendered blueprint for not only broad class-based taste hierarchies, but also for highly individualized cultural distinction."[14] That is to say that representations of foodways provide a map of global and local power inequities; that "soul food" is a byproduct of slaves making do with the scraps of the plantation,[15] the fusion curry house a consequence of British colonial rule over the Asian subcontinent,[16] cookbooks extolling the virtues of female domesticity evidence of the gendered division of labor in the home,[17] and the availability of low nutritious high-sugar snacks a mark of extreme wealth stratification.[18] Food television not only maps embodied and historical-material power inequities, it imbues them with ideological coherence. As Kathleen Le-Besco and Peter Naccarato explain, "food representations have historically been understood as mere banners of cultural sensibilities; instead, we contend that these representations actively *produce* cultural sensibilities and the possibility of transgression."[19] For most Americans, media culture is now the primary vector for knowledge about food and food*ways*. Hence, it is important at this juncture to ask: how does media culture invite American audiences to think about the relationship between food, geography, travel, and cultural difference?

This book addresses this question by examining how representations of exotic versus mundane foods in contemporary television explains the fundamental distinctions between American and global foodways, how they make sense of food as a marker of cultural pride and difference. This book seeks to understand the cultural work of food television through a close reading of popular programs about foreign and domestic culinary culture, such as *Bizarre Foods, Bizarre Foods America, The Pioneer Woman, Diners, Drive-Ins and Dives, Man v. Food*, and *No Reservations*. I suggest that these programs use foodways to construct place-based identities that map over global economic power inequities. These food-place-identities divide the globe into categories of exotic and mundane; the former signifying the mysterious identity of the foreign Other and the latter the normal and comforting rituals of everyday America. With a surge in the popularity of food culture, this study takes television seriously as a site for the reproduction of popular ideology where food becomes the commonsense of cultural difference and economic success. Through a series of polemical essays on culinary adventurism, I seek to advance the growing body of interdisciplinary work on foodways by contrasting the difference between representations of exotic eating abroad with depictions of the more pedestrian and mundane food cultures of everyday America. Examining food television as a set of cultural texts that ascribe meaning to social and geographic distance, I hope to illuminate how mediated culinary tourism makes sense of global power imbalances and addresses popular anxieties about the exceptional status of American cultural and economic power in the twenty-first century.

In the remainder of this chapter, I outline the context, theoretical approach, and scope of this book. First, I explore the relationship between food, geography, and the rhetorical construction of "taste" to explain how the mediated culinary adventure cultivates audience investments in differentiated food identities demarcated by categories such as distance, race, and class. Next, I situate this book within the growing scholarship on foodways in communication studies to both elaborate on my critical approach to studying food media texts and address the stakes of the recent critical turn in food studies. Finally, I provide an outline of the book's critical case study chapters. This book consists of five case studies: three about exotic food adventures and international travel (*Bizarre Foods*,

Bizarre Foods America, and *No Reservations*), two concerning tours of "normal" American comfort food (*The Pioneer Woman,* and *Diners, Drive-Ins and Dives* and *Man v. Food*). The first two chapters explore how representations of bizarre and exotic meals in food media mediate the putative crisis of contemporary whiteness by representing cultural difference as useful, pleasurable, even titillating to white onlookers besieged by a complicated world of fragmented and hybrid identities. The next two chapters explore the deployment of "comfort food" and how the use of nostalgia—from the family ranch or the roadside diner—celebrates the myth of unending upward mobility, economic prosperity, and American exceptionalism. The final case study chapter (*No Reservations*) examines the challenges and limitations of demanding self-reflexivity in culinary travel. The purpose of this book is to explore how American food media confronts cultural and economic anxiety in an age of neoliberal globalization.

A MATTER OF TASTE

The concept of "taste" is a central feature of contemporary food culture. Taste can be conceived of as a marker of distinction, a sign of cultural membership, a standard for enjoyment, a method of judgment. Taste signifies a specific relationship with food; palates conditioned and habituated by distinct environments, agricultural systems, and cultural rituals. Of course, the biological requirement for caloric intake makes food consumption a universal feature of human existence. From this biological fact emerge patterns of behavior that organize our social experience, structure our relationship to nature, and necessitate disparate political and economic formations across human cultures. As Joshua Frye and Michael Bruner explain, "food is central to humankind. It is a requirement for survival, but also functions as a defining element of human culture and identity."[20] Food preparation and consumption are part of the pattern of everyday life; an intimate but often shared experience that constitutes and signifies cultural belonging. Taste shapes the materiality of society, from how we organize space (the home, neighborhood, landscape, cityscape), to how we construct and relate to time (leisure and work, growing seasons, recurring social rituals). Carlnita Green and Janet Cramer explain, "food serves as a socializing mechanism by which we come to understand our cultures, our societies, and the group to which we belong."[21] Taste serves as a common point of identification, the foundation of a common set of everyday rituals organized around familiar ingredients, people, and behaviors.

Indeed, food consumption unites us through seriality, or relations of similarity made possible not by essentialism but a common experience with an external object or phenomenon; however, food also divides us through the cultural specificity of geography, gender, race, class, and, of course, taste.[22] The power of the palate to shape human history should not be underestimated. For instance, a gastronomic history of modernity illuminates how taste was one of the generative forces of Western imperialism.[23] The West's taste for exotic spices first lured the greedy great powers of Europe into economic and military adventurism in the Middle East, Africa, and East Asia to secure access to its abundance of natural resources.[24] Despite an uncanny fascination with the flavors of the non-Western world, taste also served as the symbolic boundary between the civilized palate of the Westerner and the so-called barbaric and unclean eating practices of the Other. Today, where globalization consolidates economic power in hands of Western nations, access to food itself is a global dividing line between those with privilege and the 2.8 billion people who live on less than a dollar a day.[25] Taste is as much a point of division as it is identification, and the changing nature of taste has the power to influence global flows of goods and resources.

As both material and symbolic markers of cultural difference, taste provides a useful starting point for this book's inquiry into the relationship between food and global power inequities. One such approach can be found in the controversial book *Guns, Germs, and Steel*, where anthropologist Jared Diamond advances an eco-determinist perspective of human history organized around the observation that geographic advantages—the ability to easily produce and store food crops—explain global power imbalances.[26] To make his case, Diamond contrasts the labor intensity required for harvesting wild sago in Papua New Guinea against the production of wheat and other cereal crops easily grown in the climate of North America. The geographic advantage of nourishing, high yield, and storable foodstuffs explains how Euro-Americans were furnished with a surplus of time and resources to develop the industrial, political, and military capacity for imperial conquest. Sago—which is neither easy to produce nor store, let alone export—is an insufficient basis for the development of an advanced industrial society. For Diamond, the relative positions of Europe and the United States versus Papua New Guinea are in part owed to disparate capacities for food production that are constrained and enabled by geographic position. While it might be used to explain differences, the so-called refined Western palate tells us nothing about the raw materials that constitute a food culture. To be sure, Diamond's point is not to naturalize global inequities, but rather to argue that the history of progress and colonialism might be read climatically as well as gastronomically. In other words, the accident of geographic location dictates how food is produced and consumed, and consequently, what kind of cultural and social configurations are made possible by the availability of particular foods and the relative easy of their production and consumption.

At the same, what matters as much as geostrategic location is how it is we come to define and explain the differences in food cultures in terms other than the accident of birth. When differences in food production and consumption enter into the symbolic and mediated realm of global public discourse, the world is divided once again by categories of taste. Hence, in this book I read the articulation and representation of taste as a contingent expression of judgment, preference, and hierarchy cultivated in relation to historically and culturally specific food practices. As viewers vicariously circumnavigate the globe, taste can be offered as ideological testament to the normality, convention, and appropriateness of one's own specific cultural habits. Taste is a rhetoric of social positionality that naturalizes class and racial categories, a way to rationalize difference and hierarchy according to refinement and distinction. To say that an individual or group has poor taste (in food, music, or other cultural phenomenon) is to make a moral and aesthetic judgment about their character, what Donovan Conley cunningly calls "m/orality."[27] Taking a cue from Theodore Adorno, from the position of a refined palate one might consider another's preference for what are considered low cultural forms (be it junk food, pop music, reality television, or professional wrestling) as evidence of their inferiority, their poor taste a reflection of their social undesirability and distasteful social presence.[28] Pierre Bourdieu famously argued that taste "reveals the deepest dispositions of habitus," that structuring mechanism whereby the social world is internalized and ideologies are acquired through embodied experiences with social structures.[29] "Taste" is not only a reflection of social position—race, class, gender, ability, and sexuality—but also a language that naturalizes and reinforces social divisions that are constrained and enabled by larger structural forces.[30] Taste elevates status and discernment, particular to one class, culture, race, or nation, to an objective and universal ideal. It maps hierarchy and purpose onto differences that are the byproduct of history, geography, war, conquest, migration flows, climate, trade, and so on. Whereas food consumption unites the human experience, taste forms the basis of its division.

As a device of identification and disassociation, taste is also organized around cultural conceptions of dirt and purity. Primarily, this book is concerned with how food television contrasts the clean or "normal" cuisines of mainstream American food culture with the dangerous and impure tastes of poor communities and non-Western nations. Anthropologist Mary Douglas observed that dirt is "matter out of place," and thus hygiene and cleanliness are practices of environmental organization designed to expel that which offends or pollutes our conception of order.[31] She writes that "in chasing dirt, in papering, decorating, tidying, we are not governed by anxiety to escape disease, but are positively re-ordering our environment, making it conform to an idea."[32] Dirt is culturally contingent and its peculiar particularities are subject to diverse rituals designed to manage the threat of disorder and pollution. As an intimate practice that constantly risks bodily defilement, eating is subject to taboos and thus requires a set of rituals to authorize clean consumption. In some cases, those rituals are inherited from religious doctrine such as kosher cookery and halal butchery. Food is also governed by secular rituals that, while often couched in pragmatic language, are nonetheless sacramental and ceremonial in form. For instance, American taboos about the consumption of uncooked foods require mandates about proper handling, minimum internal temperature, and minimum quality standards for serving raw or undercooked meat and fish. But, American food rituals and taboos are by no means uniform or consistent. For instance, though there are parts of the world where the consumption of insects and rodents are routine, Americans maintain a strict set of informal prohibitions against their consumption.[33] At the same time, because Americans are very distant from their food source, the corporate food industry (i.e., fast food) obscures pollution and uncleanliness in the foods they produce via out-of-sight mass production and clever antiseptic packaging.[34]

Taste, then, is a signifying practice that gives distinction to a community or culture's rituals of cleanliness. Put differently, taste creates hierarchical distinctions between culturally contingent food rituals, elevating relative distinctions to universal coordinates of difference. On food television, one way in which the world is mapped is by sorting regions into the tastes of clean and dirty eaters. Whereas the creature comforts of high-calorie semi-homemade meals on *The Pioneer Woman* convey the safety of home, a street vendor in Kuala Lumpur serving grilled organ meats on *Bizarre Foods* or *No Reservations* confronts unaccustomed American audiences with a vicarious experience of bodily defilement. Of course, taste hierarchies also manifest within cultures. For instance, the purposeful gluttony of *Man v. Food* and *Diners, Drive-Ins and Dives* transgresses the boundaries of good taste, each text an irreverent spectacle of unhealthy overconsumption. For better or worse, these two programs challenge the refined, if not elitist, trends of "foodie" culture with the more conventionally pedestrian tastes of American diner culture. Each program examined in this book implicitly asserts a particular conception of taste linked to the cultural practices and purity rituals of the assumed audience. In making implicit conjectures about good taste, each program either evokes the implied threat of uncleanliness or suggests an alternative way of conceptualizing what counts as an acceptable form of consumption. Some programs manage dirt while others invite the audience to consider what they understand to be dirt. Overall, this book suggests that taste is a framework for managing dirt, each program articulating a different point of distinction, a rhetoric of positionality by which television privileges some food rituals over others.

FOOD TELEVISION AND THE SPECTACLE OF THE OTHER

Where are these divisive and hierarchical concepts of "taste" cultivated? How does taste inform our perspectives toward cultural difference? While the differences in food cultures have natural explanations, the differences that make a difference acquire meaning in and through representation.[35] Hence, missing from the climatic account of global food inequality is an analysis of how discourse, representations, and human agency shape the cultural meaning and politics of food. As a signifier of cultural identity, *representations* of food stand in for people, places, and experiences, the familiarity of home and the exoticism of far away places.[36] When food is mediated in popular culture, it becomes enlisted in the process of "spectacular consumption," what Eric King Watts and Mark Orbe characterize as "the process through which the relations among cultural forms, the culture industry, and the lived experience of persons are shaped by public consumption."[37] That is to say that when eating and preparing meals are projected onto the public screen as entertainment, the viewer's consumption is vicarious and symbolic. Through food, audiences consume the cultural experience of others as a commodity. As Helene Shugart observed of food media, "in a consumer landscape increasingly characterized by artifice, replication, transience, and superficiality, the quest for novelty and uniqueness is endowed with greater and greater market value; to this end, cultural differences offer endless opportunities for appropriation and commodification."[38] Indeed, the commonality and intimacy of food consumption imbues the mediated food experience with a presumption of authenticity in a media landscape that appears overly commercialized, synthetic, and fake. Yet, as a mediated experience, the visceral experience of eating that we often associate with authenticity is converted into a spectacle of vicarious enjoyment, a visual pleasure commodified in an image that is consumed symbolically.[39]

In conjunction with America's food industries, food television has had an alarming effect on the public's relationship with food. As Michael Pollan contends, high quality, nutritious, farm-to-table food is more visible than ever yet has been largely replaced by cheap and convenient imitations endorsed by celebrity chefs and food TV personalities.[40] Indeed, the scope and influence of food TV can and has sustained a number of important scholarly inquiries into the economic, environmental, agricultural, and political consequences of spectacular consumption. This book narrows this inquiry to food-place-identities to draw attention to how food television invites Western spectators to view their geostrategic location in a globalized world. In doing so, I wish to highlight the specific features of food television that address the relationship between food and global cultural difference. Hence, this book's approach to food TV—and what is entailed in its construction of taste—is organized around three central propositions.

First, food TV mediates a discursive tension between global cosmopolitanism, on the one hand, and Western hegemony, on the other. Where the ceaseless flow of capital and information shrinks and flattens the globe to a close-knit yet virtual terrain, "Western" as a category of identity is conflicted between globalization's celebration of diversity, cooperation, and equality and anxieties about the singular importance of Western culture and values within that system.[41] In other words, the promise of neoliberal globalization is that the free flow of goods and services across borders, cooperation between developed and lesser-developed nations, and the spread of Western cultural and economic values will engender a global ethic of inclusion, commonality, and appreciation for human diversity. Yet, if this goal were truly achieved in practice it would require the displacement of Western hegemony and a radical openness to non-Western modernities. Thus, Raka Shome finds that the celebration of global diversity that accompanies the transnational ideology of neoliberal globalization is "so saturated by the history and temporalities of Western national cultures that it betrays its limits when placed in the context of global relations and the logics of non-Western modernities."[42] Walter Mignolo warns that discourses of development and modernization have been replaced with a transnational market ideology wherein neoliberalism has been resignified as an "emergent civilizational project," but one ultimately tethered to specifically Western interests.[43] For Mignolo and Shome, the Western coloniality that structures neoliberalism precludes the emergence of a critical cosmopolitanism that would be premised on conviviality and global citizenship. The convivial promise of globalization is thwarted by its threatening posture toward Western hegemony, an anxiety that cosmopolitanism might unfold without the West at its center.

Of course, the celebration of progressive multiculturalism, transnationalism, and globalization has done relatively little to displace Western supremacy. If anything, this anemic version of cosmopolitanism has provoked both reactionary fear of displacement along with eager anticipation of what rewards globalization might reap for the West.[44] Here, the spectacular consumption of difference plays a central role in mediating the putative crisis of the Western self that is evoked when transnational perspectives are foregrounded in the celebration of global diversity. As bell hooks suggests in her oft-cited essay "Eating the Other," cultural difference is most easily domesticated when it can be reframed as an enticing opportunity to "spice up" mainstream culture.[45] Alterity, then, can be pleasurably consumed as a form of appreciation for what it contributes to the Western experience. In terms of food culture, this perspective on cultural difference transforms the globe into a map of exotic edibles and exhilarating food rituals, a scene of adventure and conquest for the intrepid Western traveler. The mediated culinary adventure comes to signify the Westerner's simultaneous appreciation and mastery of cultural difference, a testament to both the rugged character and democratizing spirit of the Western individual. The positive and often whimsical valence of food television represents global food cultures as opportunities to overcome challenging cultural difference by rendering Otherness legible, knowable, and productive. The vicarious experience of eating the Other, then, helps manage the tensions between spectators' conflicted investments in both cosmopolitanism and Western hegemony.

Second, culinary television ascribes meaning to food-place-identities by drawing from the nostalgia and mythology of American exceptionalism. In global programming, mythology manifests in narratives of adventure against the backdrop of an exotic mise-en-scene: long treks across rugged terrain, meanderings through colorful bazaars, close encounters with fish parts and organ meat at the foreign market, wilderness hunts with local guides, and traditional meals prepared in authentically stylized home kitchens. But, this rugged pastoral image of foreign places and mysterious cuisine is ultimately the invention of the Western mind. Working from Edward Said's *Orientalism*, we find that the perspective of the camera, narrator, producers, writers, hosts, and spectators are unavoidably tethered to a conception of the non-Western world as backwards, mysterious, barbaric, romantic, and exotic.[46] With its roots in the lavish and embellished travel writing of Western colonial apologists, contemporary representations of culinary tourism invent places and people prefigured by the Western imaginary of what it possesses that the Other seems to lack.[47] In food television, seemingly authentic or unmediated encounters with exotic food cultures transform the camera into a selective instrument, a narrow way of seeing, that constructs as much as it documents its subjects. Hence, I conceive of the televised culinary adventure as a *neocolonial* discourse that adapts and refashions assumptions that once structured ideological adherence to Western colonization, namely the superiority of Western values and the imperative to extend its civilizing mission to the non-Western world.[48] Even as it celebrates difference, food television still maintains distinctions between clean, orderly, and civilized eating rituals of the First World and the strange, primal, and uncanny cuisines that define the "Third World."

By contrast, televised adventures in American food are organized around a nostalgic longing for an innocent national identity, subtly marked by the aesthetics of the frontier and mass consumer kitsch: the idyllic small town eatery, the 1950s roadside diner, and the pastoral farm. In programs such as *Diners, Drive-Ins and Dives, Man v. Food,* and *The Pioneer Woman* America is refracted through the rustic simplicity and "comfort food" found in the countryside, the small town, and the suburb. Here, working class taste is a mark of distinction that singularizes America as a humble and hard-working nation organized around small community, family values, and simple tastes. The historic American work ethic has been rewarded with abundance: large families, open landscapes, and of course, large portions.[49] The vast American frontier is both open and inviting but also a space domesticated through the hard work of turning nature into civilization. Whereas the global culinary adventure domesticates the exotic, the American-focused sojourn fortifies the homeland against external challenges by portraying America as an innocent nation capable of promulgating unending upward mobility and economic prosperity for all. In other words, the comfort food tour constructs American food-place-identities from within the logics of the American Dream where mass consumption is a national virtue. This portrait of American cuisine elides not only the structural unviability of the American Dream mythology for those valorized in such programs but also how American food cultures are themselves a reflection not of simple hard work alone but instead larger historical forces such as colonization, territorial expansion, slavery, and later mass industrialization and globalization.

Finally, food television speaks with an authoritative anthropological voice because it assimilates techniques of documentary and ethnographic filmmaking into contemporary entertainment formats. Hence, these televisual texts produce what appear to be expert knowledge about food and cultural difference derived from purported access to the everyday life experiences of individual subjects. Elsewhere I have called this phenomenon "ethnotainment" to account for the tension between the ethical self-reflectivity demanded of anthropological filmmaking and the industrial imperative to commodify and sell an entertaining product to television audiences.[50] I argued that "the Other is pressed into the service of both a consumer television market place as well as a cosmopolitan market place in which one's own identity is a commodity with rare and exotic value."[51] Ethnotainment entails close examinations of the cultural rituals and everyday lives of others to impart both sincerity and objectivity, to communicate to audiences that this is how life exists without the presence of cameras, narration, and hosts. Of course, food programming must belabor this sense of reality through techniques of mediation—from editing of raw footage to selecting local community liaisons. The appearance of authoritative and unmediated access to foreign food cultures elides how the process of selection and deflection craft an appealing image of Otherness that is adapted to the expectations of Western audiences. Hence, audiences are often treated to portraits of happy natives eager to share their food culture for interested viewers. Meanwhile, the presumed "eye/I" of the spectator is the Western cosmopolitan foodie with disposable income and consumer desires.[52] The pleasing portrait of ethnotainment reaffirms that the notion that those living in the margins of the global economy welcome Western influence.

In summary, this book proposes that the mediated culinary adventure employs techniques that invite an economically privileged and neocolonial perspective toward both global and domestic food cultures. Food transforms into a marker of both American progress and the quaint yet strange romanticism of non-Western backwardness. Food television affirms a particular version of cosmopolitanism that celebrates the richness of cultural difference without accounting for the structural inequalities that explain the distribution of global power and resources. The logics of neoliberal globalization prevail, where global uplift is enacted through the consumption of Otherness.

READING SELF AND OTHER

Stuart Hall argues that racial ideologies in media culture are promulgated and circulated inferentially. Rather than overt caricatures, "inferential racism" is the "naturalized representation of events and situations relating to race . . . which have racist premises and propositions inscribed in them as a set of *unquestioned assumptions*. These enable racist statements to be formulated without even bringing into awareness that racist predicates on which the statements are grounded."[53] One of Hall's primary examples of inferential racism entails how the concept of "adventure" was been folded into modern entertainment. He traces adventure to Euro-American colonial literature—tales of exploration, captivity, and violence—where he finds the very idea "synonymous with the demonstration of the moral, social and physical mastery of the colonizers over the colonized."[54] However, neither the formal end of colonization nor the decline in this genre of writing dislodged coloniality as a system of thought and knowledge production. Though distanced from explicitly racialized warrants for imperialist violence, Hall finds that adventure in contemporary film and television relies on traces of reworked logics, premises, and assumptions that ultimately support coloniality.[55] In Western media culture, such old tales are refashioned to produce a kind of underlying grammar to make sense of racial Others in the present.[56]

Working from Hall's notion of "inferential racism" and Kent Ono's "neocolonial rhetoric," this book approaches popular culture as a site where colonialist ideologies are translated into entertainment.[57] The texts I examine are not only structured by coloniality, but many actively participate in cultivating an affluent Eurocentric vision of the globe. Here, I use the term *coloniality* to denote the endurance of a system of thought, knowledge production, and representation that subjugates and marginalizes non-Western modernities. Colonialism entails the physical process of appropriating a people's land and resources, carrying out subjugation by imposing the colonizers' language, education, and religion.[58] Coloniality, however, is the living legacy of colonialism that endures in the present as tool of social, economic, and epistemological exclusion.[59] In Darrel Allan Wanzer's words, "coloniality is a constitutive feature of Western modernity that structures exclusionary modes of power, knowledge, and being—it is the dark underside of modernity, which influences both first and third world people."[60] While not formal academic knowledge, the rhetoric of popular ethnotainment purports to educate as it entertains its primarily affluent Western audience about the intimate cultural rituals of Americans in contrast to those largely outside of Western modernity. Coloniality provides a way of articulating a system of representations that naturalizes and normalizes power relations that are the historic byproduct of colonialism. The utility of this approach is that it accounts for the power of representation to subjugate Others even as televisual texts celebrate their cuisine and culture. Shome poignantly observes, "whereas in the past, imperialism was about controlling the 'native' by colonizing her or him territorially, now imperialism is more about subjugating the 'native' by colonizing her or him discursively."[61] Moreover, this approach accounts for how food television has difficulty escaping Eurocentric thought, particularly when the food cultures of the civilized West become its subject.

In postcolonial studies, critics often privilege history, literature, and the official institutional discourses of the state and capital as the textual sources of contemporary coloniality.[62] This is despite the fact that media institutions such as the Travel Channel, National Geographic, and the Food Network reach hundreds of millions and frame their programming as authoritative depictions of global food cultures. Scripps-owned networks alone have demonstrated immense power to drive demand, cultivate consumer trends, and shape public discourses about food and travel.[63] First, as an important site of informal knowledge production, popular culture texts mediate spectators' conceptions of place identities as much as formal hegemonic institutions such as education, religion, or news media.[64] Thus, the discourses of popular culture constitute what Henry Giroux calls a form of "public pedagogy," an extension of formal education into non-institutional settings of social learning where knowledge is generated about significant cultural politics.[65] The educative function of popular culture makes it worthy of sustaining critical attention from postcolonial critics as it cultivates knowledge, values, and aesthetic judgments about its subjects. Second, popular culture discourses also serve an important function of meaning management. Barry Brummett contends that popular texts are not merely repositories of meaning that reflect the struggles of public culture; but, rather popular texts are active and functional. They mediate, manage, and organize the meaning of the shared social experience they purport to represent. In popular culture, then, audiences are left to make meaning not from one set of official discourses but instead a series of textual fragments that circulate throughout our ubiquitous media landscape. Thus, as Kristen Hoerl articulates, "the study of how meaning is constructed in popular culture explains the processes by which communities share experience, maintain social stability, and recognize the need for social change."[66] From this perspective, food television is not simply frivolous entertainment but one of the primary mediums by which food culture is made visible and knowable to Western audiences.

In this book, I study how popular culture and political discourse about food generate and manage meaning through the arrangement of particular symbols—both verbal and visual. This book adopts an interpretive approach that views food television as a constellation of cultural texts that make implicit conjectures about the meaning of place and identity in relationship with food practices. By interpretive, I mean the use of language and symbolic action to foster audience identification, explain social phenomena, manage social conflicts, and construct meaning. I engage in a close textual analysis of television programs where I not only pay attention to production and marketing of programs, but also how food programs mobilize narrative, dialogue, on-screen interactions, voice overs, text, and other compositional elements of television to connection food, place, and culture. In my analysis, I do not make conjectures about how audiences actually interpret programs but instead what subject positions and interpretive resources are made available to audiences. I am primarily interested in how television invites identification with and naturalizes specific social ideals and categories of experience. Approached as a species of symbolic action, the language of television not only concerns aesthetics and form but also how programs "make sense" in a particular cultural context through a combination of plot, narrative causality, dialogue, characterization, narration, and mise-en-scène.

In communication studies, a series of recent books have attempted to account for the increasing visibility of foodways, attending to food culture's discourses, representations, performances, and constitutive entailments. For instance, Josh Frye and Michael Bruner's, *The Rhetoric of Food*, Janet M. Cramer, Carlnita Greene, and Lynn M. Walters's *Food as Communication: Communication as Food*, and Samuel Boerboom's *The Political Language of Food* present collections of scholarly essays that address the symbolic and representational elements of communication through and about food. While these collections are a great start, there is no sustained book-length project that examines the implications of food and travel television, which is by far the largest source of information about food in American culture, particularly when it comes to global food consumption. My focus on place and tourism is premised on the belief that travel teaches us who we are (and who we are not) through encounters—embodied and vicarious—with familiar and unfamiliar landscapes.[67] This book contributes to this growing area of research by exploring how food television advances an ideological conception of "taste" that now pervades American culture. A focus on food-place-identities elaborates on how discourse, representations, and human agency shape the cultural meaning and politics of food. As a signifier of cultural identity, *representations* of food stand in for people, places, and experiences, the familiarity of home and the exoticism of faraway places. These place identities divide the globe into categories of exotic and mundane; the former signifies the mysterious identity of the foreign Other and the latter the normal and comforting rituals of everyday America.

PLAN FOR THIS BOOK

This book offers a series of critical essays on the emerging rhetoric of culinary television, attending to how American audiences are invited to understand the cultural and economic significance of global foodways. While there are a variety of formats offered throughout the food television genre, including game shows, reality competitions, cooking demonstrations, and instruction, I focus on programs that explore food culture in its context, articulated through an emphasis of travel or situated constructions of place. Focusing on some of the most highly successful food programs, each chapter explores how audiences are invited to understand their place identities through the lens of food and the aesthetic judgments of taste. The chapters are divided between programs that explore exotic and international cuisines and programs that feature American comfort food and mass consumer traditions. This choice is to provide a contrast between how television conceptualizes cultural difference in relation to its primarily affluent Western audience.

In chapter 1 "The Neocolonial Plate" I examine the program *Bizarre Foods with Andrew Zimmern*, a one-hour travel documentary that first aired on the Travel Channel in 2006. In this program Zimmern—former chef and dining critic travels to different locales in Asia, Africa, and South America sampling foods considered "exotic" in most mainstream American food cultures. Capitalizing on synergy between Scripp's Food Network, *Bizarre Foods* was part of the Travel Channel's food-centric cosmopolitan adventure-life-style rebranding campaign. In this chapter, I examine how representations of bizarre and exotic meals mediate the putative crisis of contemporary whiteness by representing cultural difference as useful, pleasurable, even titillating to white onlookers besieged by a complicated world of fragmented and hybrid identities. The opaque politics of the Western food adventure are tainted by histories of colonialism in which the primitive mysteries of "the Orient" are consumed to season the life and palate of the Western subject. The program offers fellow culinary adventurers the opportunity to vicariously participate in consumptive excursions to exotic regions while erasing the power lines of inequity that divide the globe and commodify the cultural experience of difference in support of Western globalization.

Chapter 2 "Exoticizing Poverty" examines Zimmern's spin-off program *Bizarre Foods America*, a show that locates "strange" food cultures throughout the United States. A sojourn through the rural South and Appalachia, the program is by-and-large a poverty tour that exoticizes American food cultures born of physical and economic necessity. I contend that the program engages in "culinary slumming" where economically privileged foodies seek out, celebrate, and consume cuisines that are the byproduct of historic structural inequality. Culinary slumming represents those living in economically and geographically marginalized communities as happily content with their humble circumstances and food traditions. The appropriation, consumption, and unreflexive enjoyment of American poverty cuisines belies the structural conditions under which many must "make do" in order to survive.

In chapter 3 "From the Plantation to the Prairie," I examine the construction of American food-place-identities in Ree Drummond's *The Pioneer Woman* (Food Network), a cooking program set on a working cattle ranch. A part of the network's wholesome rebranding after the public controversy over Paula Deen's racist comments, *The Pioneer Woman* supplants southern plantation iconography—itself sutured to the history of American slavery—with the warmth and the folksy simplicity of living on the America frontier. Resituating frontier comfort food as a national tradition, woven into the mythic folklore of America's origin story, Drummond's lifestyle brand redeems an embattled national identity with a romantic vision of work and leisure. I suggest that the program's wholesomeness is belied by its reliance on American frontier mythology, an ideology once used to legitimize colonial violence, Westward expansion, and superiority of American identity.

Chapter 4, "America, the Abundant" examines two programs that revel in the excessive consumption and nostalgic consumer kitsch of American diner culture: Guy Fieri's *Diner's, Drive-Ins and Dives* (Food Network) and Adam Richman's *Man v. Food* (Travel Channel). These programs celebrate America as a land of abundance where overconsumption of high-calorie meals is a sign of both upward mobility for the working class and the spoils of a mass consumer economy. I situate both programs within a broader set of commercial discourses that conflate liberal notions of independence and liberty with the freedom, if not right, to consume. Moreover, when positioned against the "nanny state" foil, excess becomes a heroic act of resistance in defense of the American way of life. Taken together, these shows advance the mythology of the "affluent society" in which an upwardly mobile middle class can attain its portion of America's unending prosperity. These two popular programs exemplify how representations of American dining and (over)consumption are part of the rhetorical structure of the American Dream, a post-War social ideal of unbounded class mobility and affluence achieved through hard work and faith in democratic capitalism.

Chapter 5, "Going Native," explores the potentials and challenges of culinary travel narratives that privilege open-minded inquiry over frivolous pleasure-seeking. This chapter concentrates on Anthony Bourdain's *No Reservations* (Travel Channel), a show that features well-developed portraits of food in geographic, political, and economic context. Although the program is perhaps the most sophisticated, humanizing, and politically dynamic exploration of people and places often ignored or spectacularized by television, the show's emphasis on "going native," or living like the locals, is also premised on a fixed and binary notion of culture, that behind the smokescreen of staged tourism is an authentic and knowable Other. Moreover, "going native" exempts the traveler from critiques of cultural commodification and globalization while the naive tourist foil remains duped by the façade and political economy of the multicultural spectacle. Yet, *No Reservations* is a powerful polemic against global tourist culture, a program structured like a long-form argument against closed-minded ethnocentric forms of food tourism. While this tension in many ways limits the possibility that travel might dissolve imperialist conceptions of self and Other, it might also transform cosmopolitanism as it is currently conceived by inviting audiences to reconsider their own desires for mastery and the limitations of their Eurocentric worldviews. The attempt to escape the conventional logics of tourism often proves illusive, but this should not preclude us from developing food television that directs us toward new ethics of global citizenship.

Finally, in the conclusion, I discuss the implications of food television in the context of global structural inequality and inquire into the possibilities for restructuring our food-place-identities. Though this book is critical of food television's spectacularization of foreign Others, I conclude that the commonality and universality of food provides some unique opportunities for bridging the cultural differences and structural inequalities that are characteristic of life under late capitalism.

NOTES

1. See David Bell, "Fragments for a New Urban Culinary Geography," *Journal for the Study of Food and Society* 6.1 (2002): 10–21.
2. See Cheri Ketchum, "Tunnel Vision and Food: A Political Economic Analysis of *Food Network*," in Sarah Banet Weiser, Cynthia Chris, and Anthony Freitas, *Cable Visions: Television Beyond Broadcasting*, pp. 158–176 (New York, NY: New York University Press, 2007); and "The Essence of Cooking Shows: How the Food Network Constructs Consumer Fantasies," *Journal of Communication Inquiry* 29.3 (2005): 217–234.
3. Nancy Gagliardi, "Is the Food Network Still Relevant?" *Forbes*, November 17, 2014. Accessed from http://www.forbes.com/sites/nancygagliardi/2014/11/17/is-the-food-network-still-relevant/#58ad7d4c168e
4. *The Chew* stars Mario Batali, Carla Hall, Clinton Kelly, Daphne Oz, and Michael Symon. It won a daytime Emmy in 2015. It premiered on September 26, 2011 and replaced *All My Children*. The show released its first cookbook *The Chew: Food. Life. Fun* and *The Chew: What's For Dinner* (2013) and *The Chew: A Year of Celebrations* (2014).

5. Justin Bergh, "Food Magazines," in Ken Albala (ed.), *SAGE Encyclopedia of Food Issues* (587–591) (London, UK: Sage Reference, 2015).

6. "Cookbook Publishing in the US Market Research," *IBISWorld*, October 2014, http://www.ibisworld.com/industry/cookbook-publishing.html.

7. See Michael Pollan, *Cooked: A Natural History of Transformation* (New York: Penguin Books, 2014); and Lindsey P. Smith, Shu Wen Ng, and Berry M. Popkin, "Trends in US Home Food Preparation and Consumption: Analysis of National Nutrition Surveys and Time Use Studies from 1965–1966 to 2007–2008," *Nutrition Journal* 12 (2013), http://link.springer.com/article/10.1186%2F1475-2891-12-45.

8. Michael Pollan, "Out of the Kitchen, Onto the Couch," *New York Times*, July 29, 2009. Accessed from www.nytimes.com/2009/08/02/magazine/02cooking-t.html?pagewanted=all&_r=0.

9. Quoted in Time Carman, "Bourdain Declares Celebrity Chef Shows the 'New Pornography.'" *The Washington City Paper*, May 28, 2009. Accessed from www.washingtoncitypaper.com/blogs/youngandhungry/2009/05/28/bourdain-declares-celebrity-chef-shows-the-new-pornography/.

10. Amanda Fortini, "The Pioneer Woman Gets Lost on the Range," *The New Yorker*, February 3, 2012. Accessed from http://www.newyorker.com/culture/culture-desk/the-pioneer-woman-gets-lost-on-the-range.

11. See Ree Drummond, *The Pioneer Woman Cooks: Recipes from an Accidental Country Girl* (New York, NY: William Morrow Cookbooks, 2009).

12. Linda Keller Brown and Kay Mussell (eds.), *Ethnic and Regional Foodways in the United States: The Performance of Group Identity* (Knoxville, TN: University of Tennessee Press, 1984), 5.

13. For work on "food pedagogies" and epistemologies see Elaine Swan and Rick Flowers (eds.), *Food Pedagogies* (Burlington, VT: Ashgate, 2015).

14. Sarah Murray, "Food and Television," in Ken Albala (ed.) *Routledge International Handbook of Food Studies*, 187–198 (London, UK: Routledge, 2013), 190; See also Pauline Adema, "Vicarious Consumption: Food, Television, and the Ambiguity of Modernity," *Journal of American and Comparative Cultures* 23, no. 3 (2000): 113–124; and Isabelle De Solier, "TV Dinners: Culinary Television, Education and Distinction," *Continuum: A Journal of Cultural and Media Studies* 19.4 (2000): 465–481.

15. See Herbert C. Covey and Dwight Eisnach, *What the Slaves Ate: Recollections of African American Food and Foodways from the Slave Narrative* (Santa Barbara, CA: ABC-CLIO, 2009); and Frederick Douglass Opie, *Hog and Hominy: Soul Food from Africa to America* (New York, NY: Columbia University Press, 2013).

16. See Cecilia Leong-Salobir, *Food Culture in Colonial Asia: A Taste of Empire* (London, UK: Routledge, 2011).

17. See Sherrie A. Inness, *Secret Ingredients: Race, Gender, and Class at the Dinner Table* (New York, NY: Palgrave Macmillan, 2005); and Jessamyn Neuhaus, *Manly Meals and Mom's Home Cooking: Cookbooks and Gender in Modern America* (Baltimore, MD: Johns Hopkins University, 2012).

18. See Eric Schlosser, *Fast Food Nation: The Dark Side of the All-American Meal* (Boston: Mariner Books, 2012).

19. Kathleen LeBesco and Peter Naccarato, *Edible Ideologies: Representing Food and Meaning* (Albany, NY: SUNY Press, 2012), 2.

20. Joshua Frye and Michael Bruner, *The Rhetoric of Food: Discourse, Materiality, and Power* (New York, NY: Routledge, 2012), 1.

21. Carlnita P. Greene and Janet Muriel Cramer, "Beyond Mere Sustenance: Food as Communication/Communication as Food," in Janet M. Cramer, Carlnita Greene, and Lynn M. Walters, *Food as Communication: Communication as Food* (New York, NY: Peter Lang, 2011), xi.

22. Here I draw from John Paul Sartre's explanation of individual belonging to social classes wherein collective identities are formed not based on essence but relationship with common experience with capitalist production. Individuals are positioned in a series of relationships by phenomenon external to the self. See Jean-Paul

Sartre and Fredric Jameson, *Critique of Dialectical Reason, Volume One*, ed. Jonathan Ree, trans. Alan Sheridan-Smith (London; New York: Verso, 2004).

23. See Carolyn de la Peña and Benjamin N. Lawrence, "Introduction: Foodways, 'Foodism,' or Foodscapes? Navigating Local/Global and Food/Culture Divides," Benjamin N. Lawrance and Carolyn de la Peña, *Local Foods Meet Global Foodways: Tasting History*, pp. 2–15 (New York, NY: Routledge, 2013); and Wenying Xu, *Eating Identities: Reading Food in Asian American Literature* (Honolulu, HI: University of Hawaii Press, 2008).

24. This argument is particularly supported by many recent microhistories of specific foods and spices such as Mark Kurlansky, *Salt: A World History* (New York, NY: Penguin Books, 2003); *Cod: A Biography of the Fish That Changed the World* (New York, NY: Penguin Books, 2010); Marjorie Shaffer, *Pepper: A History of the World's Most Influential Spice* (New York, NY: St. Martin's Griffin, 2014); Jack Turner, *Spice: The History of a Temptation* (New York, NY: Vintage, 2005).

25. "United Nations Resources for Speakers on Global Issues," accessed January 12, 2016, http://www.un.org/en/globalissues/briefingpapers/food/vitalstats.shtml.

26. Jared Diamond, *Guns, Germs, and Steel: The Fates of Human Societies* (New York, NY: W. W. Norton & Company, 1999).

27. Donovan Conley, "M/orality," *Communication & Critical/Cultural Studies* 12, no. 2 (2015): 224.

28. See Theodor W. Adorno, *The Culture Industry: Selected Essays on Mass Culture*, ed. J. M. Bernstein (London ; New York: Routledge, 2001).

29. Pierre Bourdieu, *Distinction: A Social Critique of the Judgment of Taste* (London: Routledge, 1984), 190; and James Arnt Aune, "The Scholastic Fallacy, Habitus, and Symbolic Violence: Pierre Bourdieu and the Prospects of Ideology Criticism," *Western Journal of Communication* 75, no. 4 (2011): 430.

30. See Pierre Bourdieu, *Distinction*; and *Masculine Domination* (Palo Alto, CA: Stanford University Press), 60.

31. Mary Douglas, *Purity and Danger: An Analysis of the Concept of Pollution and Taboo* (New York, NY: Routledge), 50.

32. Douglas, *Purity*, 3.

33. See Psyche Williams Forson and Carole Counihan, *Taking Food Public: Redefining Foodways in a Changing World* (New York, NY: Routledge, 2013).

34. See Eric Schlosser, *Fast Food Nation: The Dark Side of the All-American Meal* (New York, NY: Houghton Mifflin Harcourt, 2001).

35. See Stuart Hall, *Representation: Cultural Representations and Signifying Practices* (London and Thousand Oaks, CA: Sage Publications, 1997); and *Policing the Crisis: Mugging, the State and Law and Order* (New York, NY: Palgrave Macmillan, 2013).

36. See Graham Huggan, *The Postcolonial Exotic: Marketing the Margins* (New York, NY: Routledge, 2001); Peter Mason, *Infelicities: Representations of the Exotic* (Baltimore, MD: The Johns Hopkins University Press, 1998); and Edward W. Said, *Orientalism* (New York, NY: Vintage, 1979).

37. Eric King Watts and Mark P. Orbe, "The Spectacular Consumption of 'True' African American Culture: 'Whassup' with the Budweiser Guys?," *Critical Studies in Media Communication* 19, no. 1 (2002): 1.

38. Helene A. Shugart, "Sumptuous Texts: Consuming 'Otherness' in the Food Film Genre," *Critical Studies in Media Communication* 25, no. 1 (2008): 73.

39. See Guy Debord, *Society of the Spectacle* (Detroit, MI: Black & Red, 2000).

40. Pollan, *Cooked*; and *The Omnivore's Dilemma: A Natural History of Four Meals* (New York, NY: Penguin, 2007).

41. See Raka Shome and Radha Hegde, "Culture, Communication, and the Challenge of Globalization," *Critical Studies in Media Communication* 19, no. 2 (2002): 172–89.

42. Raka Shome, "Mapping the Limits of Multiculturalism in the Context of Globalization," *International Journal of Communication* 6 (February 2012): 161.

43. Walter Mignolo, "The Many Faces of the Cosmo-polis: Border Thinking and Critical Cosmopolitanism," Carol A. Breckenridge et al., *Cosmopolitanism*, pp. 157–188 (Durham, NC: Duke University Press, 2002).

44. Richard Dyer, *White: Essays on Race and Culture* (New York, NY: Routledge, 1997).

45. bell hooks, *Black Looks: Race and Representation* (Boston, MA: South End Press, 1992), 21-40. For more on the appropriation and consumption of racial identities in popular culture see Stuart Hall, "What Is This 'Black' in Black Popular Culture?," *Popular Culture and Cultural Theory: A Reader*, ed. John Storey, pp. 374-381 (New York: Routledge, 2009).

46. Said, *Orientalism*.

47. See Debbie Lisle, *The Global Politics of Contemporary Travel Writing* (London: Cambridge University Press, 2006); Kristi Siegel, *Issues in Travel Writing: Empire, Spectacle, and Displacement* (New York, NY: Peter Lang, 2002); and David Spurr, *The Rhetoric of Empire: Colonial Discourse in Journalism, Travel Writing, and Imperial Administration* (Durham, NC: Duke University Press, 1993).

48. See Derek T. Buescher and Kent A. Ono, "Civilized Colonialism: Pocahontas as Neocolonial Rhetoric.," *Women's Studies in Communication* 19, no. 2 (1996): 126–53; and Kent A. Ono, *Contemporary Media Culture and the Remnants of a Colonial Past* (New York, NY: Peter Lang, 2009).

49. See Carlnita P. Greene, *Gourmands and Gluttons: The Rhetoric of Food Excess* (New York, NY: Peter Lang, 2015).

50. Casey Ryan Kelly, "Strange/Familiar: Rhetorics of Exoticism in Ethnographic Television," in *Communicating Colonialism: Readings on Postcolonial Theory(s) and Communication*, ed. Rae Lynn Schwartz-DuPre (New York, NY: Peter Lang, 2013). See also Karl G. Heider, *Ethnographic Film: Revised Edition* (Austin, TX: University of Texas Press, 2009); and David MacDougall, *The Corporeal Image: Film, Ethnography, and the Senses* (Princeton, NJ: Princeton University Press, 2006).

51. Kelly, "Strange/Familiar," 196.

52. This phrasing is borrowed from Greg Dickinson, Brian L. Ott, and Eric Aoki, "Spaces of Remembering and Forgetting: The Reverent Eye/I at the Plains Indian Museum," *Communication & Critical/Cultural Studies* 3, no. 1 (2006): 27–47.

53. Stuart Hall, "The Whites of Their Eyes: Racist Ideologies in the Media," *Gender, Race, and Class in the Media: A Text-Reader*, ed. Gail Dines and Jean M. Humez, pp. 89–93 (Thousand Oaks, CA: Sage, 2003), 91.

54. Hall, "Whites," 91.

55. See also Yvonne Tasker, *The Hollywood Action and Adventure Film* (New York: Routledge, 2004); Hernan Vera and Andrew Gordon, *Screen Saviors: Hollywood Fictions of Whiteness* (Lanham, MD: Rowman & Littlefield, 2003).

56. For applications of Hall's approach to inferential racism in film and television see Michael Ryan and Douglas Kellner, *Camera Politica: The Politics and Ideology of Contemporary Hollywood Film* (Bloomington, IN: Indiana University Press, 1988); and Casey Ryan Kelly, "Neocolonialism and the Global Prison in National Geographic's Locked Up Abroad," *Critical Studies in Media Communication* 29, no. 4 (2012): 331–47.

57. See Ono, *Colonial Past*. Michael Ryan and Douglas Kellner call this process "transcoding," where the struggles of broader culture are teased out, managed, and given ideological coherence in fictional mediated texts. See Ryan and Kellner, *Camera Politica*.

58. This definition is borrowed from Buescher and Ono, "Pocahontas."

59. See Aníbal Quijano, "Coloniality and Modernity/Rationality," *Cultural Studies* 21, no. 2–3 (2007): 168–78; and Walter D. Mignolo and Arturo Escobar, *Globalization and the Decolonial Option* (New York, NY: Routledge, 2013).

60. Darrel Allan Wanzer, "Delinking Rhetoric, or Revisiting McGee's Fragmentation Thesis through Decoloniality," *Rhetoric & Public Affairs* 15, no. 4 (2012): 647–57.

61. Raka Shome, "Postcolonial Interventions in the Rhetorical Canon: An 'Other' View," *Communication Theory* 6, no. 1 (1996): 42.

62. A well-articulated literature review in support of this argument is made in Jessamyn Neuhaus, "Colonizing the Coffee Table: 'National Geographic' Magazine and Erasure of Difference in the Representation of Women," *American Periodicals* 7 (1997): 1–26.

63. Ketchum, "Tunnel Vision"; Allen Salkin, *From Scratch: The Uncensored History of the Food Network* (New York, NY: Penguin, 2014).

64. Television is "hegemonic" in the Gramscian sense that it helps cultivate ideological adherence to ruling class notions of "common sense." See Antonio Gramsci, *Selections from the Prison Notebooks of Antonio Gramsci* (New York: International Publishers, 1971). For secondary applications of hegemony to popular culture see Dana L. Cloud, "Hegemony or Concordance? The Rhetoric of Tokenism in 'Oprah' Winfrey's Rags-to-riches Biography," *Critical Studies in Mass Communication* 13, no. 2 (1996): 115–37; and Herman Gray, *Watching Race: Television and the Struggle for Blackness* (Minneapolis, MN: University of Minnesota Press, 2004).

65. Henry A. Giroux, "Cultural Studies, Public Pedagogy, and the Responsibility of Intellectuals," *Communication and Critical/Cultural Studies* 1, no. 1 (March 1, 2004): 59–79.

66. Kristen E. Hoerl, "Criticism of Popular Culture and Social Media," *Rhetorical Criticism: Perspectives in Action, 2nd Edition*, ed. Jim Kuypers, pp. 269–288 (Lanham, MD: Lexington Books, 2016).

67. See Phaedra C. Pezzullo, *Toxic Tourism: Rhetorics of Pollution, Travel, and Environmental Justice* (Tuscaloosa, AL: University of Alabama Press, 2008); and Gregory Clark, *Rhetoric Landscapes in America: Variations on a Theme from Kenneth Burke* (Columbia, SC: Univerity of South Carolina Press, 2004).

ONE

The Neocolonial Plate

Bizarre Foods with Andrew Zimmern

Whiteness, that invisible and unnamed center from which all others are marked with the category of race, can be best characterized as a space of abundance. That is to say that from an unmarked position of whiteness flows the private accumulation of unearned and often unacknowledged privileges. As Peggy McIntosh so aptly observes, white privilege is like an "invisible knapsack of special provisions, maps, passports, codebooks, visas, clothes, tools, and blank checks."[1] Indeed, whiteness can produce a surplus of material and cultural capital, including the ability to navigate the world with ease, discernment, ethos, confidence, and relative comfort without the constraint of skin color.[2] Yet, in a globalized world where transnationalism and multicultural identities are celebrated as the new progressive features of a cosmopolitan marketplace, the invisible center of whiteness can seem like a cultural-less void, a bland dish desperately in need of seasoning.[3] Richard Dyer suggests that this white identity crisis is less attributable to the material demise of white hegemony (whose homogenizing cultural forms he suggests are actually still in ascendance) but instead to the mistaken perception that the imperatives of multiculturalism and globalization have displaced white supremacy. He writes, "postmodern multiculturalism may have genuinely opened up space for the voices of the other, challenging the authority of the white West . . . but it may also simultaneously function as a side-show for white people who look on with delight at all the differences that surround them."[4] In other words, the challenges of multicultural diversity and transnational identity to white hegemony are quite often diffused by commodifying difference into a surplus, or by absorbing racial Others into a system of white abundance. Through appropriation and consumption, bell hooks observes, "ethnicity becomes spice, seasoning that can liven up the dull dish that is mainstream white culture."[5] The threat of Otherness is converted into both desire and opportunity: to assimilate the authentic experience of culture and color into the mundaneness of white identity without fundamentally challenging white Eurocentric privilege[6]; to assuage the collective guilt of our racial history with narratives of progress and transcendence[7]; to govern culture and identity by the logics of a Western capitalist marketplace[8] ; and, above all, to show Others how enlightened white Westerners have become by putting their appreciation and tolerance for foreign cultures on public display.[9]

This chapter takes the metaphor of consumption quite literally by examining the relationship between food, consumption, and *adventure*. Culinary adventurism is, in hook's words, the practice of "eating the Other": vicariously experiencing cultures other than one's own through the consumption of food indigenous to a particular locale or people.[10] While the practice revels in an exhilarating and open-armed celebration of difference, culinary adventurism reveals the ambivalence that is at the heart of contemporary whiteness: an identity that is at once the assumed norm, the generic template for humanity, and yet remains a lack, an absence, a meaningless void. Among many other practices of cultural appropriation, "eating the other" manages this crisis of white ambivalence by giving white Westerners the illusion of experiencing authentic Otherness through a practice that is both intimate and universal. Whites can retain the privilege of being unmarked while experiencing, and ultimately domesticating, the exhilaration of the exotic. Laura Lindenfeld suggests that when the experience is mediated, and therefore vicarious, culinary adventurism allows white Westerners to consume the Other "without ever coming into contact with actual, potentially fear-invoking racialized bodies."[11] Moreover, culinary adventurism offers white audiences a pleasant and celebratory image of the globe, one in which race, geographic location, nationality, class, and gender are no longer barriers to global upward mobility. Instead, exotic cultures and their bizarre edibles seem poised to compete in the global cosmopolitan marketplace forged by the imperatives of neoliberal globalization and sustained by the insatiable demands of a Western consumer economy.[12] But without addressing structural global inequities, Elspeth Probyn adds that it is this "hearty enthusiasm for 'foreign food' that is supposed to hide the taste of racism."[13] Thus, examining culinary adventurism, its representational and rhetorical dynamics, offers a profile of how consumption (a market metaphor, bodily function, and audience viewing practice) helps stabilize whiteness that is at once under siege by multiculturalism but delighted by its potential abundance.

Culinary adventurism has long been a popular ritual among Western tourists, as has been their effort to document, represent, and understand the experience.[14] In the past ten years, there has been an explosion of popular ethnographic and tourist television that explores global culture through the culinary experience.[15] These "sumptuous texts" illustrate a broader latent desire among Westerners to domesticate Otherness through the experience of food.[16] In light of the genre's popularity, this chapter examines how the "exotic" food adventure manages the racial and cultural differences that threaten white supremacy in a globalized, postcolonial world. As an exemplary case study, I examine the Travel Channel's hit program *Bizarre Foods with Andrew Zimmern*, a lighthearted chronicle of a Western culinary explorer sampling foods considered to be "acquired tastes," otherwise exotic, inedible, or disgusting to most mainstream white audiences. First, I argue that host Andrew Zimmern's delighted consumption of mealworms, grubs, spiders, rodents, and other foods considered to be inedible in most parts of the Western world mediates the crisis of white identity by constructing and then assimilating the exotic into the abundance of white privilege. Second, consuming radical Otherness, even if it disgusts, contributes to a narrative of Western exceptionalism in which tolerance and cultural appreciation signal the transcendence of global power inequities and validate the superiority of Western democratic values. Finally, because the Other must be rendered exotic enough to be considered authentically cultural when contrasted with the blank slate of whiteness, *Bizarre Foods* ultimately reinforces the difference between self and Other; an Other permitted to exist according to what suits the Western palate. In accordance with the goal of this volume, I show how the commodification and cultural appropriation of Otherness evinces the durability and resilience of white hegemony and contemporary Orientalism against the globalizing forces of cosmopolitanism that might uproot its dominance.

AN APPETITE FOR DIFFERENCE

Thomas Nakayama and Robert Krizek explain that whiteness is a "strategic rhetoric," a malleable set of discourses, performances, and everyday talk that imply the normalcy and desirability of white identities and experiences.[17] Whiteness is operative, often unconsciously, in discourses that mark Others as different by virtue of their deviation from the implied norm of white skin color, geography, history, cultural practice, and even consumer items. As whiteness exempts white identities from the scrutiny of visibility, it privileges non-racialized bodies with the structural capacity to navigate the world with presumption and superiority. As a strategic rhetoric, whiteness not only operates through the negation of racialized bodies, but also through feel-good tropes of reverence and appreciation for authentic racial difference. Put differently, when the privileged normality of whiteness transforms into an experience that is dull and prosaic, when the world's diversity seems on the precipice of

displacing the invisible center, white culture eradicates the threat
through assimilation and domestication. Bringing racial and cultural difference within the fold enables mainstream white culture to transcend
and disavow its racial ambivalence without seceding its privilege. Eric
King Watts and Michael Orbe suggest that the consumption of racial
difference and cultural authenticity as *sameness* disguises how "blackness
as *otherness* is annexed and appropriated as a commodity and hides from
view the fact that American culture exhibits a profound ambivalence
toward 'authentic' blackness."[18] Paradoxically, consuming the cultural
forms of people of color allays white ambivalence by rendering the experiences and expressions of others to be both universal and distinct. Watts
and Orbe therefore suggest the importance of attending to "how the act
of consumption transforms the relation between the consumer and the
consumed."[19] What pleasures are amplified by the consumption of "authentic difference"? Does incorporating difference into mainstream culture contribute to the long-term durability of whiteness? Indeed, the ability of white culture to simultaneously incorporate racial difference as a
kind of universality and yet still mark Others as distinctive and authentic
speaks to the strategic flexibility of whiteness. Moreover, this movement
also reflects white ambivalence not only about racialized subjects, but
also about the privileges and inadequacies of whiteness itself. Thus, this
chapter considers how mediated consumption of Otherness in popular
culture seeks to replenish whiteness by embracing the discourses and
experiences that might displace white hegemony as the global norm.

Many critical communication scholars suggest that the rhetoric of
Western imperialism and otherwise overt defense of white hegemony
have been eclipsed by the representational celebrations of authentic difference, progressive democratic narratives extolling the emancipatory
forces of neoliberal globalization, declarations of universal human rights,
and appeals to benevolent humanitarianism, only to name a few.[20] These
scholars suggest that whiteness and Western privilege are now most effectively maintained by discourses that accommodate, rather than explicitly prohibit, Otherness. Difference can therefore be rendered useful,
pleasurable, even titillating to white onlookers besieged by a complicated
world of fragmented and hybrid identities. Others can be permitted to
exist by virtue of what they can productively contribute to white Western
experiences.[21] With consumption also comes the power to manage and
regulate what differences are allowed to be a part of the cosmopolitan
marketplace. Wendy Brown suggests that tolerance, a prominent feature
of contemporary neoliberal governance, is "a posture of indulgence toward what one permits or licenses, a posture that softens or cloaks the
power, authority, and normativity in the act of tolerance."[22] Ultimately,
white Western culture will determine which kind of cultural differences
are authentic, meaningful, and tasteful. Meanwhile, the magnanimity
and earnestness with which white culture conducts this exercise disguise

the power and privilege of deciding which cultural differences constitute a world that remains entertaining and safe for white Westerners. For instance, in a program like *Bizarre Foods*, the portly white host invites his Western audience to vicariously taste the bounty of the lesser-developed world and decide what is edible and what is revolting to the Western palate. Here, globetrotting tests the boundaries of Western tolerance by discerning which cultural practices are permissible within the universal experience of food.

Paradoxically, to consume and celebrate difference under the banner of sameness and unity requires that differences be so distinct and authentic that it clearly demarcates self from other. Thus, for the contrast to be stark, the logical limits of consumption extend into the realm of the exotic, a vision of racial Others as mysterious, primitive, bizarre, and romantic. The history of representing the exotic "Orient" in literature, art, anthropology, journalism, travel writing, and later in film and television, satisfies the desire to domesticate and ultimately control Otherness while confirming the superiority of Euro-American modernities. As Said argues, the Orient itself is a construct of Western discourse, invented as a way "dealing with it by making statements about it, authorizing views of it, describing it by teaching it, settling it, ruling over it."[23] The Orient is a geography constructed in discourse alone, a place that is at once barbaric, mysterious, exotic, romantic, primitive, threatening, repulsive, and alluring. While consumption contributes to a narrative of difference as sameness, for whiteness to be replenished the exotic must be continually renewed and held at arm's length. Anthropologist Stephen William Foster explains that "to domesticate it [the exotic] exhaustively would neutralize this aspect of its meaning and regretfully integrate it into the humrum of everyday routines."[24] The primitive, the "exotic," or the experience of non-Western modernity must continually be invented so that it can adequately provide adventure, "spice," and diversity to the white Western world without fundamentally challenging the categories of us/them, modern/primitive, light/dark, first world/third world, and civilized/savage that have historically licensed the West to colonize and dominate the globe. In this way, the televised food adventure can be read as a neocolonial rhetoric, a masked and updated discourse shaped by assumptions and inferences derived from the long history of Western colonialism. Beneath Zimmern's hearty and quite earnest embrace of global food cultures lie a set of colonialist assumptions that the non-Western world is a place of mystery, torn between tradition and modernity, and the starting point for romantic adventures.[25]

The mediated culinary adventure is a useful site at which to examine how whiteness remains durable in a world that increasingly commemorates, if at least nominally, our supposed "post-racial" multicultural moment.[26] Scholars who study the communicative and cultural practices surrounding foodways explain that food is a significant marker of cultural identity and is therefore a conspicuous symbol of global power differentials. Patterns of food consumption often represent vast disparities in income, geography, accessibility, and cultural values. For instance, the United Nations recently advocated the consumption of insects as an alternative sustainable protein source but acknowledged that "consumer disgust" in the West remains the primary impediment to their adoption.[27] In parts of Asia, South America, and Africa insects have long been a significant protein source because they are cheap and widely accessible. The Western palate remains a significant force in not merely determining global food trends, but as a marker for what cultural practices are allowed to participate in the spirit of multiculturalism. Moreover, discourses about global food cultures and consumption patterns access the tensions between universality (i.e., the *sameness* of food needs) and difference (i.e., the *otherness* of exotic foods). An increasing number of scholars explain that the intimacy of food makes consumption practices an important site that marks the separation between Western self and exotic Other. In his study of Western attitudes toward the notorious durian fruit, Alan Han argues that, "food consumption works to construct a distinction between race-abject-Other-bodies, and clean white eaters"[28] Scholars such as Michael Dietler, Lisa Heldke and Laura Lindenfield explain that food is the primary means by which Westerners begin to exoticize and essentialize the differences between themselves and others.[29] Shugart adds that representations of culinary adventurism are at root "templates for the desire and consumption of otherness more broadly, including as market practices, establishing the terms for them in such a way as to restabilize privilege against the threat that they pose."[30] I add that representations of food and global culinary experience serve as one of several primary vehicles by which white Westerners are invited to embrace their position of superiority in a globalized world. That is to say, the televised food adventure positions that Western audience to see a globalized, cosmopolitan world as an emporium of exotic delights, exhilarating experiences, colorful people, romantic traditions, and pastoral landscapes seemingly untouched by Western modernity. Instead of seeing a world plagued by famine and poverty, white Western audiences are invited to see the world as a source of titillating food trends that spice up the drab dish that is mainstream culture. They are given the power to symbolically carve up the world according to taste, choosing which culture and their edibles to integrate and which to keep at arm's length. Food consumption and the consumption of food television mediate, manage, and reproduce difference in a controllable form. Here, the consumption of Otherness establishes a multicultural world that helps stabilize, sanitize, and replenish the privilege of whiteness.

Thus, the growing popularity of exotic culinary adventurism and foreign food television in the United States reflects the emerging multicultural and cosmopolitan ethos of contemporary neoliberal globalization.[31] Where corporate globalization seeks to open new markets, globally source inexpensive labor, and internationalize global capital flows, its leads the way in extolling the virtues of multiculturalism; a diverse world community united by what is presented as a common economic imperative.[32] The construction of a delightful world of digestible cultural experiences renders the practice of consumption a progressive endorsement of multiculturalism. Scholars such as Henry Giroux, Bradley Jones, Roopali Mukharejee, Raka Shome, Radha Hedge, and Darrel Enck-Wanzer among others suggest that this discourse of "neoliberal multiculturalism" presents a world in which race and culture are valuable commodities in a cosmopolitan marketplace, as opposed to a time when they were substantive barriers to social and economic justice.[33] Thus, in the discourse of neoliberal multiculturalism, Western consumerism positively monetizes the Western experience of the global South while elevating the act of consumption to racial transcendence. The problem with this rhetoric goes beyond its unproblematic faith in market capitalism as the solution to many of the long-standing global inequalities it, in part, helped to create. The larger failure is that this rhetoric is entirely ahistorical, silent on the legacies of Western colonialism and exploitation that continue to structure the relationship between "first" and "third" world. As Shome and Hegde elaborate,

> The liberal approach to multiculturalism is couched in a sanitized version of difference where the unspoken centers of power, and the normativity of whiteness, remain unquestioned. This cosmetic approach to multiculturalism does not question the systemic structures of power nor does it touch the contradictions and tensions written into the realities of everyday life. This is the colonial legacy that postcolonial criticism marks, unpacks, and questions.[34]

When adventurous consumption, cultural appropriation, and fascination with the exotic are situated within ongoing histories of colonialism, the discourses of neoliberal multiculturalism show themselves to be driven by the same set of assumptions and imperatives: to absorb the threat and allure of difference. Therefore, Lindenfield argues that the consumption of Otherness—as both a bodily process and experience of mediated voyeurism—must be "considered within the framework of racist, sexist, and, neocolonialist society."[35] As such, the remainder of this chapter explores the dynamics of whiteness, consumption, and neoliberal multiculturalism in *Bizarre Foods* to show how the seemingly innocuous televised food adventures contribute to a much larger process of stabilizing a world order that is sanitized for racism and colonialism, exciting but ultimately secure for white privilege.

THEY ARE WHAT *YOU* EAT

Bizarre Foods with Andrew Zimmern is a serial one-hour travel documentary in which former chef and dining critic Andrew Zimmern seeks out, samples, and explains the production processes of regional cuisines around the globe that might be considered strange or disgusting to many Americans. The program is shot on location, narrated by Zimmern, and focuses on a specific region of the globe in each episode. The producers of the program put Zimmern in contact with local guides, restaurateurs, chefs, food manufacturers, and translators to help him find foods that according to the show "stray far from the normal culinary path." Episodes typically feature visits to local food markets and street vendors, a home-cooked meal with a local family, and a wilderness or ocean hunt for delicacies that are more difficult to find in urban markets. Each show provides an interactive map that charts Zimmern's travels over a multiday journey and on-screen texts appear throughout the episode to provide background information such as country demographics, explanations of cultural rituals witnessed on camera, and facts about the production of a specific food items. After originally airing as a highly rated stand-alone one-hour documentary titled *Bizarre Foods of Asia*, the Travel Channel began production of the first season in 2006. Since 2007, *Bizarre Foods* has aired six seasons that includes seventy-six episodes. The program's success has resulted in several spin-off programs hosted by Zimmern, including *Bizarre World*, *Bizarre Foods America*, and *Border Check*. *Bizarre Foods* is one of the most popular programs on the Travel Channel. Along with *No Reservations* and *Man v. Food*, *Bizarre Foods* is credited by Channel spokespersons with boosting the networks ratings by 35 percent in their first two years (up 46 percent with its 18–49 audience).[36]

Since making the leap from chef and dining columnist to television, Zimmern has become an evangelist and unofficial US ambassador for "exotic" global cuisine.[37] In 2010, Zimmern was awarded the James Beard Foundations Award for Outstanding TV Food Personality.[38] He is now a popular columnist, blogger, celebrity endorser, talk show guest, and go-to expert on adventurous food. As an international brand, Zimmern now promotes everything from Eyebob Eyewear to Pepto-Bismol.[39] With slogans like "if it looks good eat it!" and "experiencing food, sharing culture," Zimmern's intrepid persona fits perfectly within the cosmopolitan brand identity cultivated by the Travel Channel.[40] Indeed, *Bizarre Foods* benefits from not only a growing interest in culinary tourism and food programing, but also the growing media brand of Scripps networks. *Bizarre Foods* is embedded in a lineup of similar adventure-style programming targeted at relatively affluent American consumers interested in domestic and international travel, human interest, food, geography, and foreign culture. In short, the Travel Channel and *Bizarre Foods* are marketed to a highly educated, progressive, and cosmopolitan consumer.

The Travel Channel boasts that their brand "is a place for consumers to experience great storytelling, shared human connections, and engaging talent that celebrate the surprising encounters that happen right here and right now. The Travel Channel personality is authentic, inquisitive, surprising and fun. It's open-eyed and open-minded, living in the moment, and finding surprises where others might not see them."[41] *Bizarre Foods*, its audience, and the paratexts that surround it make it an exemplary program with which to explore the relationship between culinary adventurism and the mediation of whiteness. In this analysis, I examine the first season of *Bizarre Foods*, which includes 12 episodes and the one-hour documentary pilot titled *Bizarre Foods of Asia*. The first season offers a template of the program's generic features that are replicated throughout the later seasons, including plot, style, framing choices, production values, and dialogue. I examine the recurring patterns throughout the season, each episode a fragment contributing to a larger narrative about food and culture. I analyze the ways in which Zimmern contextualizes and translates his experiences to the audience, attending to narration as well as dialogue deployed by Zimmern as a sense making device. Piecing together these fragments evinces a kind of patterned response in Western culture to the challenges of confronting difference, showing how the program implicitly accesses much larger discourses of neoliberal multiculturalism, whiteness, and neocolonialism.

The Abject/Exotic

To authenticate a world of excitement and cultural diversity beyond the invisible center, *Bizarre Foods* seeks out cuisine and experiences that are perhaps the most incommensurate with Western norms of cleanliness and appropriateness. As Zimmern quips, "there's nothing like gnawing on a turtle leg to immerse yourself in another's culture."[42] The program gauges the authenticity of the Other by how much their cultural rituals and foodways test the limits of the white West's most sacrosanct food taboos. While the program tries to maintain a stance of objectivity and reserve judgment, the audience is positioned as the assumed norm from which all-else deviates. Regardless of Zimmern's enjoyment or displeasure, the invisible audience, or what one might call the vicarious voyeur, is the implied auditor of the pleasure and authenticity of the experience. The program is less interested in the everyday and the routine then it is the extremes of another's food culture. After all terms like "bizarre" and "strange" only acquire meaning when they are contrasted against a state of normalcy, natural order, or a set of acceptable behaviors. By seeking out the most extreme forms of deviance from the experience of the audience (and in many cases the region itself), the program engages the Other at the moment in which they might seem the most repellent, primitive, and backwards.

The program finds a kind of radical Otherness that can be vicariously consumed without being fully incorporated. To remain exotic, a foreign culture must be continually tethered to a feeling of strangeness and disease that cannot be assimilated into the norm. *Bizarre Foods* continually renews this sense of exoticism by aligning authentic difference with disgust. To use a metaphor of consumption, the program constructs a kind of difference that can be consumed with nose held, but will eventually be expelled. In fact, *Bizarre Foods* revels in disgust. The menu includes but is not limited to pig testicles, chicken uterus, frog heart, lizard sake, poisonous blowfish, turtle, bird's nests, unfertilized duck eggs, putrid lamb meat, coconut grubs, mosquito eggs, ant larva, organ meat, intestines, stomach, blood, and bile. By "bizarre," it is clear that the program means foods that will likely provoke revulsion in a mainstream Western audience. In this regard, the program finds foods that are threatening, dangerous, polluting, taboo, and above all, abject. Abjection is a state of filth, degradation, and monstrosity, a hidden or taboo element that has been cast off from the self.[43] Julia Kristeva explains that the abject is the "immoral, sinister, scheming, and shady: a terror that dissembles, a hatred that smiles, a passion that uses the body for barter instead of inflaming it, a debtor who sells you up, a friend who stabs you."[44] Food revulsion sets aside or expels unclean and improper elements from the self, forming the subject "I" that separates it from "other." As Kristeva writes, "food loathing is perhaps the most elementary and most archaic form of abjection" (p. 2). In *Bizarre Foods*, the abject serves as a form of demarcation between the Western audience and its unclean Other. As fascinating as their culture may be, the authentic Other is rendered disgusting; lacking refinement, manners, and above all taste. The consumption of exotic culture flirts with but ultimately demands that the Other be cast off as a reaffirmation of the Western self. Moreover by conflating authentic culture with disgust, the program confirms the controlled and civilized nature of Western eating practices while relegating the filth and monstrosity of more primitive consumption cast off by the West when it embraced modernity.

Throughout the program, disgust and exoticism transform the cultures and places depicted in each episode into a spectacle of primitive eating. This process is enhanced by a number of common tropes featured in each episode. First, the program constructs non-Western cultures as being closer to their food sources and, therefore, more connected to primitive traditions, ancient rituals, and the premodern past. For instance, when viewing bugs and live fish at a Tokyo market, Zimmern generalizes that "Asians are very close to their food source."[45] In the Philippines he explains how the open-air market is a sign of culinary "pride . . . without any modern trappings."[46] Delighted by a traditional meal of coconut grubs and cow's stomach soup he remarks "for me making traditional dishes . . . brings us closer to our past and reconnects us to our food source."[47] While greater awareness of where our food comes from seems to be a valuable insight, it is framed as a practice associated with a premodern way of life, a deviation from a fast-paced civilized existence. Additionally, people in South America, Africa, and Asia are depicted as more in tune with nature and, therefore, more willing to accept food that is considered unclean in most parts of the United States. For instance, in Ecuador he remarks, "like most cultures around the world, Ecuadorians eat all parts of the animal."[48] If this is indeed the case, then why is Ecuadorian cuisine considered bizarre at all? If anything, the repetition of experiences involving the "whole animal" throughout the series should lead one to conclude that Western nations are perhaps wasteful and deviant in contrast to global food culture. Yet, for *Bizarre Foods*, being close to one's food source and using the whole animal are romanticized as being part of an idyllic past; a history the Euro-American world discarded in the process of building an industrialized civilization. Its deviance from modernity, not from the accepted foodways of most of the world, is what makes head-to-tail cuisine "bizarre." As Zimmern quite frequently laments, modern conveniences are "slowly replacing traditional ways."[49] It is this perception of Western temporality that explains why he instinctively knows "with a larger indigenous population it's also home of some of the most bizarre foods."[50] What the show ultimately marks is the difference between clean, modern cuisine and primitive rituals of eating that involve knowledge and respect for the food source.

Second, the program suggests that there are some foods that Westerners are literally unable to consume. This contention not only saves Zimmern from eating exceptionally bizarre foods but, more importantly, confirms the incommensurability of Western and non-Western cuisine. Even the most seasoned and intrepid adventurer will have their limits tested, and ultimately reestablished. When transitioning from commercial, Zimmern often provides a teaser in which he suggests that he is going to find "the most bizarre foods we can stomach."[51] While showing respect for the practice, Zimmern explains that saving all parts of the animal "goes a bit too far for me."[52] He even turns down sausage at an open market because there is "too much funky stuff in there for my Western system."[53] After he attempts to consume fermented tofu in Taiwan he concedes that "its just too putrid and foul for me."[54] In another episode, when confronted with the pungent durian fruit in Thailand, Zimmern gags while proclaiming that "it tastes like completely rotten mushy onions."[55] At the end of the episode, Zimmern jests that, "all I feel like right now is just a cheese burger."[56] Viewing Zimmern's limits helps allay any audience's fears that their own tastes may be too pedestrian and mundane for a cosmopolitan society. At the same time, it also confirms that some food cultures are simply beyond the pale. In other words, even an open-armed embrace of the Other has limitations and some differences are insurmountable. Even though Zimmern and his audience may celebrate the difference that he encounters, they can remain certain that there are indeed significant differences that demarcate the first and third world. The fantasy of the cheeseburger at home provides a remedy for the spectacle of primitive eating and confirms the safety and comfort of modern amenities not available to most of the world. Representations of abject/exotic cuisine help mark the separation between modern/ primitive, civilized/savage, and clean/unclean.

Imperialist Nostalgia

Renato Rosaldo argues that one of the many ironies of imperialism is that it produced in Western nations an antithetical yet romantic longing for the things and people it destroyed.[57] "Imperialist nostalgia" was a way by which Westerners could absolve their feelings of guilt associated with conquest and transform from "responsible colonial agent into an innocent bystander."[58] Nostalgia of this kind is operative in discourses that romanticize the beauty and simplicity of the precolonial world and lament the seemingly inevitable yet tragic onslaught of Western modernity.[59] It is also a discourse that implicitly excludes the survivors of colonialism from modernity. Whereas Western civilization evolves as it marches forward, the authentic cultural traditions of non-Western societies are seen as ancient, unchanging, and part to a distant and irretrievable past.

Bizarre Foods is symptomatic of a long history of imperialist ambivalence toward the cultures it eradicated. To make Zimmern's encounter with traditional foods more meaningful, the program embraces a sentimental posture toward cultural practices that are in jeopardy of extinction. Whereas Western civilization is dynamic and universalizing, non-Western culture clings to tradition, moves slowly, and resists change. This posture is expressed in program through voice over narration in which Zimmern attempts to summarize (often overgeneralizing) the culture and history of the country or region he has explored. For instance, in Thailand Zimmern describes "mystical Chang Mai" as a place with "enthralling scenery, ancient temples, [and] elephant rides."[60] He explains that here one would find "a simpler way of life" and feel as if they were "going back in time," an experience "exotic to most Westerners."[61] In the Philippines, he expresses admiration for the "quaint" villages that populate the countryside, remarking that the country's lack of paved roads made it a kind of "prehistoric setting from a dinosaur movie."[62] Similarly, while surrounded by snake charmers and carnival performers in an open-air market, Zimmern notes that Morocco is a nation that "embraces its Berber history" and is "mysterious and exotic."[63] Despite all the pressures of modernity, "the lifestyle here [Morroco] has remained unchanged for a thousand years."[64] In the context of the bizarre, Zimmern's contextualizing explanations position these regions outside of modernity.

They provide a present-day referent for a simple and bucolic world that existed before the imposition of Western colonialism.

Though his tone is reverent, Zimmern's narration implicitly consigns non-Western traditions to the ancient past. For these regions to be considered "modern" would require them to update or abandon their "primitive traditions" altogether. This is evident in Zimmern's description of non-Western societies as trapped between two worlds. He frequently refers to foreign places as lands of "contrast," suggesting that non-Western nations have yet to reconcile their primitive traditions with modern living. For example, he contends that the Japanese "revere tradition but worship trend setting."[65] He also describes Quito as "a tale of two cities: old town and new town" a city with a "more modern way of life" that "still celebrates food culture despite its surroundings."[66] In a romantic tone, he explains that Ecuador's proximity to the Amazon Rainforest provides an opportunity for Westerns to still "experience that way of life."[67] Moreover, the persistence of traditionalism amidst modern amenities implies the ongoing presence of pre-modern beliefs in magic and mysticism. In Taiwan he notes that, "many Taiwanese feel a spiritual connection to the land."[68] As the camera depicts a bustling financial district contrasted with a background of tropical mountains bathed in fog, Zimmern says, "contrast that vibe with the symbols of modern Asia."[69] He marvels at their engineering and financial feats while expressing amazement that the Taiwanese have "a keen sense of upholding tradition" and that "the Taiwanese food scene looks forward and backwards."[70] As he meanders through markets of medicinal foods, he surmises that Taiwan is a "magical blend of ancient and modern."[71] Similarly, in Vietnam the show depicts a man who believes that the consumption of cobra hearts and blood has "magical" healing properties.[72] Overall, the East is represented by stereotypes of mysticism, torn between its primitive medicinal culture and its modern acumen for engineering and finance. Throughout each episode, Zimmern locates the bizarre in the ancient and mysterious traditions "handed down from generation to generation."[73] Indeed, there seems to be nothing magical or mystical about modern mass-produced cuisine or foreign foods already appropriated by Western nations. In sum, when the show is in Asia, Africa, or South America, it only considers cuisines that can be linked to the region's ancient past or reflects a struggle between primitive and modern eating. The show romanticizes primitive eating and laments the modern industrial society that destroyed it.

Yet, the program is relatively silent about the consequences of historic colonialism on each region's culture and cuisine. If colonialism is referenced, it is always as something that adds "spice" to the local cuisine and explains the beauty and diversity of the region's people. In Trinidad and Tobago, Zimmern explains that the beauty of the buildings harkens "back to the colonial occupation."[74] This "picturesque place" shows the

audience how European colonials "all left their mark on the island."[75]
Today, the audience is told the country is "melting pot of cultures . . .
celebrating our common cultural love for great food."[76] In the Philippines, he praises the nation's cultural hybridity for enhancing the local
cuisine. From the "remnants of the Spanish occupation" the audience is
offered a "spicy Chex mix" or figurative "melting pot."[77] As these examples illustrate, colonial histories are only referenced as advantageous for
each region and the tourists who take in its natural beauty. Though the
show cannot give an exhaustive history of each region it visits, glib references to colonialism and culture hybridity as alluring features for the
adventurous eater elide the pain and suffering inflicted by colonization.
Zimmern becomes a passive bystander who remains unconnected to the
colonial legacies he casually references. His romantic posture keeps the
darker histories of colonialism out of the picture, leaving the audience
with images of happy natives serving tourists unaffected by histories of
imperialism.

The Modern Bizarre and the Primitive Within

Bizarre Foods features several episodes in the United States and Europe. This includes an episode in Spain, the United Kingdom, Alaska, the
US Gulf Coast, and New York City. These episodes vacillate between
exoticizing the poor, marginalized, and otherwise unincorporated populations within modern nations and announcing the triumphant and quite
scientific mastery of the bizarre by elite Euro-American restaurateurs. For
the former, the program seeks out cuisines of necessity, born of poverty
and oppression. Throughout his tour of the Gulf Coast—which includes
some of the poorest rural regions in the United States—Zimmern focuses
on "soul food," a food tradition that traces its roots to American slavery.[78] "Soul food" refers to cuisine made up of the "lesser cuts" of meat
and produce deemed inedible by whites and thus left to the slave class.
Historically, cooking soul food is about making do with the scraps of the
slaveholder and white bourgeois society. Zimmern's tour of the
American South involves samplings of chitterlings (pig intestine), nutria,
squirrel, alligator, and other foods historically considered inedible by the
white Southern elite. Though soul food has a more mainstream presence
in the United States today, it is "bizarre" because it represents the experience of those excluded from modern America: African Americans, the
poor, and the dispossessed. Like the exotic abroad, the bizarre within are
closer to their food source, cling to tradition, and defy assimilation into
mainstream culture. Zimmern describes the rural South as a place with
"mystical bayous" and where "the people are spicy, earthy, and full of
character."[79]

In Alaska, Zimmern spends a majority of his time exploring the cuisine of Alaskan Native and Aleutian nations. Here he also finds a land of

"mystery" populated by food traditions based in basic survival. In this episode, Zimmern samples several varieties of seal, whale (and whale fat), preserved white fish, moose, and other wild game. He describes Alaska as a "final frontier, raw, rugged," where the people "retained customs" by "living off the land."[80] As a result, it is "a land that is as wild as the food provides."[81] In this episode, Alaska's exoticism is derived from the fact that it has not been fully conquered and subdued by its inhabitants. Its Native residents "make do" to survive the harsh landscape. What makes Alaska bizarre is its likeness to the regions of South America, Africa, and Asia in the episodes discussed earlier in this analysis. Alaskans remain tied to a primitive past, rich in tradition, and unable to be fully assimilated by Western modernity. By exoticizing the cuisine and culture of the poor, the marginalized, and the unassimilated, *Bizarre Foods* invites the audience to view the program's subjects from a position of privilege and abundance. In other words, what makes soul food "bizarre" is that it repurposes the scraps of elite white cuisine; yet, it offers a new realm of cuisine once discarded by mainstream culture. It could only be considered deviant or exotic from the position of someone who has not been forced to consider eating the lesser cuts. Thus, the primitive within is the subject marked by food habits of those without racial and economic privilege. At the same time, white culture would like a second chance to sample the cuisine it discarded.

By contrast, Europe is valorized for both its technical mastery of the bizarre and its ability to update their traditions to modern times. In Spain, Zimmern is treated to five star meal at a restaurant (El Bulli) renowned for molecular gastronomy, a modern cooking technique that creates flavor profiles, textures, and appearance of ingredients by manipulating their physical and chemical properties.[82] Zimmern describes the restaurant as a "flavor laboratory" led by the "father of molecular gastronomy." His experience was "scientific" and "beyond comprehension."[83] Spain's food culture is praised for harnessing Western scientific know-how to master the bizarre, to control and manipulate ingredients to produce any flavor or texture the chef desires. El Bulli is portrayed as an industrial machine, staffed by food engineers and technicians testing, observing, manipulating, and torturing each morsel until it produces the exact taste they desire. In modern Spain, bizarre is an intentional result of academic discipline, advanced knowledge of chemistry and physics, and complete mastery of the craft of cooking. In the show's depiction of Europe, the bizarre symbolizes the triumph of modernity and its ability to enliven the mundane experience of eating. A key distinction is how European chefs see the role of tradition. Whereas in places like Morocco, Ecuador, and the Philippines traditions tether people to their primitive pasts, in Spain, Zimmern explains, they "understand the values of tradition but embrace the unique and the bizarre."[84] For Europeans, to be bizarre is a choice and privilege, not an innate characteristic that defines their history and identity.

In the United Kingdom, however, *Bizarre Foods* suggests that the triumph is in the country's ability to bring back spice and exoticism to what was notoriously bland cuisine. Zimmern suggests that British food has experienced a renaissance that makes it both familiar and intriguing. He proclaims that the United Kingdom is "back on top of the food chain," primarily because a "populist food movement" is reviving traditions that give British food character.[85] The bizarre aspects of new British cuisine are presented as familiar, comforting, and non-threatening. For instance, Zimmern remarks that, "even if you've never been to the UK before, the moment you arrive it feels familiar."[86] After a five star meal, consisting of wild hare and poultry, he explains "if game birds were cooked like this in other countries, more people would eat them."[87] This comment suggests that what seems to be remarkable about new British cuisine is its ability to make bizarre foods palatable to Westerners. He describes this upscale eatery as a "food palace" the "Mt. Olympus of food" yet steeped in "heritage" and "tradition."[88] Indeed, the Europeans have not only mastered and tamed the bizarre, but they have fashioned their traditions to make the bizarre both familiar and exciting. As Zimmern concludes, "It's the Brits that are finally having the last laugh."[89]

Eating as Tolerance

In the recurring introduction to *Bizarre Foods*, Zimmern stands in the center of a circular conveyor belt, stocked with bowls, plates, and containers of what appear to be different cuisine. Zimmern rubs his hands together with a look of excitement and randomly opens different dishes as they pass him. To his delight, he finds and shows off to the audience a large insect, a plate of brains, and other animated and exotic ingredients. A whimsical jingle plays with the repetitive lyrics "bizarre . . . its so bizarre." Zimmern stands over a world of abundance. The world is an emporium of exotic edibles and fascinating cultures that all promise to spice up the life of the global consumer. Zimmern—white, portly, lighthearted—symbolizes the Western consumers' appetite for dishes and experiences that confirm their status as progressive, tolerant, cosmopolitan individuals. Through vicarious consumption the audience is invited to view global food consumption as a kind of test, a conspicuous sign of their own embrace of neoliberal multiculturalism. Western audiences get to vicariously consume the Other without the risk of encountering threatening racialized bodies. What the audience consumes directly is tolerance for the Other; a feeling that they have assimilated them into their own experience and in doing so display the progressivism of the new Western self.

In *Bizarre Foods*, consumption is the test of tolerance. In other words, Zimmern's ability to consume exotic ingredients is a testament to his good nature, his respect for other cultures, and his liberal sensibilities. For the audience, their ability to bear with him throughout his journey validates their status as cosmopolitan citizens, without all the risks. In many episodes, he reminds the audience "if you really want to under-stand the culture of a country, you try everything, you eat everything."[90] In many ways, he sells the entire experience as an adventure, that which at times may test your limits but will ultimately make you stronger and more interesting. In *Bizarre Foods of Asia*, he even suggests that culinary adventurism is "a real life Indiana Jones adventure for those of us from the other side of the world."[91] The culinary adventure is the ultimate test of one's own personal tolerance. While facing down a plate of organ meat in Morocco, Zimmern asserts, "if you consider eating a full contact sport, this is the stuff that makes a champion seasoned."[92] Often, he goads his audience by saying things like "this is not wimp food," this is "not for the tame-minded eater," and "to some people this kind of stuff is scary, to me, it's just good."[93] He testifies to his own endurance by eating with courage and encouraging the audience to face their food taboos directly. The show suggests that one's willingness to accept the bizarre is a marker of their enlightenment. Moreover, the white Western experience is en-hanced more by assimilating difference rather than excluding it. The show fortifies the Western self by testing the limits of their tolerance, and showing them all the options of a life of privilege and abundance.

In the last episode of the season, Zimmern returns to his hometown of New York City. This episode marks a homecoming to "the world's great-est food town" where bizarre foods are "all just comfort food."[94] New York is portrayed as a "melting pot of lifestyles and cultures" with neigh-borhoods that are "hip, bohemian, [and] gritty."[95] Zimmern visits iconic sites such as the Carnegie Deli and unique pubs in Brooklyn where you can grill your own dinner. The foods he consumes in this episode are less abject than they are the greatest hits of Zimmern's hometown favorites. After eleven episodes of consuming food that many Westerners would consider repulsive, the familiarity of New York provides an interesting point of contrast. New York is represented as a cosmopolitan city that encompasses the entirety of global cuisine, including the bizarre. The city symbolizes the overwhelming advantages of assimilating difference, the limitless choice and experiences that it offers to an audience with means and privilege. New York City also symbolizes that tolerance for differ-ence is what makes Western societies exceptional. In New York, Zim-mern contends that he feels "recharged" and "energized" by his return home.[96] Zimmern's return is also a reminder that it is possible to experi-ence and display one's acceptance of the Other without giving up their privilege or creature comforts.

A NEW PALATE

The Food and Agriculture Organization reports that 925 million people do not have enough food to eat, which is "more than the combined populations of the USA, Canada and the European Union."[97] This is hardly the whimsical and romantic world that we vicariously experience through Zimmern's travels. Many of the world's bizarre foods are born of necessity and are consumed for their life-saving calories not their taste. Yet, *Bizarre Foods* invites its audience to see the world as full of abundance, rich in exotic edibles and people happy to share their culture with Western culinary adventurers. This chapter is less concerned with the capacity of *Bizarre Foods* to accurately represent the challenges of global food consumption than it is the tropes it employs to cultivate care and interest in the world. The globe as an exotic playground that tests the will and endurance of the Western individual is, in fact, a discourse with a long history. The concept of adventure requires a proving grounds, a terrain that can test the constitution of the rugged Western individual, a frontier that can be conquered. Though guided by a magnanimous spirit, culinary adventurism is an updated and refashioned justification for consuming and controlling the globe. Of course, *Bizarre Foods* is unlikely to be cited as a justification for economic or military conquest by this or any future governmental administration. The central concern of this essay is how representations of culinary adventures are embedded in a series of larger discursive practices that prevent neoliberal multiculturalism from becoming global economic equilibrium. The adventure belies the substantive task of eradicating structural economic inequalities that allow nearly a billion people to go to bed hungry every night. Given that global hunger is a clear divide between North and South, the cultural differences of the world are not yet assets that can be sold for gain in a global cosmopolitan marketplace.

Bizarre Foods and the culinary adventure certainly construct a new frontier; however, it is a boundary that exists within the Western mind. How much difference can the white Westerner endure? How far are they willing to go to prove they are as tolerant and progressive as they claim to be? What kind of adventures can adequately season their experience? This chapter suggests that *Bizarre Foods* illustrates the ambivalence of white society, both toward itself and Others. The program illuminates how whiteness cultivates a desire to consume racialized Others as both a form of domestication and self-affirmation. The requirement that difference always be authentic and communicate stark contrasts between self and Other mandates that foreign cultures be continually exoticized until they reach the point of incommensurability. The vicarious consumption of difference then enables Westerners to incorporate cultural diversity into their experience without sacrificing their accumulated privileges. This chapter suggests that the world can be engaged without words like "mystical," "exotic," and "bizarre." The non-Western world need not be a resource for white Westerners to work out their anxieties about themselves and the perceived decline of their own cultural forms. Instead of being continually replenished, whiteness and white privilege need to be exposed, deterritorialized, and injected with self-reflexivity. White hegemony has proven to be a durable and quite flexible system, resistant and adaptive to the challenges of globalization and multiculturalism. Travel television, food culture, and entertainment are all popular venues in which white hegemony continually replicates itself as the taken-for-granted norm, the invisible center of the universe. Perhaps, popular programming about global food and culture can find a way to move forward in acknowledging one another, rather than just looking at ourselves.

NOTES

1. Peggy McIntosh, "White Privilege: Unpacking the Invisible Knapsack" in Paula S. Rothenberg, *White Privilege: Essential Readings on the Other Side of Racism* (New York: Worth Publishers, 2005), 109.

2. See also George Lipsitz, *The Possessive Investment in Whiteness: How White People Profit from Identity Politics* (Philadelphia: Temple University Press, 1998); and Thomas K. Nakayama and Robert L. Krizek, "Whiteness: A Strategic Rhetoric," *Quarterly Journal of Speech* 81 (1995): 771–807.

3. See Ruth Frankenberg, *White Women, Race Matters: The Social Construction of Whiteness* (Minneapolis, MN: University of Minnesota Press, 1993).

4. Richard Dyer, *White* (London and New York: Routledge, 1997), 3–4.

5. bell hooks, *Black Looks: Race and Representation* (Boston, MA: South End Press, 1992), 21.

6. For instance, see Rachel E. Dubrofsky, "*The Bachelor*: Whiteness in the Harem," *Critical Studies in Media Communication* 23, no. 1 (2006): 39–56.

7. See Kent A. Ono, *Contemporary Media Culture and the Remnants of a Colonial Past* (New York: Peter Lang, 2009).

8. See Amy A. Hasinoff, "Fashioning Race for the Free Market in *America's Next Top Model*," *Critical Studies in Media Communication* 25, no. 3 (2008): 324–343; Eric K. Watts and Michael Orbe, "The Spectacular Consumption of 'True' African American Culture: 'Whassup' with the Budweiser Guys?," *Critical Studies in Media Communication* 19, no. 1 (2002): 1–20; and David C. Oh and Omotayo O. Banjo, "Outsourcing Postracialism: Voicing Neoliberal Multiculturalism in *Outsourced*," *Communication Theory* 22, no. 4 (2012): 449–470.

9. See Casey Ryan Kelly, "Strange/Familiar: Rhetorics of Exoticism in Ethnographic Television," in *Communicating Colonialism: Readings on Postcolonial Theory and Communication*, ed. Rae Lynn Schwartz (New York: Peter Lang, 2013).

10. hooks, *Black Looks*, 21.

11. Laura Lindenfeld, "Visiting the Mexican American Family: *Tortilla Soup* as Culinary Tourism," *Communication and Critical/Cultural Studies* 4, no. 4 (2007): 303–320.

12. See Henry Giroux, "Beyond the Biopolitics of Disposability: Rethinking Neoliberalism in the New Gilded Age," *Social Identities* 14, no. 5 (2008): 587–620.

13. Elspeth Probyn, *Carnal Appetites: Foodsexidentities* (New York: Routledge, 2002), 2.

14. For more on the history of Western travel writing and its relationship with colonialism see Mary B. Campbell, *The Witness and the Other World: Exotic European Travel Writing, 400-600* (Ithaca, NY: Cornell University Press, 1991); Mary Louis Pratt, *Imperial Eyes: Travel Writing and Transculturation* (New York and London: Routledge,

2007); and David Spurr, *The Rhetoric of Empire: Colonial Discourse in Journalism, Travel Writing, and Imperial Administration* (Durham, NC: Duke University Press, 1993).

15. Breeanna Hare, "Obsessions: Getting Our Fill of Food TV," *CNN*, May 6, 2011, http://www.cnn.com/2011/SHOWBIZ/TV/05/06/food.television.shows/index.html (accessed May 30, 2013).

16. Helene A. Shugart, "Sumptuous Texts: Consuming 'Otherness' in the Food Film Genre," *Critical Studies in Media Communication* 25, no. 1 (2008): 68–90.

17. Nakayama and Krizek, "Whiteness," 771.

18. Watts and Orbe, "Spectacular," 3.

19. Watts and Orbe, "Spectacular," 3.

20. For a partial list of works not cited a various points throughout this essay see Dana Cloud, "'To Veil the Threat of Terror': Afghan Women and the 'Clash of Civilizations in the Imagery of the US War on Terrorism," *Quarterly Journal of Speech* 90, no. 3 (2005): 285–306; Radha Hegde, "Disciplining Spaces and Globalization: A Postcolonial Unsettling," *Global Media and Communication* 1, no. 1 (2005): 59–62; Raka Shome, "Mapping the Limits of Multiculturalism in the Context of Globalization," *International Journal of Communication* 6 (2012): 144–165; and Raka Shome, "Postcolonial Interventions in the Rhetorical Canon: An 'Other' View," *Communication Theory*, 6, no. 1 (1996): 40–59.

21. Marianna Torgovnick makes a similar argument about the pleasure of the "primitive" in Western mythology of the Other. In art, literature, anthropology, film, and consumerism, so-called primitive peoples and objects are animated not only to draw power lines between the Western and non-Western world, but to gratify the Western "us" in seeing what is thought to be the ancient roots of "ourselves." See Marianna Torgovnick, *Gone Primitive: Savage Intellects, Modern Lives* (Chicago: University of Chicago Press, 1990).

22. Wendy Brown, *Regulating Aversions: Tolerance in an Age of Identity and Empire* (Princeton, NJ: Princeton University Press, 2006), 26.

23. Edward Said, *Orientalism* (New York: Vintage Books, 1979), 3.

24. Stephen William Foster, "The Exotic as a Symbol System," *Dialectical Anthropology* 7, no. 1 (1982): 22.

25. For work on neocolonial rhetoric see Derek Buescher and Kent A. Ono, "Civilized Colonialism: Pocahontas as Neocolonial Rhetoric," *Women's Studies in Communication* 19, no. 2 (1996): 127–153; Stuart Hall, "The Whites of Their Eyes: Racist Ideologies in the Media," In *Gender, Race, and Class in Media: A Text-Reader*, ed. G. Dines and J.M. Humez (Thousand Oaks, CA: Sage, 2003/1981); Casey Ryan Kelly, "Neocolonialism and the Global Prison in National Geographic's *Locked Up Abroad*," *Critical Studies in Media Communication* 24, no. 4 (2012): 331–347; Kent A. Ono, *Contemporary Media Culture and the Remnants of a Colonial Past* (New York: Peter Lang, 2009); and Gayatri Chakrovorty Spivak, "Neocolonialism and the Secret Agent of Knowledge," *Oxford Literary Review* 13 (1991): 220–251.

26. See Catherine Squires, Eric King Watts, Mary Douglas Vavrus, Kent A. Ono, Kathleen Feyh, Bernadette Marie Calafell, and Daniel C. Brouwer, "What Is This 'Post' in Postracial, Postfeminist . . . (Fill in the Blank)?" *Journal of Communication Inquiry* 34, no. 3 (2010): 210–253.

27. Jemma Crew, "UN has new nutritional, sustainable diet for hungry world: insects" *The Independent*, May 13, 2013, www.independent.co.uk/news/world/politics/un-has-a-new-nutritional-sustainable-diet-for-a-hungry-world-insects-8614691.html (accessed June 1, 2013).

28. Alan Han, "'Can I Tell You What We Have to Put Up With?': Stinky Fish and Offensive Durian," *Continuum: Journal of Media & Cultural Studies* 21, no. 3 (2007): 361–377.

29. Michael Dietler, "Culinary Encounters: Food, Identity, and Colonialism," in *The Archaeology of Food and Identity*. ed. K. Twiss (Carbondale, IL: Southern Illinois University Press, 2007); Lisa Heldke, "Let's Cook Thai: Recipes for Colonialism," in *Food and*

Culture: A Reader, eds. Carole M. Counihan, Penny Van Esterik (New York: Routledge, 2012); and Lindenfield, "Tortilla Soup."

30. Helene Shugart, "Sumptuous Texts: Consuming 'Otherness' in the Food Film Genre," *Critical Studies in Media Communication*, 25, no. 1 (2008): 73.

31. Accounts of the social history of American culinary commodification and the present popularity of adventurous foreign cuisine can be found in Andrew P. Haley, *Turning the Tables: Restaurants and the Rise of the American Middle Class, 1880-1920* (Chapel Hill, NC: University of North Carolina Press, 2011); and Jennifer Jensen Wallach, *How America Eats: A Social History of U.S. Food and Culture* (New York: Rowman & Littlefield, 2013). In addition, the Travel Industry Association reports that 17 percent of American tourists seek out culinary activities while on vacation and a large portion (89 percent) reported enjoying their food adventures. See Sarah Peters, "Adventurous American Eaters Going Abroad," *The Daily Pilot*, August 23, 2010, http://articles.dailypilot.com/2010-08-23/news/tn-dpt-0824-mcdonald-20100823_1_travel-agents-american-leisure-travelers-culinary-tourism (accessed May 31, 2013).

32. See Raka Shome and Radha Hegde, "Culture, Communication, and the Challenges of Globalization," *Critical Studies in Media Communication* 19, no. 2 (2002): 172–189; and Raka Shome and Radha S. Hegde, "Postcolonial Approaches to Communication: Chart the Terrain, Engaging the Intersections," *Communication Theory* 12, no. 3 (2002): 249–270.

33. See Giroux, "Disposibility"; Bradley Jones and Roopali Mukherjee, "From California to Michigan: Race, Rationality, and Neoliberal Governmentality," *Communication and Critical/Cultural Studies* 7, no. 4 (2010): 401–422; Darrel Enck Wanzer, "Barack Obama, the Tea Party, and the Threat of Race: On Racial Neoliberalism and Born Again Racism," *Communication, Culture, and Critique* 4, no. 1 (2011): 23–30. For scholarship from outside communication studies see David Goldberg, *Threat of Race: Reflections on Racial Neoliberalism* (Malden, MA: Wiley Blackwell, 2007).

34. Shome and Hegde, "Postcolonial Approaches," 263.

35. Lindenfield, "Tortilla Soup," 305.

36. Andy Fixmer and Sarah Rabil, "Food Is New Real Estate as Cooking Show Ratings Jump (Update 3)," *Bloomberg News*, August 20, 2009, www.bloomberg.com/apps/news?pid=newsarchive&sid=aq3rYSGydhJ0 (accessed June 2, 2013).

37. It is important to note that when I refer to Andrew Zimmern throughout this essay, I am not referring to the flesh-and-blood individual but instead to the persona of Zimmern that is constructed and mediated by television. Celebrity identities are the product of writing, editing, camera work, make-up, and other elements of television production. Zimmern, the private individual, is distinct from the brand constructed around his personality by himself, the producers of *Bizarre Foods*, his publicists, agent, and advertisers. In her critique of Oprah Winfrey's rags-to-riches biography, Dana Cloud also makes this distinction between the celebrity and the private citizen, focusing her analysis not on an individual Oprah Winfrey but the rhetorical construction of Oprah the billion-dollar brand. See Dana Cloud, "Hegemony or Concordance?: The Rhetoric of Tokenism in 'Oprah' Winfrey's Rags-to-Riches Biography," *Critical Studies in Mass Communication* 13, no. 2 (1996): 115–137.

38. Jeff Gordinier, "Waiter, There's soup in my bug," *New York Times*, September 22, 2010, D1.

39. "Adventure Traveler Andrew Zimmern Partners with Pepto-Bismol to Share How to Have a Taste for Adventure," *Health Business Week*, November 7, 2008, p. 1533.

40. "If It Looks Good, Eat It!: Interview with Andrew Zimmern," *South Coast Today*, July 30, 2008, http://www.southcoasttoday.com/apps/pbcs.dll/article?AID=/20080730/SC24705/80730008/-1/SC24705 (accessed May 30, 2013); and see http://andrewzimmern.com (accessed May 30, 2013).

41. The Travel Channel, "About Us," http://www.travelchannel.com/about/about-us (accessed May 31, 2013).

42. *Bizarre Foods*, "Bizarre Foods of Asia," Travel Channel, November 1, 2006, written by Andrew Zimmern.

43. While derived from psychoanalytical and poststructural theories of subject formation, here I provisionally use the abject to explore how disgust and revulsion help demarcate the Western self (a collection of "clean eaters") from the Other that is unclean, defiled, and monstrous.

44. Julia Kristeva, *Powers of Horror: An Essay on Abjection*, trans. Leon S. Roudiez (New York: Columbia University Press), 4.

45. *Bizarre Foods*, "Asia."

46. *Bizarre Foods*, "Phillippines," Travel Channel, February 26, 2007, written by Andrew Zimmern.

47. *Bizarre Foods*, "Asia."

48. *Bizarre Foods*, "Ecuador," Travel Channel, March 12, 2007, written by Andrew Zimmern.

49. *Bizarre Foods*, "Ecuador."

50. *Bizarre Foods*, "Mexico," Travel Channel, July 16, 2007, written by Andrew Zimmern.

51. *Bizarre Foods*, "Asia."

52. *Bizarre Foods*, "Asia."

53. *Bizarre Foods*, "Asia."

54. *Bizarre Foods*, "Taiwan," Travel Channel, July 30, 2007, written by Andrew Zimmern.

55. *Bizarre Foods*, "Asia."

56. *Bizarre Foods*, "Asia."

57. Renato Rosaldo, "Imperialist Nostalgia," *Representations* 26 (1989): 107–122.

58. Rosaldo, "Nostalgia," 108.

59. Randall Lake explains how American apologists for American Indian genocide often lamented the destruction of the "noble savage" as a necessary though tragic result of historical forces beyond their control. The nineteenth-century "cult of the noble savage" was an oratorical and literary tradition of commemorating the tragic loss of American Indian peoples. While its adherents romanticized American Indian life before encounter, they often made appeals to what Lake calls "time's arrow," the belief that time is a linear and one-directional force that moved Western civilization forward (and quite often was accompanied by a divine mandate). See Randall Lake, "Between Myth and History: Enacting Time in Native American Protest Rhetoric," *Quarterly Journal of Speech* 77, no. 2 (1991): 123–151.

60. *Bizarre Foods*, "Asia."

61. *Bizarre Foods*, "Asia."

62. *Bizarre Foods*, "Asia."

63. *Bizarre Foods*, "Morocco," Travel Channel, March 5, 2007, written by Andrew Zimmern

64. *Bizarre Foods*, "Morocco."

65. *Bizarre Foods*, "Asia."

66. *Bizarre Foods*, "Asia."

67. *Bizarre Foods*, "Ecuador."

68. *Bizarre Foods*, "Taiwan."

69. *Bizarre Foods*, "Taiwan."

70. *Bizarre Foods*, "Taiwan."

71. *Bizarre Foods*, "Taiwan."

72. *Bizarre Foods*, "Vietnam," Travel Channel, August 13, 2007, written by Andrew Zimmern.

73. *Bizarre Foods*, "Trinidad and Tobago," Travel Channel, July 9, 2007, written by Andrew Zimmern.

74. *Bizarre Foods*, "Trinidad and Tobago."

75. *Bizarre Foods*, "Trinidad and Tobago."

76. *Bizarre Foods*, "Trinidad and Tobago."

77. *Bizarre Foods*, "Philippines."

78. *Bizarre Foods*, "Gulf Coast," Travel Channel, March 26, 2007, written by Andrew Zimmern.

79. *Bizarre Foods*, "Gulf Coast."

80. *Bizarre Foods*, "Alaska," Travel Channel, July 23, 2007, written by Andrew Zimmern.

81. *Bizarre Foods*, "Alaska."

82. *Bizarre Foods*, "Spain" Travel Channel, March 19, 2007, written by Andrew Zimmern.

83. *Bizarre Foods*, "Spain."

84. *Bizarre Foods*, "Spain."

85. *Bizarre Foods*, "United Kingdom," Travel Channel, April 2, 2007, written by Andrew Zimmern.

86. *Bizarre Foods*, "United Kingdom."

87. *Bizarre Foods*, "United Kingdom."

88. *Bizarre Foods*, "United Kingdom."

89. *Bizarre Foods*, "United Kingdom."

90. *Bizarre Foods*, "Spain."

91. *Bizarre Foods*, "Asia."

92. *Bizarre Foods*, "Morocco."

93. *Bizarre Foods*, "Morocco"; *Bizarre Foods*, "Spain."

94. *Bizarre Foods*, "New York City," Travel Channel, August 6, 2007, written by Andrew Zimmern.

95. *Bizarre Foods*, "New York City."

96. *Bizarre Foods*, "New York City."

97. Food and Agriculture Organization of the United Nations, September 2010, "Global Hunger Declining, But Still Unacceptably High," http://www.fao.org/docrep/012/al390e/ al390e00.pdf.

TWO

Exoticizing Poverty

Bizarre Foods America

A subgenre of the culinary adventure, "culinary slumming" refers to the unreflective enjoyment of adventurous cuisine that is by-and-large the product of poverty and marginalization.[1] In the United States, taco trucks, gas station delis, cafeterias, juke joints, barbecue shacks, open-air markets, and country cook-offs all provide affluent culinary tourists with an exhilarating opportunity to sample the cuisine of the Other, or in bell hooks's words, season "the dull dish that is mainstream white culture."[2] Slummers, repelled yet fascinated, venture into the country or the ghetto seeking out exotic dishes that challenge the most intrepid of foodies: neck bones, ears, skin, snouts, tails, brains, intestines, organ meat, foraged vegetable greens, insects, garbage fish, rodents, invasive species, birds, and other scraps and lesser cuts that reflect histories of economic subjugation. The rhetorical construction of these dishes as chic food trends ultimately masks the legacies of exclusion and exploitation that force communities living in poverty to "make do" with society's leftovers. For their temporary disavowal of privilege, however, slummers are putatively availed of the authentic experience of America's dispossessed.[3] Such adventurous eating fortifies this progressive cosmopolitan subject through joyful displays of tolerance and multicultural consumption. While sojourners invest money into struggling local economies, they implore the inhabitants of modern-day hush harbors and hidden vernacular spaces to confess their secret recipes and make their food and culture part of the next culinary trend.[4] The slummer, therefore, forgoes their luxury cuts to appreciate what society once discarded; yet, their reverent, touristic gaze elides the economic force of capitalism, slavery, and colonialism that produced cuisines of poverty and necessity.

47

In the past decade, the lived practice of culinary slumming has been supplemented by the popular ascendance of the food television industry. In dozens of programs across a variety of networks, celebrity chefs, travel writers, and television food personalities offer fellow slummers the opportunity to vicariously participate in culinary excursions to exotic regions across the globe without leaving the comfort of their living room.[5] Hosts engage in embodied performances of slumming, acting as a tour guide who shapes and guides audiences experience with the foodways of foreign cultures. In one sense, the slummer is invited to move outside of their comfort zone and face their fear of Otherness. In another sense, slummers are disciplined to experience foreign cultures through a framework of exoticism that keeps Otherness at arm's length. As I argued in the previous chapter, programming that depicts culinary tourism is part of a larger shift in documentary television that employs ethnographic filmmaking to represent people, places, and cultural traditions as they exist.[6] Driven by the imperative to both educate and entertain cosmopolitan viewers, ethnotainment employs the gaze of a hobby anthropologist or tourist, exoticizing the foodways and cultural practices of subaltern communities.[7]

This chapter seeks to explain how celebratory depictions of culinary slumming address the structural dynamics of American poverty. With a slight change in emphasis from the previous chapter, I argue that televisual discourses on culinary slumming assimilate food cultures of poverty into the pantheon of contemporary haute cuisine. Food television represents "making do" as a set of proud choices, tied to deep investments in cultural heritage, that symbolizes the happy contentment of poor and dispossessed communities who seemingly prefer their humble traditions to the private accumulation of wealth. For an audience of predominantly middle class and affluent consumers, images of vibrant food cultures in the rural countryside and zones of suburban triage are made to attest to the sustainability of the growing wealth gap and an economic system premised on a politics of disposability.[8] Culinary slumming not only overlooks the economic and cultural factors that have shaped cuisines of necessity, but glorifies those cuisines as the proud and exotic traditions of simple but ingenious people who live off the land without pretense.

This chapter explores Zimmern's spin-off program *Bizarre Foods America*, attending to exotic representations of poor rural communities. Here, I contend that *Bizarre Foods America* exoticizes America's rural poor by celebrating food traditions that actually bespeak persistent economic inequalities. With 46 million Americans living in poverty at the time of the program's premier, I read the show as a post-recessionary acquiescence to historic rates of income inequality.[9] Representing cuisines of necessity as evidence of the nobility of poverty, *Bizarre Foods America*'s fixation with the exotic delights of the rural poor obscures the growing pervasiveness of rural hunger as well as the dwindling economic opportunities among America's permanent underclasses. The program's emphasis on food as an embodiment of heritage, tradition, and authenticity reduces rural poverty to nativist lifestyle politics. In other words, poverty cuisine becomes the representative anecdote for a culture adopted by choice in resistance to the excesses of capitalism.[10] The selective visibility and vicarious consumption of folksy communities from the Ozarks to the Mississippi Delta—happily stuck in time but willing to share their secrets with the chic culinary world—disguises the taste of economic exploitation. The program confirms that the table scraps, the nasty bits, the waste products relegated to America's rural poor are a source of enjoyment, something converted by the dispossessed into a hot commodity that adds diversity and deliciousness to the bourgeois American palate. In my analysis, I focus on the episodes that sojourn into some of the poorest regions of the American South, paying attention to how discourses of heritage belie the structural exploitation of America's permanent underclass that traces its roots to the colonization of North America.

EXOTICIZING POVERTY IN AN AGE OF AUSTERITY

In 2012, the income gap in America reached an all time high.[11] One in seven Americans now lives below the poverty line. Rural poverty is particularly acute. According to the Southern Rural Development Center at Mississippi State University, the poverty rate in rural America is 16.6 percent and the poverty rate for rural children is approximately 27 percent.[12] The National Poverty Center found that four hundred rural counties have rates over 20 percent and nearly 60 percent of those living in poverty are racial minorities.[13] As Congress considers $4 billion in cuts to the Supplemental Nutrition Assistance Program (SNAP), children living in rural communities continue to be the most likely to experience food insecurity.[14] Despite the persistence of rural poverty, the public is woefully under-educated on the subject and overwhelmingly lacks empathy toward those living in such conditions. For instance, the Salvation Army found that nearly half of Americans believed that those living in poverty could find a job or improve their circumstances if they were properly motivated.[15]

Kenneth L. Deavers and Robert A. Hoppe surmise that "the current gap between reality and public beliefs about the incidence of poverty results largely from the close contact between city people and the urban poor and from the prominence given to the urban poor by national broadcast media. In contrast, the rural poor, who live in many small scattered settlements in apparently 'picturesque' country surroundings, are relatively invisible."[16] Indeed, the lack of attention to rural poverty is a byproduct of not only invisibility, but also the perception that rural living is bucolic, rustic, simple, and romantic. As Michael Harrington

observed, "seeing in them a romantic image of mountain life as independent, self-reliant, and athletic, a tourist could pass through these valleys
and observe only quaintness."[17] Unfortunately those living in poverty
outside of urban and suburban landscapes "suffer terribly at the hands of
beauty."[18] That is to say that while the sight of urban poverty might
inspire reflection on the harsh realities of life in a postindustrial society,
rural poverty is often misread as a rustic country lifestyle that embraces
simplicity and even offers a hopeful escapism from urban blight.

To the extent that it is made visible, representations of rural poverty
can take a variety of stereotypical forms, including imagery of "rednecks" and "White trash," backwater racists who remain willfully (and
sometimes comically) ignorant and downtrodden.[19] For instance, a variety of reality television programs such as *Duck Dynasty, Here Comes Honey
Boo Boo, Hillbilly Handfishing, Moonshiners, Redneck Island, Redneck Wed-
dings, Rocket City Rednecks*, and *Swamp People* position audiences to laugh
at rednecks' contentment with impoverishment or total lack of cultural
refinement. Elsewhere in media culture, rednecks are portrayed as dangerous and primitive (e.g., *Deliverance*, 1972).[20] At the same time, representations of rural black poverty frequently accentuate the wisdom derived from "making do," or the mythical freedom of living outside of
civilization (e.g., *Beasts of the Southern Wild*, 2012).[21] This chapter, however, is concerned with how efforts to counter misconceptions of rural culture with authentic portrayals of simple rustic lifestyles romanticize what
are by-and-large difficult living conditions.[22] To their credit, programs
like *Bizarre Foods America* use the long-standing food traditions of rural
Southern communities to demonstrate that the aforementioned cultural
stereotypes are in many ways misleading. The program offers a vicarious
experience of culinary slumming through exotic and misunderstood cuisines as evidence that rural communities adapt and preserve traditions in
response to economic challenges.

Yet, *Bizarre Foods America*'s vision of rural life leaves audiences with
the underdeveloped perception of a tourist interloper who is invited to
accept the "staged authenticity" of proud food traditions as an "illusion
of familiarity with that culture."[23] The façade of country folk who are
happy to share their fascinating yet challenging cuisine presents an image of rural life as humble, traditional, frozen in time, and free from the
confines of modern civilization. The audience is invited to consume the
rural South's proud heritage, to better understand rural life through a
soulful, reverent valiance toward foods and lifestyles born of necessity. In
this way, *Bizarre Foods* engages in "poverty tourism," a practice Biana
Freire-Medeiros argues "is a by-product of Western fascination with the
exotic 'Other,' of a middle-class romanticism of the poor."[24] Poverty tourism and culinary slumming are the providence of the heritage industry,
which converts the authentic cultural experience of marginalized communities into an opportunity to educate and profit from middle-class

consumers' desire for authentic Otherness.[25] Poverty tourism is an experience in navel gazing that Stephan Palmie characterizes as "catering to consumers economically capacitated to engage in a sumptuary politics of self-authentification [*sic*]."[26] The experience of communities living in poverty is commodified into a celebratory image that satisfies the consumers' desires to affirm their cosmopolitan, multicultural ethos. The spectacle of proud and delighted eaters—seemingly unburdened by the histories of their cuisine—replaces old stereotypes with a pleasing image of happy concordance.

Mediating the rural South through the lens of the bizarre and exotic also keeps the program's subjects at arms length from the tourist/spectator. The production and consumption of Otherness requires that the show's producers find the most extreme version of "making do," including the most unpalatable dishes found in poor communities. The rhetoric of exoticism is marked by ambivalent desires, the coexistence of fascination, curiosity, and revulsion toward difference.[27] Julia Kristeva contends that food taboos are the first source of childhood encounter with the abject, a site at which we learn through bodily expulsion to separate the self from Other.[28] This observation frames the significance of food traditions in demarcating the Western civilized self from the unclean and disgusting food habits of people living in poverty. Focusing on the most challenging cuisine helps audiences mark their separation from the program's subjects and confirms the authenticity of their Otherness.

Indeed, the poverty cuisines celebrated in *Bizarre Foods America* are byproducts of slavery and segregation, the colonization of American Indians, and the impoverishment of poor white laborers. They are also reflections of the invisible structural inequalities that continue to impinge rural upward mobility.[29] From this approach, poverty tourism is a neocolonial practice, driven by the same "colonial desire to fix the identity of the other in order that it remains . . . distinct from tourist identity."[30] The exoticization of poverty draws from hidden colonialist assumptions about the primitive and nostalgic beauty of life outside the metropole, the mastery of knowledge of unconquered frontiers, and superiority of Western civilization, the universal desirability of capital and consumerism. In this case, the glorification of poverty cuisine is an extension of economic colonialism that lends authority to the discourses of self-reliance and private initiative that uphold the myth of unlimited upward mobility for all regardless of race and class. The glorification of poverty cuisine narrates a history of rural life where the predations of colonialism and capitalism play no fundamental part. Representations of ingenuity, self-reliance, and proud heritage invite audiences to take delight in humble traditions without reflection on the historic forces that created and sustain a permanent underclass in the United States.

THE EXOTIC AT HOME

Bizarre Foods America is a one-hour documentary style program that chronicles the culinary tours of host Andrew Zimmern. Following the same format as the original *Bizarre Foods* (2006–2011), the program is shot on location in different destinations throughout the United States. Each episode showcases different local and regional cuisine that deviates from what the producers assume to be a standard American diet, including wild fish and game, lesser cuts and organ meats, foraged greens, and other foods that might be considered challenging to unfamiliar audiences. All episodes typically involve trips to scouted locations such as local bars and restaurants, butchers, farmer's markets, food festivals, food-processing facilities, and other purveyors of exotic ingredients. Zimmern also typically shares a meal with local residents, prepared in a family's home or community center. In episodes shot in rural locations, Zimmern is often invited to participate in a hunt or fishing expedition, followed by a sampling of local traditional meal preparations. Like its predecessor, the episodes are celebratory and lighthearted in tone, a feeling accentuated not only by the use of a playful score but also Zimmern's whimsical affect. To his credit, Zimmern is always cordial, respectful, and willing to try any cuisine. The network produced *Bizarre Foods with Andrew Zimmern* for six seasons and *Bizarre Foods America* for six seasons (2012–2014. The channel has also produced an additional original series with Zimmern titled *Bizarre Foods: Delicious Destinations.*[31] The success of the *Bizarre Foods* franchise attests to both widespread public interest in culinary slumming as well as the cultural influence of food television.

This chapter analyzes episodes of *Bizarre Foods America* across seven seasons that showcase the cuisine of the rural American South. This includes episodes shot in Appalachia, the Ozarks, the Mississippi Delta, Central Florida, Alabama, West Virginia, and the Gulf Coast. I selected these episodes because they are locations that currently experience some of the most disproportionately high rates of poverty and food insecurity in the United States. They are also places still affected by the legacy of slavery, segregation, Jim Crow, as well as the economic subjugation of poor white laborers.[32] Despite Zimmern's demonstrable commitment to philanthropy and cultural education through food, the program's potential positive contributions are eclipsed by the demands of the ethnotainment format. Zimmern candidly attests to the fact that the program deviates from what he originally proposed to the network.[33] Recalling a conversation with a Travel Channel executive, Zimmern explains, "He said, 'If you do the show for us, you need to invert that model, and it has to be 80 percent entertainment and 20 percent intellectual gravitas.' I remember looking at him and saying, 'As long as I get to keep the 20 percent intellectual gravitas, you got a deal.'"[34] Dispensing with deeper intellectual engagements with culture and geopolitics adopted in a program like

CNN's *Parts Unknown* with Anthony Bourdain, Zimmern is often re-duced to feel good tropes and folksy witticisms that provide shallow insights into the economic and historical conditions that shape rural com-munities' relationship with food traditions. Thus, it is important to note that this chapter is not a criticism of Andrew Zimmern the private indi-vidual but the program as a cultural text subject to techniques of media-tion and the commercial forces exerted on cable programming. In this analysis I attend to three specific moves that emerge throughout these episodes. First, I examine how the program ties exotic rural food tradi-tions to a simple, rustic way of life that elide the conditions under which the food continues to be produced and consumed. Second, I explore how the program cultivates faux intimacy with its subjects, inviting the audi-ence not to see themselves as interlopers but instead welcome guests who are entitled to only positive and self-affirming encounters with happy natives. Finally, I analyze how the program assimilates poverty cuisine into the establishment of haute cuisine and bourgeois food culture, a commodity of the new south unburdened by economic disparities.

Simple Country Folks

Each of the episodes examined in this chapter asserts that food tradi-tions are a cultural medium, a type of heuristic that can be used to evalu-ate and understand why specific rural communities organize around par-ticular rituals, modes of work, and ways of life. For instance, when visit-ing the Gulf Coast (Season 4, Episode 3) Zimmern declares "my greatest joys in traveling is actually getting to taste a culture."[35] While foodways clearly reflect specific cultural histories and traditions, the practice of consuming a culture through a medium requires reduction and conden-sation. How food is produced and consumed becomes the representative anecdote for all elements of culture represented on and off screen. Throughout the program, the ingenuity, hard work, and survival skills that go into some aspects of rural food production represent the proud traditions of living off the land. Terms like "heritage" and "tradition" are frequently associated with the difficult labor of hunting, growing, or for-aging a meal not available in grocery stores. In the process, the difficult labor of "making do" becomes tied to a romantic ideal of living simply and without pretense. Heritage and tradition are reflections of lifestyle choices and contentment, rather than structural economic conditions. In-deed, for every happy hunter and self-reliant mountain person depicted on screen there are countless others living with persistent food insecurity.

First, the program uses the ingenuity of Southern food cultures as testaments to the benefits and freedom of self-help. For instance, in the Ozarks of Arkansas (Season 3, Episode 8), with happy hunters and an-glers dressed in camouflage and navigating rural swamps portrayed on screen, Zimmern explains in voice over, "People here treasure their freedom, their family, and the timeless heritage of living off the land."[36] He notes that while modernity is a part of Arkansas's landscape, there is "pluck and self-reliance . . . everywhere you look."[37] Through meals of Bear cracklings, bacon-wrapped crow, rabbit legs, and suckerfish, the difficulty of attaining these hard to find proteins is framed as a purposeful and joyful enactment of personal agency. The episode also emphasizes the festive and communal elements of hunting and cooking exotic cuisines. Zimmern is invited to participate in a suckerfish fish fry and squirrel cookoff with diverse home preparations. The reason that these communities can make "the unpalatable, palatable" is because they put "a high value on preserving the skills and the wisdom handed down from generations of mountain living."[38] While the festive atmosphere depicted on-screen is undeniable, the framing of these events as representations of "folksy Arkansas" transform temporary moments of community enjoyment into summations of the joyful freedom experienced by living only on what the land provides.[39] Without denying the pride of those who hunt and fish as a way of life, the repetition of "freedom" and "self-reliance" assimilates cuisines of necessity into the grand narratives of late capitalism in which private initiative, hard work, and independence are envisioned as replacements for the welfare state. The subjects depicted as happily and even defiantly living off the land, harnessing survival skills developed under conditions of absolute freedom, provide a plausible portrait of alternatives to public assistance. Self-reliance is a rational and empowered choice, not one born of necessity. As Zimmern concludes, food in the Ozarks is "a perfect example of how one culture's trash becomes another's culinary treasure."[40] He makes a similar argument when visiting the Mississippi Delta, noting that the food represents "a very old tradition of making a little go a long way."[41] In other words, the ingenuity of the rural South is a fitting example of how socioeconomic status need not be a barrier to unlimited upward mobility. This episode in particular imparts the lesson that society's culinary wastes are a treasure trove of edible delights. Through hard work and self-reliance, table scraps can become as delicious as high-end cuisine.

Second, *Bizarre Foods America* represents poverty cuisines as signs of a fiercely defended way of life. The program's romantic portrayal of declining food traditions that rely on hunting, fishing, and gathering laments the wane of noble poverty, of cultures content with living off the land. This portrayal is most prominently foregrounded in episodes featuring the cuisine of the Gulf Coast, the Mississippi Delta, and rural Florida. In these episodes, Zimmern continually highlights these are places "you can taste a vanishing way of life."[42] During a community dinner of various exotic fish and organ meat with Isleno descendants of early immigrants from the Canary Islands, he explains: "only a few families still hold on to this way of life."[43] For Zimmern, dish after dish represents "another vestige of a lost way of life."[44] In Clarksville, Mississippi (Season 2, Episode 7), Zimmern calls the Delta "a place standing outside of time."[45] In the rural outskirts of New Orleans (Season 1, Episode 2), Zimmern observes country home cooking with optimism that "grandma's favorite food hasn't faded into the sunset quite yet."[46] In these episodes, romantic attachment to the old South encases these communities behind museum glass, so to speak, rendering them a kind of curated living display of doomed cultures. The food of the rural South is represented as primitive, preserved for its quaint and sentimental attachment to bygone eras. Specifically, the rural South is both spatially and temporally remote from contemporary civilization. For instance, the Gulf Coast is "a corner of the country forgotten by most,"[47] while in the Mississippi Delta "time has more or less stopped."[48] Nonetheless, rural Southerners cling to their exotic and outdated traditions. In fact, for those who "proudly call themselves crackers," "living off the land the way their ancestors did is just a practical way of life."[49]

In these episodes Zimmern explains the pride rural Southerners feel in defending ways of life that are ostensibly pre-modern. Meanwhile the camera cuts between shots of local residents in camouflage outfits, loading hunting and fishing gear, and preparing to head into forests, swamps, and bayous. The subjects are framed by the program as holding emphatic attachments to tradition in spite of modern conveniences. Thus, the framework of the program sustains a modern/primitive binary in which poverty cuisines exist out of a charming refusal to integrate into the mainstream consumer economy. Again, the rhetoric of heritage and tradition explains access to wealth and resources as phenomena structured by how cultures relate to modernity. Exotic food traditions in the rural South are the product of parochial cultures choosing to live outside of time's passage, deciding instead to live off pig entrails, junk fish, and squirrel meat.

Finally, the program represents rural Southern cuisine as the savage and playful spirit of primitive America. On the Gulf Coast, Zimmern employs a lighthearted tone to introduce "a cast of characters [who] fight to preserve their way of life."[50] These "characters" are frequently characterized as "rowdy," "rough," or "wild" and depicted happily touting guns, drinking beer, and smoking mystery meats in makeshift contraptions. For instance, Zimmern describes the residents of Hurricane Alley, Alabama as "rough and tumble," "armed to the teeth," and "rowdy."[51] And while they work hard, they enjoy "having a damn good time while they're at it."[52] Outside New Orleans, Zimmern praises the "rough and ready country cooking."[53] He also visits what he characterizes as a "rowdy road house" that serves turtle and raccoon. While harvesting bullfrogs in the Everglades he observes the "rugged way of life" of the rural Gladesman.[54] In many ways, this frame provides a positive elaboration on the standard redneck caricature that is ubiquitous in American popular culture. But, the image presented here is also of happy savages unaware and unconcerned about modern refinement, standards of cleanliness, and convenience. The wild and challenging nature of the cuisine symbolizes a culture with seemingly child-like maturity and aspirations. That is to say that in the rural South we see the humble yet unrefined cuisines of the poor and less civilized. The audience is assured, however, that these rowdy individuals are quite content, if not overjoyed by the difficult task of scrounging for a meal. Their culture is proudly primitive and continues to be passed on and adopted by choice. As Zimmern watches a peaceful sunset over the Everglades he tells his backwater hosts, "you've got it pretty good, my friend."[55] Here, the sincere admiration for primitive ways of life overshadows the implicit assumption that, in general, eking out a meager existence on difficult to obtain protein sources is the preference of those who do. Certainly, the subjects with whom Zimmern visits express pride and enjoyment, but audiences are left to positively generalize about rural life in general, saved from having to observe the harsher side of making do.

Faux Intimacy and Family Meals

In each episode, Zimmern is invited to join a local family for a home cooked meal. During the preparation of the meal, Zimmern interacts with the cook, samples ingredients, and explains cooking processes to the audience. Throughout the preparation and meal, Zimmern asks his hosts questions about their family history, life circumstances, and the significance of particular rituals and ingredients. While the conversations are ostensibly about unique and exotic foods, the dialogue often unfolds the cook's personal and family history, their stature in the local community, and how food relates to their cultural heritage. While many of the festival and hunting scenes turn poverty cuisine into spectacle, the family dinner sequences are profoundly intimate and work to humanize the program's subjects. They offer a glimpse into how model rural families structure their lives around exotic foods. Though these recurring sequences build familiarity and comfort with the food customs of rural families, they also ensure that the presence of the exotic does not fundamentally disturb the audience's privilege. Like Zimmern, the audience is entitled to be welcome guests in the rural Southern kitchen, to have exotic subjects make them feel at ease, comforted, and taken care of as they experience difference. This sense of intimacy is an invitation to engage in culinary slumming. It reminds viewers that for the price of a temporary disavowal of privilege, tasting the South's exotic edibles provides unmediated access to the authentic cultural experience of the Other. The audience is not forced to confront the unpleasant power lines that divide them from the program's subjects. The Other is made present to confirm that the world is open and accessible for the upwardly mobile food aficionado.

In particular, two meal sequences demonstrate how the program cultivates comfort and welcomeness for the adventurous foodie. First, in Bayou La Batre, Alabama, local community organizer David Pham brings
Zimmern to lunch in the home of first generation Vietnamese immigrants
Min and Ho Tran. Bayou La Batre has a large Vietnamese community
that predominantly makes a living in the local seafood industry.[56] As an
unofficial ambassador for the Vietnamese community, Pham secures
Zimmern and his cameras entrance into Buddhist temples, Vietnamese
markets and groceries, and even the homes of local residents. The Ho
family provides Zimmern with a tour of their garden of Vietnamese vegetables, their prized roosters, and homespun varieties of dried and fermented fish. A majority of the preparations are unavailable in local restaurants because the Food and Drug Administration prohibits the fer-
mentation processes employed by the Ho family. Zimmern's delight with
this fact suggests that the audience is privy to the most challenging and
authentic experience with Southern-Vietnamese fusion. They are treated
to the most secret and mysterious cuisine that the South has to offer.

The dangers of fermented fish are made comforting and delightful by
how the program cultivates intimacy between Zimmern and the host
family. During home meal sequences, Zimmern provides voice over narration where he explains the family's history and cuisine over old black
and white portraits. The experience has the documentary quality of rum-
maging through old family photo albums. Throughout the meal, Zimmern spends as much time describing the meal as he does expressing
reverence for the family's traditions of making the unpalatable, delicious.
At the conclusion of the meal, Zimmern embraces the family's matriarch
with a high level of familiarity and comfort. He compliments David for
how well he negotiates being "trapped between two cultures" and compliments Min and Ho for the authenticity of the meal.[57]

In a second example, Zimmern visits a family cookout with the Chow
family of Clarksdale, Mississippi. He is treated to "a showcase of the
wonderful things that can happen when the Far East meets Deep South,"
including traditional Southern dishes like pigs feet and tails with Chinese
spices and cooking techniques.[58] While in the previous example the
Trans were portrayed as a relatively lower income immigrant family
making the best of their circumstances, the Chows are fourth generation
immigrants who came from humble roots to become "a family of white
collar professionals."[59] This episode contrasts black and white photos of
the family's humble beginnings with their present day success, including
a vibrant family with the creature comforts of affluence. Zimmern is invited to participate in the kitchen, sample ingredients, and even join the
family in prayer before the meal. Again, the family's openness to Zimmern provides a portrait of a welcoming South, eager to share its culinary
secrets with the affluent consumers on the other side of the camera.
Above all, the program's emphasis on the family's assimilation into

American culture and their adherence to the American Dream mythology makes servings of pig feet more palatable. Though the family once relied on poverty cuisine to survive, evidence of their hard work and perseverance makes their festive celebration of pig feet and crawfish safely accessible to those with the privilege to choose how they wish to dine. This intimate portrayal of a successful immigrant family also confirms that the consumption of bizarre foods may have at one point been about necessity, but today they are a part of family heritage and community traditions. The invitation that the audience be part of the family attests to the welcomeness of culinary slummer. Images of happy natives, opening their homes to be observed, give the viewer tacit approval to gawk for their pleasure. In other words, the program's subjects seemingly consent to be studied and examined; rendered knowable and consumed for the edification of viewers at home. The feeling of closeness is, however, staged as a device to ease audience fears of Otherness and authorize their pleasurable consumption of poverty cuisines.

New South Cuisine

Bizarre Food America portrays poverty cuisine as part of the chic new food trends that are revitalizing contemporary Southern cuisine. Here, techniques born of necessity and survival are used to spice up and add exotic qualities to mundane restaurant fare. Assimilating poverty cuisine into the fine dining experience extends the experience of slumming beyond the tour to the everyday life of the adventurous eater. In this way, the audience can capture the experience of Otherness at their local farmer's market, the specialty grocer, or the neighborhood gastro-pub. In these spaces, poverty cuisines can be consumed without a discomforting confrontation with the historical and economic context of the cuisine. With an expert chef at the helm and pleasant like-minded patrons as company, the nasty bits and lesser cuts can be experienced with the comfort of refinement. The program's promise that these exotic elements will be coming to a hip new restaurant near you provides reassurances that an authentic encounter with Otherness can be obtained without self-risk or liberal guilt. In another sense, the high price of these exotic new menu items assuages the guilt associated with slumming by bringing them under the canopy of elite taste. Representations of new Southern cuisine offer transcendence from the "old South," a place where lines of race, class, and gender dictate access to food and capital.

In several episodes, Zimmern showcases popular Southern chefs who have turned to rural cuisine to update the menus at their high-end eateries. In the episode eponymously named "The New South" (Season 1, Episode 2), Zimmern spends time with Chef Chris Hastings of the James Beard Award winning Hot and Hot Fish Club in Birmingham, Alabama.[60] The episode follows Zimmern and Hastings's adventures through the aisles of local butchers and international markets where they ponder the relative merits of everything from blood cake to dried and fermented fish. Through voice over, Zimmern remarks, "this isn't your grandma's Piggly Wiggly," and declares, "Birmingham food and cultural scene are evolving."[61] Hastings observes that new Southern cuisine is about assimilating and fusing classics with rare and undiscovered ingredients. Observing the influence of local foods and international markets, Hastings explains, "us white guys started showing up and saying this is the coolest thing ever."[62] Similarly, in Oxford, Mississippi, Zimmern shops with Chef John Currence of the critically acclaimed City Grocery where the two ponder combinations like Japanese miso and locally sourced pig's ear and testicles. Zimmern remarks that the market "is a monument to changing times."[63] His exotic excursions with local celebrity chefs put the privileged practice of cultural appropriation on display. Here, the hallmark of great Southern chefs is their ability to turn the unfamiliar and even distasteful ingredients of first generation immigrants and country rednecks into contemporary haute cuisine. The kitchens of Hot and Hot Fish Club and the City Grocery are portrayed as places where teams of trained professionals make the nasty bits pleasurable to those who have not likely had the need to eat ingredients like testicles out of necessity. Most importantly, the food is made to tell a different story that harkens vaguely to heritage and tradition with no reference to history and context.

For those who do not typically dine in James Beard award-winning restaurants, new Southern cuisine is also supposedly the rising tide that lifts all boats. That is to say that the program suggests that the demands of affluent consumers for new and exotic ingredients might provide economic support to communities who hunt, trap, and raise wild game to survive. These individuals are now poised to use their unique set of skills and traditions to profit from the rise of culinary tourism. The most profound example can be found in Zimmern's discussion of the unique ingredients harvested by the Seminole Indian nation of central Florida. In a tour through the exotic game preserves to the Brighton reservation, Zimmern suggests that Seminole business success in supplying wild game to the region means "hunting for food is not a necessity anymore."[64] Casinos notwithstanding, the demand for Seminole ranching is responsible for "keeping their culture alive."[65] Implicitly, the emergence of an affluent class of exotic eaters is responsible for improving the lives of the marginalized and dispossessed. The purveyors and consumers of rare and bizarre foods are now presented with the kind of upward mobility that affords a more discerning and refined palate. Again, the Seminole are offered as evidence that self-reliance and tradition can be marshaled by underclasses to market their quaint and charming lifestyle to the upper-class consumer. While the Seminole's success is well documented, the program presents self-help, cultural commodification, and entrepreneurialism as the pathway out of poverty and marginalization. In essence, the show suggests that the exotic tastes of affluent consumers can, in part, alleviate centuries of economic dislocation caused by their ancestors.

THE POLITICAL ECONOMY OF DIET

Despite Zimmern's best efforts to show rural Southerners as they live, *Bizarre Foods America* provides an inadequate account of the economic realities of food production and consumption. For every self-reliant country family depicted as living happily off the land; every charming food culture poised to compete in the new cosmopolitan marketplace; and every culinary slummer invited into home kitchens where secret recipes are divulged, there are countless individuals living with the legacies of capitalism. This chapter demonstrates that glorification of poverty cuisine masks the discontent of America's rural underclass. Pride, heritage, and charm obscure the profound lack of choices and the severe limitations on upward mobility that characterize the modern crisis of rural poverty. While those living in poverty are adept, skillful, and resilient, the celebratory exoticization of their foodways overlooks the need for a more equitable distribution of material resources. Attention to the historic legacies of "soul food," and other cuisines fashioned from the scraps and leftovers of the haves, would do more to contextualize the parallel development of different food classes in America. Perhaps Zimmern's original formula for the program could have provided the context audiences need to understand the implications of culinary slumming and appropriation. With attention to the relationship between food, capitalism, and American empire, this analysis brings attention to how the televised food adventure dispenses with an analysis of economic colonialism to placate the new cosmopolitan eater.

In this program, the rural South is quite literally domesticated and its food cultures contorted to tell a narrative of humble contentment with existing social and economic structures. Indeed, economic austerity has profoundly impacted the Southern diet. For instance, while high rates of obesity are attributed to high fat protein sources and deep fried treats, the unfortunate reality is that systemic poverty is primarily responsible. The new poverty cuisines of the South are fast food and cheap carbohydrates sold at discount chains such as Walmart.[66] Decades of depressed wages and declining employment opportunities have also changed attitudes toward physical fitness and healthy eating. The self-reliant family living off the land is an idyllic image that obscures the proliferation of low priced processed foods, produced by companies that have taken advantage of economic austerity. While more affluent culinary tourists consume what is presented as the authentic South, many rural Southerners either go hungry or fill up on low nutrition fillers. If anything, these chemically enhanced and artificially sweetened treats more appropriately deserve the label of "bizarre foods." This chapter shows how reverence and exoticization push aside the economic realities of food for a self-affirming portrait of an exhilarating food adventure, complete with servile natives, rustic beauty, and challenging tests for the intrepid foodie. In *Bizarre Foods America*, the culinary slummer remains unburdened by the painful histories of the cuisines they vicariously consume. Ultimately, those same foods will be featured at a local fine dining establishment, marketed as new Southern cuisine, to be enjoyed without the disturbing presence of Others.

NOTES

1. Doris Witt, *Black Hunger: Soul Food and America* (Minneapolis: University of Minnesota Press, 2004), 101; See also Jeffrey Pilcher, "From 'Montezuma's Revenge' to 'Mexican Truffles': Culinary Tourism Across the Rio Grande," pp. 76–96 in *Culinary Tourism*, ed. Lucy M. Long (Lexington: University Press of Kentucky, 2013).

2. bell hooks, *Black Looks: Race and Representation* (Boston, MA: South End Press, 1992), 21.

3. Biana Freire-Medeiros, *Touring Poverty* (London and New York: Routledge, 2013), 3.

4. For instance, Frederick Douglass Opie traces the history of "soul food" to the secret cultural practices and religion of African American slaves. See *Hog and Hominy: Soul Food from Africa to America* (New York: Columbia University Press, 2010); Also see Jessica Harris, *High on the Hog: A Culinary Journey from Africa to America* (New York: Bloomsbury, 2011); Rachel Lauden, *Cuisine and Empire: Cooking in World History* (Berkeley, CA: University of California Press, 2013); Adrian Miller, *Soul Food: The Surprising Story of an American Cuisine One Plate at a Time* (Chapel Hill: University of North Carolina Press, 2013); Andrew Warnes, *Savage Barbecue: Race, Culture, and the Invention of America's First Food* (Athens, GA: University of Georgia Press, 2008).

5. On the Travel Channel alone there is *Bizarre Foods with Andrew Zimmern, Dangerous Grounds, Man v. Food, Man v. Food Nation, No Reservations, Samantha Brown,* and *The Layover*.

6. See also Casey Ryan Kelly, "Strange/Familiar: Rhetorics of Exoticism in Ethnographic Television." In *Communication Colonialism: Readings on Postcolonial Theory and Communication*, ed. Rae Lynn Schwartz-Dupre (New York: Peter Lang, 2013).

7. Kelly, "Strange/Familiar," 196.

8. See Henry Giroux, "Beyond the Biopolitics of Disposibility: Rethinking Neoliberalism in the New Gilded Age." *Social Identities* 14, no. 4 (2008): 587–620.

9. Ruth Manthell, "Household Income Falls as 46 Million in Poverty," *MarketWatch*, September 12, 2012. Accessed October 13, 2014 at www.marketwatch.com/story/household-income-falls-as-46-million-in-poverty-2012-09-12.

10. The "representative anecdote" is borrowed from Kenneth Burke, *Grammar of Motives* (Berkeley, CA: University of California Press, 1969). For its application in media criticism see Barry Brummett, "Burke's Representative Anecdote as a Method in Media Criticism." *Critical Studies in Mass Communication* 1, no. 2 (1984): 161–176.

11. Don Lee, "U.S. Income Gap Between Rich, Poor Hits New High," *Los Angeles Times*, September 12, 2012. Accessed October 13, 2014 at http://articles.latimes.com/2012/sep/12/business/la-fi-census-poverty-rate-20120913.

12. Thomas D. Rowley, "Food Assistance Needs of the South's Vulnerable Populations," August 2000. http://srdc.msstate.edu/publications/archive/218.pdf; See also

Tom Zeller Jr., "Rural Minorities Ponder the American Dream from the Bottom Rung of the Economic Ladder," *The Huffington Post*, September 20, 2012. Accessed October 13, 2014 at www.huffingtonpost.com/2012/09/20/rural-poverty-minorities_n_1829911.html.

13. Daniel T. Lichter, Domenico Parisi, and Michael C. Taquino, "The Geography of Exclusion: Race, Segregation, and Concentrated Poverty," *National Poverty Center Working Paper #11-16*, May 2011. Accessed October 13, 2014 at http://npc.umich.edu/publications/u/2011-16%20NPC%20Working%20Paper.pdf.

14. Rural child food insecurity rates have been as high as 46 percent. See Alan Pyke, "REPORT: Child Hunger Is Concentrated in Rural America," *ThinkProgress*, June 10, 2013. Accessed October 15, 2014 at http://thinkprogress.org/economy/2013/06/10/2132331/report-child-hunger-is-concentrated-in-rural-america/; and Feeding America, "Map the Meal Gap, Food Insecurity in Your County," 2001. Accessed October 15 at http://map.feedingamerica.org/county/2014/overall.

15. The Salvation Army, "Perceptions of Poverty: The Salvation Army's Report to America," October 2012. Accessed October 13, 2014 at http://salvationarmynorth.org/wp-content/uploads/2012/10/2012SAPovertyReportWEB.pdf.

16. Kenneth L. Deavers and Robert A. Hoppe, "Overview of the Rural Poor in the 1980s," ed. Cynthia M. Duncan, *Rural Poverty in America* (Westport, CT: Greenwood Publishing, 1993), 3. This point extends Michael Harrington's foundational work on poverty in the United States, in which he argues that the interstate highway system enables most to travel without ever seeing the grim realities of structural poverty that exists just minutes from the on ramp. See Michael Harrington, *The Other America: Poverty in the United States* (New York: Touchstone, 1962).

17. Harrington, *Other America*, 41.

18. Harrington, *Other America*, 41.

19. See Diana Elizabeth Kendall, *Framing Class: Media Representations of Wealth and Poverty in America* (Lanham, MD: Rowman & Littlefield, 2011).

20. See Derek Nystrom, *Hard Hats, Rednecks, and Macho Men: Class in 1970s American Cinema* (London: Oxford University Press, 2009).

21. With the exception of civil rights and Blaxploitation films, most of popular culture looks past the public memory of poverty, slavery, segregation, the Ku Klux Klan, and Jim Crow.

22. See Paul J. Cloke and Jo Little, *Contested Countryside Cultures: Otherness, Marginalization and Rurality* (New York: Psychology Press, 1997).

23. Lucy M. Long, *Culinary Tourism* (Lexington: University Press of Kentucky, 2013), 2; See also Dean MacCannell, *The Tourist: A New Theory of the Leisure Class*, 2nd ed. (New York: Schocken Books, 1989); and J. Urry, *The Tourist Gaze* (London: Routledge, 1990).

24. Biana Freire-Medeiros, *Touring Poverty* (London and New York: Routledge, 2013).

25. See C. Michael Hall and Hazel Tucker, "Tourism and Postcolonialism: An Introduction," ed. C. Michael Hall and Hazel Tucker, *Tourism and Postcolonialism: Contested Discourses, Identities, and Representations*, pp. 1–24 (London and New York: Routledge, 2004).

26. Stephan Palmie, *The Cooking of History: How Not to Study Afro-Cuban Religion* (Chicago: University of Chicago Press, 2013), 240.

27. See Stephen William Foster, "The Exotic as Symbol System." *Dialectical Anthropology* 7 (1982): 22–30; Said, *Orientalism*; and Marianna Torgovnick, *Gone Primitive: Savage Intellects, Modern Lives*. Chicago: University of Chicago Press, 1990.

28. See Julia Kristeva, *The Powers of Horror: An Essay on Abjection*, translated by Leon S. Roudiez (New York: Columbia University Press, 1984).

29. The colonial roots of "soul food" and country cooking are explored in Opie, *Hog and Hominy*.

30. Urry, *The Tourist Gaze*, 17.

31. Kent Gibbons, "Travel Channel Adds New Andrew Zimmern Show," *Broadcasting & Cable*, October 7, 2014. Accessed October 15, 2014 at www.broadcastingcable.com/news/programming/travel-channel-adds-new-andrew-zimmern-show/134636.
32. See David Roediger, *Wages of Whiteness: Race and the Making the American Working Class* (New York: Verso, 1999).
33. See "Foodies, Fun and Philanthropy," *Star Tribune*, March 14, 2014. Accessed October 15, 2014 at http://www.startribune.com/local/248299801.html.
34. Tim Carman, "Andrew Zimmern's 'Bizarre Foods America,' Returns Monday with D.C. Episode," *The Washington Post*, February 8, 2013. Accessed October 15, 2014 at http://www.washingtonpost.com/blogs/going-out-guide/wp/2013/02/08/andrew-zimmerns-bizarre-foods-america-returns-monday-with-d-c-episode/.
35. *Bizarre Foods America*, "Third Coast," Travel Channel, July 15, 2013, written by Andrew Zimmern.
36. *Bizarre Foods America*, "The Ozarks," Travel Channel, April 1, 2013, written by Andrew Zimmern.
37. *Bizarre Foods America*, "The Ozarks."
38. *Bizarre Foods America*, "The Ozarks."
39. *Bizarre Foods America*, "The Ozarks."
40. *Bizarre Foods America*, "The Ozarks."
41. *Bizarre Foods America*, "The Blues Trail," Travel Channel, August 20, 2012, written by Andrew Zimmern.
42. *Bizarre Foods America*, "Third Coast."
43. *Bizarre Foods America*, "Third Coast."
44. *Bizarre Foods America*, "Third Coast."
45. *Bizarre Foods America*, "The Blues Trail."
46. *Bizarre Foods America*, "New Orleans," Travel Channel, January 30, 2012, written by Andrew Zimmern.
47. *Bizarre Foods America*, "Third Coast."
48. *Bizarre Foods America*, "The Blues Trail."
49. *Bizarre Foods America*, "The Other Florida," Travel Channel, August 27, 2012, written by Andrew Zimmern.
50. *Bizarre Foods America*, "Third Coast."
51. *Bizarre Foods America*, "Third Coast."
52. *Bizarre Foods America*, "Third Coast."
53. *Bizarre Foods America*, "New Orleans."
54. *Bizarre Foods America*, "The Other Florida."
55. *Bizarre Foods America*, "The Other Florida."
56. In this episode, Pham's role as political advocate for Southeast Asia immigrants is backgrounded to his role ambassador for the community's cuisine.
57. *Bizarre Foods America*, "Third Coast."
58. *Bizarre Foods America*, "The Blues Trail."
59. *Bizarre Foods America*, "The Blues Trail."
60. *Bizarre Foods America*, "Birmingham (The New South)," Travel Channel, July 29, 2013, written by Andrew Zimmern.
61. *Bizarre Foods America*, "Birmingham."
62. *Bizarre Foods America*, "Birmingham."
63. *Bizarre Foods America*, "The Blues Trail."
64. *Bizarre Foods America*, "The Other Florida."
65. *Bizarre Foods America*, "The Other Florida."
66. Patrik Jonsson, "Mississippi Most Obese State: Southern Diet or Culture on the Skids," *Christian Science Monitor*, August, 14, 2012. Accessed October 16, 2014 at http://www.cs monitor.com/USA/Society/2012/0814/Mississippi-most-obese-state-Southern-diet-or-culture-on-the-skids.

THREE

From the Plantation to the Prairie

The Pioneer Woman

In June 2013, Lisa Jackson filed a race and sex discrimination lawsuit against her former employer, Food Network star Paula Deen.[1] Jackson alleged that Deen used racial epithets in the presence of her employees and, on one occasion, expressed her wish to plan a Southern slave plantation-themed wedding for her brother Bubba. Though the suit was dismissed, Deen's record of casual racism had become a matter of public record. Despite Deen's emotional public apologies, the Food Network cancelled her popular programs (*Paula's Home Cooking, Paula's Best Dishes*) and her corporate sponsors, including retailers such as J.C. Penney, Sears, and Walmart, withdrew their endorsements.[2] Previously, Deen had served as the Food Network's ambassador to a quaint but decadent version of Old Southern cuisine, saturated in unhealthy amounts of fat and sugar but nonetheless endearing as an exemplar of "Southern hospitality." But, the lawsuit generated public discomfort with her romanticized portrait of Southern life and culture, a lifestyle brand that elided the historic exploitation of black labor in the Southern "home" and the production and consumption of regional cuisine. As Anjali Vats keenly observes, "her sanitized portrayals of Southernness, while characteristic of the Food Network, ignore Southern hospitality's antebellum roots, when house slaves cooked and served while their masters and masters' guests enjoyed leisurely eating."[3] Deen's tarnished image partially exposed the thinly veiled unconscious racism of Southern myth and the extent to which romanticism of Southern hospitality is premised on erasure, or at the very least, the past-ness of racism.[4]

The home of the Old South, denuded of its quaint charms, could no longer serve as the basis for Food Network's sentimental portrait of

American food culture and domestic life. While the network did not wholly disavow the Southern kitchen, it did seek to rebrand its relationship with comfort food by developing new programs that were more generically "American country" or "New South" than plantation-chic.[5] The network's purging of Deen, however, was less of a courageous indictment of post-racism than a well-timed pivot toward a more wholesome and innocent portrait of American food identities. The transition away from Deen as the face of the network was perhaps inevitable in light of her declining ratings and criticisms of her bacon and butter-laced cuisine—punctuated by her confession that she had been living with Type-2 diabetes.[6] In addition to programming that reflected popular interest in both urbane gastronomy and competitive cooking, the network had also begun grooming stars who could adapt Deen's format of homespun classics delivered with folksy charm from the country family kitchen.[7]

In 2010, the Food Network discovered Ree Drummond, author of the popular and award-winning blog entitled "The Pioneer Woman," a lifestyle website devoted to domestic advice mixed with photography and stories about her transition to life on her husband's Oklahoma ranch.[8] Drummond was also the best-selling author of *From Black Heels to Tractor Wheels: A Love Story* and *The Pioneer Woman Cooks: Recipes from an Accidental Country Girl*.[9] Her cookbooks were lauded by critics for their lack of pretension; even Julia Moskin of the *New York Times* wrote that "vegetarians and gourmands won't find much to cook here, but as a portrait of a real American family kitchen, it works."[10] Drummond first appeared on *Throwdown! With Bobby Flay* in November 2010 and in April 2011 the network announced that she would host her own daytime cooking program from her home. *The Pioneer Woman* adapted many aspects of Deen's format, including an emphasis on rural aesthetics, a family kitchen setting, dialogue composed of country anecdotes, appearances from family members, and, of course, oversized portions of high-calorie comfort food. A key difference was that Drummond's recipes were designed for hungry cowboys rather than Southern gentlemen. Promoting Drummond's brand of Western ranch cooking enabled the Food Network to exchange the tainted legacy of the Southern hospitality for the seemingly more benign mythology of the American frontier.

In the context of Deen's racist transgressions, this change in setting took on redemptive qualities. In the public imaginary, the idyllic Western frontier is a romantic ideal seemingly far removed from the violent legacies of slavery and Jim Crow.[11] By contrast, the pioneer homesteader and the intrepid cowboy of America's vast interior remain enduring and positive symbols of national identity: self-reliance, rugged individualism, the Protestant work ethic, and personal liberty all heightened through an encounter with open landscapes awaiting domestication.[12] The adoption of Drummond's prairie lifestyle brand helped sanitize the Food Network's representation of American comfort food with a pleasing and wholesome portrait of American country living, and one with mythic cultural status. In all its forms, the frontier myth is a type of American origin story that is less formal history than a set of ideological narratives used to explain America's distinct political, cultural, and economic development.[13] According to the myth, the arduous process of turning nature into civilization is the foundation of American national identity and, therefore, explains the success of American empire.[14] Traveling to the frontier, if only vicariously, is a redemptive act that enables Americans to "experience a 'regression' to a more primitive and natural condition of life so that the false values of the 'metropolis' can be purged and a new, purified social contract enacted."[15] But, as Richard Slotkin explains, the end of Westward expansion meant that the frontier became "primarily a term of ideological rather than geographical reference."[16] The contemporary frontier is more of a conceptual than a physical geography.

Indeed, *The Pioneer Woman* reenacts this cycle of frontier redemption, whisking viewers away to the rugged landscape of Oklahoma where life and work have been stripped of pretense and corruption. Drummond's story—the overall framework for her program—evokes the redemptive spirit and fortune of the frontier: an "accidental country girl," an urban woman whose life was transformed when she married a cowboy and was forced to simplify her lifestyle and adjust her priorities to the rhythms of a working cattle ranch. The show offers a nostalgic fantasy of ancestral return to an innocent American identity characterized by honest hard work rewarded with the comforts of family and home-cooked meals. In contrast to the Southern leisure class who exploited the labor of others, the pioneer harnessed their own free labor to transform nature into capital. In moving from Southern hospitality to the rugged Western frontier, the Food Network exchanged one set of myths for another; the new mythology symbolizing equal opportunity and, thus, more plausibly inclusive of people of color.

While distancing the network from the distinct heritage of Southern racism, the network's valorization of frontier food identities escapes neither America's history of racial violence nor the contemporary politics of post-racial America. In one sense, Deen's dismissal exemplifies how structural racism has been reduced to an issue of personal responsibility and those few racists who remain in the post-Civil Rights era are relics of a distant past.[17] In another sense, replacing Deen with an idyllic portrait of white pioneer family life also sanitizes the colonialist history of Westward expansion that required the displacement or extermination of American Indians in the name of progress.[18] Nostalgia for frontier life and foodways is yet another form of colorblind revisionism, or what Kristen Hoerl calls "selective amnesia": a form of collective remembrance that silences or negates any narrative that might rupture or contest the myth of American exceptionalism.[19] With Deen's transgressions threatening to disrupt hegemonic narratives of postracial progress, *The Pioneer Woman* reconnected audiences with a familiar mythology that remains nearly impervious to the force of counternarratives. The program's emphasis on comfort food classics and domestic bliss contribute to its wistful vision of American life. Though seemingly innocuous, the meaning of comfort food in American culture is sutured to the politics of nostalgia, a desire to return home via sensory experience. As one cookbook puts it, comfort food "fills us up emotionally and physically, connecting us back to our first eating experiences that sooth hunger pangs and puts us cozily in the arms of our caregiver."[20] As a cultural construct, comfort food promises to transport us to the innocent moment of our origins, to gaze backward with sentimentality and reverence. As an articulation of a comforting food place identity, *The Pioneer Woman* provides a warm affirmation of American history and identity—swiftly closing the rupture created by the Deen controversy. In this way, a concept of simple taste counters the complexity of Deen's racially coded expressions of Southern hospitality. Put differently, Drummond's frontier recipes function as a kind of national palate cleanser, disguising the taste of historic racism with something more clean, wholesome, and untainted. While her recipes are not that fundamentally different from Deen's, the change in setting helped reorganize dirt and disorder through ritual purification.

This chapter shifts attention from Otherness to constructions of sameness, attending to how comfort food is articulated as a part of American frontier ideology. Resituating comfort food as a national tradition, woven into the mythic folklore of America's origin story, Drummond's lifestyle brand redeems an embattled national identity with a romantic vision of work and leisure. *The Pioneer Woman's* revisionist portrait of frontier life and history compensates for the sins of the South while expunging the crimes of nation-building associated with westward expansion. What's left is an innocent portrait of American individualism in which hard work is rewarded with opportunity and abundance. In this sense, simple tastes reflect a return to simple values; where the honest hard work of a white pioneer family redeems the nation.

The program's construction of authentic American identity is implicitly racialized, located exclusively in the intrepid and heroic white settler overcoming the dark forces of the rugged frontier.

THE COWBOY MYSTIQUE

Ree Drummond's brand is organized around the simple tastes and everyday pleasures of life on the ranch. The Drummond property is located in Osage Country near Pawhuska, Oklahoma, a town with a population of 3,666. As a blogger, in 2006 she began posting lighthearted "confessions" about the travails of country living, homemaking, and her hectic life raising four children. Often humble and self-effacing, her posts convey a sense of domestic bliss that is at ease with messiness and imperfection. Her site is infused with playful humor, country witticism, and motherly gests such "now I have to go water my children, iron my vegetables, and feed my laundry."[21] Her posts feature stock characters such as her children, the family basset hound, her husband Ladd who she affectionately refers to as "The Marlboro Man," their ranch hand "Cowboy Josh," her sister Betsey and brother Mike, best friend Hyacinth, father-in-law Chuck, and an assortment of extended family and friends. Her photography captures the aesthetics of rural life: horses and livestock, cowboys and cowpokes, trucks, tractors, barns, fences, dirt roads, grasslands, eastern redbuds, and hay bails among others. She describes her recipes as "rib-sticking" or "meat and potatoes" comfort food for cowboys. Simple tastes.

Drummond's website launched her Food Network career, receiving nearly 23.3 million visits per month and generating over $1 million in advertising revenue per year.[22] Shortly after the premier of the *Pioneer Woman*, the program became one of the network's top Nielsen performers, particularly popular with women 25–54.[23] *The New Yorker's* Amanda Fortini explains Drummond's broad appeal: "The Pioneer Woman is like an artifact from a more wholesome era: Ozzie and Harriet on a ranch. Even the graphics look vintage—flowers and filigreed letters in the muted colors of an antique map. There is no serious conflict, no controversy, no cynicism, no snark. . . . What anyone else would call banality or drudgery is, for her, humorous, dramatic, and valuable. Drummond makes an average life look heroic."[24] While her program includes cooking demonstrations and recipe secrets, the food is used to narrate her family life. Each episode begins with the preface "Here's what's happening on the ranch." Acting as a kind of an everyday life correspondent, Drummond narrates how each meal fits into the demands of ranch life. She adapts recipes for both work and leisure: from cattle shipping and fence-building days to family cookouts and church potlucks. The program is a perfect simulacra of idyllic pioneer life, a testament to the modern existence of a work and family ideal that by and large never existed outside of film and television.[25] The program resolves the tensions between work and family life by retreating to an imagined past where the home was the center of production and the sole source of fulfillment for both women and men. Here, the problems and complications of the outside world ostensibly do not exist.

Before turning to the program's use of aesthetics and narrative, it is important to note the ideological significance of its underlying mythology. The frontier myth and the cowboy mystique are essential components of American nationalist discourse, invoked as explanations for America's power and status on the global stage. American presidents from Theodore Roosevelt and John F. Kennedy to Ronald Reagan and George W.

Bush have praised the cowboy as the quintessential American hero, at times even adopting his persona, aesthetic, and speech patterns.[26] From nineteenth-century dime novels to modern Hollywood Westerns, the cowboy is the single most valorized profession in American culture.[27] Will Wright argues that the cowboy is the "definitive hero, the symbolic frontier individualist. He is still that hero today, long after the open frontier has vanished from American society. He still rides from the western wilderness to create a civil society, and he still portrays the individualist promise, the promise of freedom and equality."[28] The cowboy is a repository of traditional American values, an icon that lends itself to a variety of political projects, "romantic and modern, individualistic and communal, nostalgic and progressive."[29]

Yet, Slotkin's body of work on frontier mythology suggests that the cowboy image has been most often employed to legitimate American conquest in the name of progress—from Manifest Destiny to the invasion of Iraq and Afghanistan. In its most conservative iterations, the cowboy is an icon of hegemonic masculinity, capitalism, and militarism—a ruggedly virile, individualistic entrepreneur with a penchant for spectacular violence.[30] The success of Buffalo Bill Cody's Wild West and cowboy dime novels in the 1880s gave rise to the cowboy as a symbol of American virtues such as "honor, chivalry, individualism, and the triumph of right over wrong."[31] According to popular lore, the cowboy would use violence judiciously to maintain law and order on the frontier. In his extensive writings on the subject, Teddy Roosevelt romanticized the cowboy as part of a recovery of American manhood at a time in which rapid industrialization and economic instability had separated Americans from the character-building hard work and toil of early American agrarianism.[32] While central to his vision of national virility, Roosevelt also considered ranching to be the most noble of American professions because it symbolized the virtues of free market individualism. Replacing the figure of the trader and the adventuring scout, the rancher was a more visionary entrepreneur who took full advantage of cheap land to cultivate livestock, eventually reaching markets beyond their regional economy. And though ranch hands were waged workers, they were still considered models of austerity, stoicism, and honest hard work, the traits that comprised the ideal Protestant worker. Neither the rancher nor ranch hand were victims of mass industrialization; the alienation of labor and the isolation of living in an urbanized mass society. Open spaces signified unlimited opportunity and upward mobility, "the epic imperial reach of taking and then making land."[33]

As testaments to the core tenets of free market ideology, it makes sense that the cowboy lifestyle continues to be romanticized in American culture. In the twenty-first century, cowboy imagery remains a staple of literature, Hollywood Westerns, advertising, professional sports, video games, magazines, and contemporary fashion. As Evelyn Schlatter puts it, "you no longer have to make a physical pilgrimage to prove yourself out West."[34] And while the cowboy is a romantic figure, cultural nostalgia for his rugged lifestyle elides the darker side of his mythology. For instance, Schlatter finds that frontier nostalgia supports a revisionist historical narrative of triumphant white imperialism. She explains that "invariably, all one has to do is mention 'red-blooded American' and the image that jumps to mind is that of a white man engaged in various masculine pursuits such as settling the West, building a city, surveying a landscape studded with oil derricks, going to war, or perhaps riding a horse into the sunset. The essence of this 'American character,' no matter the medium through which it is expressed, it itself a frontierist construction, and its archetype encodes race (white), gender (male), and place (frontier - out West)."[35] Indeed, ranching itself was an enterprise made possible by the violent expropriation of Texas and other territories from Mexico, and later, US cavalry and paramilitary campaigns against the native nations of the Great Plains and the Southwest.[36]

After the Civil War, reservation allotment and homesteading policies displaced American Indians to make space for white settlers to move West where nations such as the Pueblo and Pima had been successfully ranching for generations.[37] Cowboy romanticism erases imperial violence and the displacement of Native peoples from the history of western settlement. Moreover, while historic ranchers were also Native American, black, Latino, and women, contemporary romanticism constructs cowboys as civilizing white male heroes.[38] A nostalgic gaze sanitizes the history of westward expansion of colonialist violence while preserving heroic national identity of white men.

The contemporary cowboy mystique has its own distinct (post)racial politics that is as troubling as contemporary Southern myth. The white cowboy is celebrated by the Tea Party movement as an anti-government hero who courageously fights the "nanny state" and its tyrannical land-use policies. The Obama administration, representing ideas that are putatively foreign and un-American, constitutes a racial and racist threat to the way of life the cowboy has been anointed to protect.[39] In 2014, Nevada rancher Cliven Bundy became a Tea Party icon, even receiving praise from some members of Congress, when he refused to pay $1 million in federal grazing fees and threatened armed violence against BLM workers.[40] In 2015, his son Ammon Bundy and a group of fellow ranchers temporarily occupied the BLM headquarters at the Malheur National Wildlife Refuge in Oregon in a similar act of protest.[41] Cliven drew significant attention for his public statements about race and President Obama, including comments that African Americans were better off under slavery.[42]

As Darrel Enck-Wanzer notes, Tea Party racism is rarely so overt. Instead the movement's rhetoric is more subtly Otherizing, coded, and inferential.[43] Referring to President Obama as a "Kenyan socialist" or the

"food stamps President" among other racially coded derisions, the movement "articulate[s] Obama to racial threat, which has significant consequences in the neoliberal fantasy and imagining the U.S. body politic."[44]
The Tea Party represents a kind of white identity politics that appeals to
individuals who feel embattlement by progressive social change and believe their country has been taken from them by foreign ideas and foreign
people.[45] Constructed as a rugged individualist with a distaste for big
government, the cowboy is the fitting icon of a movement that resists
progressive social change and adheres to a triumphantalist revision of
American history.[46] The cowboy represents a libertarian America that
will not stand for a foreign tyrannical government dictating to the people
how to use their land and live their lives.

This political and historical context suggests that the cowboy represents a very narrow vision of American national identity. The cowboy
has transformed into an implicitly white defender of traditional
American values: free enterprise, self-reliance, and liberty. He is an oppo-
nent of government dependency and so-called entitlement culture, a racially coded discourse that implies that civil rights, affirmative action,
and government assistance redistributed white America's hard earned
wealth to indolent minorities.[47] He is what Richard Dyer calls the "Great
White Protector," an invincible and unassailable hero who, while he
takes a variety of forms in Western culture, defends white people and
culture against the dark forces of barbarism.[48] At its most extreme, a
cowboy nation is racially and politically homogeneous, committed to an
exceptional and teleological view of history in which white culture forms,
economic systems, and political organization inevitably triumph over all
other alternatives. Of course, this was never the cowboy's mandate nor is
it the only way in which his mystique can be deployed, but in contemporary public culture it is an icon that has become attached to a culturally
regressive vision of American life. Thus, Drummond's innocent romanticism of the cowboy life is not without consequence. While sentimental,
her vision of pioneer life aligns with the "take our country back" ethos of
contemporary white identity politics. The cowboy mystique sanitizes and
reclaims traditional American values in the wake of progressive forces
that continue to challenge the mythology of an innocent America; that
American history is replete with militarism and racial violence, that the
American free market system has impoverished millions of Americans,
and that countless demands for equality and justice remain unmet.

"WELCOME TO MY FRONTIER"

And so, with the above preface, begins each episode of *The Pioneer
Woman*. The opener establishes an idyllic image of contemporary pioneer
living, a modern update of classic frontier mythology. The narrative

framework mirrors the mythic tales of frontier settlers who left the Eastern industrial city or the European metropole to make their fortune in the West. In this myth, regression to a more natural state on the frontier strips away the artifice of civilization and reveals the true character of the individual. Drummond introduces her story in similar fashion: "I'm Ree Drummond. I'm a writer, blogger, photographer, mother, and I'm an accidental country girl. I live on a ranch in the middle of nowhere and I've got hungry mouths to feed. My style of food is simple but scrumptious. All my recipes have to be approved by cowboys, hungry kids, and me." This introduction references a backstory of country romance that brought Drummond to rural Oklahoma, which she details on her blog and in *Black Heels*. Drummond, recently graduated from the University of Southern California, was on the path to law school in Chicago when she met Ladd in a bar in her hometown of Bartelsville, OK. Their ensuing courtship and marriage inspired her to abandon her career ambitions and the big city to raise a family on the ranch. Like the mythology, Drummond's story is fundamentally about the simplification of values, priorities, and lifestyle. Country tastes are a marker of distinction. Now in the "middle of nowhere," Drummond is shown to have happily purged the misguided ambitions associated with modern urban living. On the prairie, the conditions of life and work radically alter what is vital to one's personal fulfillment. Here, raising children and maintaining the homestead appear to be more natural and innately fulfilling duties and life objectives.[49] And while Drummond is an extraordinary successful entrepreneur, blogging, writing, and photography are framed as mere dispatches from the frontier, forms of correspondence to the fast-paced world she left behind for simpler ambitions, and of course, simpler food.

The opening is addressed as a letter or communique to the audience—the outside world—which prefaces regular updates about "what's happening on the ranch." Each episode follows new developments on the ranch, family milestones, relationships with stock characters, and special events. Filmed on location, the program is profoundly intimate, each recipe an opportunity to share updates about the status of their close friends and family, including the family dogs. While the audience is temporarily transported into the Drummond home, their distance from the frontier imbues her stories with the mythic qualities of frontier correspondence.[50] That is to say, that the program mediates contemporary pioneer life according to the fantasy structure of a mythical ideal, a simulacra of frontier living informed by the folk legends of those who romanticized the all-American pioneer family. Thus, the framework of the program is a dispatch to the metropole about the travails and rewards of life after the overland journey.

Since it appears on the Food Network, *The Pioneer Woman* is ostensibly a cooking show in which Drummond re-creates recipes from family and church cookbooks.[51] But the comfort food recipes featured in the pro-

gram primarily advance a rhetoric of space and place, articulating connections between open spaces, simplicity, hard work, and freedom. The
frontier is a marker of distinction, the site of quintessentially American
tastes and values. First, most of Drummond's recipes are extraordinarily
high in fat and sugar, including such "cowboy tested" dishes as country-
fried steak, short ribs and cheese grits, chicken cordon bleu casserole,
pizza burgers, cheese steak sandwiches, creamed vegetables, pies, cakes,
and so on. As Drummond explains in the pilot episode, "my family is a
meat and potatoes family and my husband is a meat and potatoes kind of
guy."[52] Bucking health food trends, Drummond's unabashedly decadent
cuisine is portrayed as a return to simplicity, food without the pretension
and vanity that accompanies complicated calorie-counting diets and fig-
ure-conscious meal regimens. In conjunction with the program's emphasis on the liberating simplicity of country life, Drummond's unhealthy
recipes free the audience from the airs of the metropole where overindul-
gent food and large portions are subject to regulation and ridicule by
public health officials. Nor is the food overcomplicated by cosmopolitan
interests in the molecular gastronomy and exotic ingredients that comprise contemporary haute cuisine. There is an emphasis on simplicity, on
revisiting modest comforts. Drummond often characterizes her high-
calorie dishes as a return to basics, inspired by the tastes of her cowboy
husband. For instance, while baking a chocolate pie she comments "he's a
man of simple wants," and "Ladd likes it plain and unadorned."[53] While
making quintessential cattle drive food, she notes "Ladd has always really liked a simple pot of beans."[54] Frontier living forces individuals to
simplify their everyday life practices; however, such a transition is as
liberating as the open mise-en-scene of the Oklahoma prairie. That is to
say that real American cuisine signifies enjoyment without prohibition,
no one to chastise individuals for neither possessing unsophisticated
taste nor consuming in abundance. For those who might balk at such
cuisine, Drummond retorts "don't be alarmed, I have a large family to
feed."[55]

Second, Drummond frequently contrasts her ruggedly Oklahoman
tastes with the more feminized health-conscious cuisine that reflects her
time living in the city (Los Angeles). Thus, the program maintains a facile
distinction between country and urban tastes. The contrast is often in
terms of a dish's quotient of meat protein; frontier food is ruggedly masculine whereas urban California cuisine is dainty and feminine. Thus, her
"meat and potatoes" cuisine affirms that the frontier is a masculine space
where men's work requires "something to stick to their ribs."[56] When
making a "girly" peaches-and-cream dessert for her female guests, she
remarks "can you imagine cowboys eating ice cream and peaches? Not in
Osage County."[57] Elsewhere she describes her lighter dishes such as tofu
and kale salad as something reminiscent of her time in California, during
her "vegetarian days," something she has largely abandoned.[58] In an

episode entitled "Girl Time and Burger Time" Drummond makes vegetarian pasta primavera for her daughters, but when the boys return home she cooks burgers.[59] Pasta, she explains, is "the quintessential dish the boys won't eat because it doesn't have meat in it."[60] Hence, she is forced to "bring the food back down to earth."[61] Barely acknowledging Ree except to express hunger, Ladd and her sons Todd and Bryce return home in full cowboy regalia and begin immediately consuming their large portions of meat. Note that California cuisine is lofty and pretentious, whereas meat-heavy Oklahoma meals are "down to earth." Thus, Drummond saves her dainty California recipes for herself, daughters, and girlfriends. While expressing a fondness for the urban cuisine of her past, she frequently notes that she has adopted her husband's Oklahoma palate. For instance, she expresses an appreciation for sushi but quickly jokes, "no sushi is ever going to show up at one of our anniversary dinners."[62] The recurring message throughout the program is that meat recipes are more suited for the frontier than the "girly food" she only serves when the men are away (salads, quiches, cupcakes). Plainly stated, "out here on the ranch, it doesn't get more cowboy friendly than chicken fried steak."[63] Drawing from the longstanding cultural association between masculinity and meat-eating, Drummond's protein-heavy version of Oklahoma cuisine constructs a place-identity grounded in the conquest of nature and the feminine, aligned with Roosevelt's masculine vision of frontier virility.[64] If the frontier is a place that reveals what can be characterized as authentic subjectivity, our de facto national identity is hyper-masculine.

Finally, Drummond frames her decadent and protein-centered cowboy recipes as the spoils of frontier labor.[65] In other words, overindulgence in high-calorie food is permissible if it is an incentive or reward for a commitment to hard work. As such, the program defends its food as part of the American Dream wherein hard work unlocks the individual benefits of a free market capitalist society.[66] Of course, the cowboy is the quintessential portrait of free market labor as he transforms nature into useful capital by hard work alone. A vast majority of the episodes revolve around the entailments of ranch work and matching meals to suit distinct tasks. Work is a vital component of the program's narrative, emphasized by Ree and Ladd's narration of projects such as feeding and herding alongside visual demonstration of those tasks. These verbal and visual cues confirm for the audience that although the ranch is serene and bucolic, hard labor is relentless and ongoing. The program stresses that the Drummond children—particularly their oldest Alex and Todd—are learning the value of hard work, punctuated with scenes of tutelage and training in how to run the ranch.[67] These episodes intersperse shots of fence building, hay hauling, cattle feeding, herding, shipping, and grass burning between recipe segments that feature Drummond cooking in the kitchen. After the first season, the program even gives more screen time to ranch labor by truncating recipe segments or directing the audiences to more information on the Food Network's website.

Work episodes typically begin with pre-dawn shots that remind the audience that the boys and Ladd's crew are awake at five a.m. to begin their long day of physical labor. Next, Drummond introduces her meal plans as a necessary feature of specific ranch labor. For instance, she begins with statements such as "we've been hauling hay, building fences, and shipping cattle," "it's a hardworking morning of cooking and feeding with me and my hardworking husband," and "we are always busy around here, between ranch work, school work, and everything else life throws at us."[68] Drummond then narrates each meal in terms of earned entitlements. In an episode entitled "All Work and Some Play," she tells the audience that "we're rolling up fence, it's the tougher, less romantic side of ranching. They deserve a treat."[69] In a later episode she reaffirms "there's always fence to fix, miles and miles of it, so everyone needs a rib-sticking lunch to look forward to."[70] In another episode about shipping cattle she quips "that's the kind of work that really builds up an appetite," thus, they will need "a scrumptious breakfast after a morning of hard work on the prairie."[71] Indeed, her "hard-working crew" seems to be continually in "need [of] their protein."[72] Ree even implores her son Todd to "pig out and that's an order!"[73] The message is that high-calorie food is not gluttony or excess if it is either fuel or compensation for the completion of physical tasks.

While such high-calorie meals are often associated with rising obesity rates—particularly in Oklahoma where the rate is a staggering 30 percent—the Drummonds appear relatively fit and healthy.[74] It is, therefore, unlikely that the Drummonds cook and eat how they are depicted on screen. But, the appearance that the Drummonds are unaffected by obesity and the health complications of high fat and sugar diets implies that they either do not eat such cuisine as a part of their regular diet or that the family's work ethic somehow overcomes the health challenges posed by the pioneer diet. Drummond only addresses the health consequences of recipes when she assures the audience that what appears to be excessive amounts of fat are in proper ratio to the large size of the recipe. What, then, accounts for such high rates of obesity among those who enjoy a similar diet? Although the American Dream myth praises hard work, it is important to note that it also holds the individual responsible for their failures—even if they are the result of structural inequalities. Inferentially, obesity is the byproduct of a diminished work ethic. Indulgence without taxing physical labor represents gluttony or shows a fundamental lack of self-restraint. Within the structure of the American Dream, "pigging out" becomes a reward for sacrifice and persistent labor. Yet, it punishes the bodies of those lacking in pioneer spirit. The program's silence on health consequences implies that it is hard work that enables the cowboys to transcend the physical limitations of an unhealthy diet. In a broader sense, hard work enables the cowboy to transcend structural limitations to success that might prove barriers for others who lack his rugged character. Drummond's food builds on the mythic status of the frontier, a place where masculine labor conquers the limitations of nature and even the body.

THE ALL-AMERICAN FAMILY

While work is paramount, the program also celebrates a homogeneous and parochial conception of familial community. In *The Pioneer Woman*, the frontier is a proto-nationalist space, a version of America that is more distinctly patriotic, hard-working, family-oriented, and pious than other parts of the country. Here, community is organized around family gatherings, football, homeschooling, Fourth of July celebrations, and church. The show holds up country life as exemplar of traditional American values, consummated through a fantasy of return to the small-scale tightly knit communities of American life that predate the alienation of urbanization and industrialization. If the frontier represents a simplification and clarification of core values, the program's representation of community is privileged with an air of authenticity, as something more quintessentially American than a plurality of diverse places and communities throughout the country. The program makes no explicit political overtures; however, its representation of community resonates with populist strands of conservative and Tea Party discourse. In 2008, Vice Presidential candidate Sarah Palin infamously suggested that rural communities were more fundamentally pro-American than others. She contended that "we believe that the best of America is in these small towns that we get to visit, and in these wonderful little pockets of what I call the real America, being here with all of you hard working very patriotic . . . pro-America areas of this great nation. This is where we find the kindness and the goodness and the courage of everyday Americans."[75] Palin's valorization of small town America reflects some conservatives' disdain for the secularization and diversification of American life following the political upheaval of the 1960s.[76] This romanticization of rural life is a way for conservatives to recast authentic American identity as something embodied in the hard work, Christian principles, and family values of the 1950s small town. Accordingly, this vision of "real America" negates and silences "urban America," a postracial inference to people of color.

The Pioneer Woman ultimately affirms this conservative caricature of frontier life as exclusively American. First, the program celebrates church as an authentic expression of American small town community. While church plays a very important role in many rural communities, the program's frontier populism contests the post-1960s secularization of American society with a valorization of Christian values as an exclusive cultural adhesive of authentic America. Throughout the program, Sunday brunches and church potlucks signify the unification of a dispersed and atomized rural public. One such episode features extended scenes of Ree, Ladd, and the children attending an early morning church service. Shots featured the family singing hymns and paying careful attention to a minister's sermon.[77] The camera pans throughout the modest church to capture an eclectic congregation of working class characters, including farmers and fellow ranchers. The potluck to follow features scenes of parishioners sitting around large tables engaged in pleasant and gregarious conversation. Ree makes the rounds, greeting fellow members of her congregation and doing her best to impress their church's minister, who is delighted to sample her recipe of "Mormon funeral potatoes." The family takes their seat at the table and enjoys a meal made possible through a collection of small efforts by every member of the congregation. Smiling with contentment, Drummond concludes the episode by directly addressing the camera: "food made by church people, it don't get any better." The camera cuts to Todd who resounds "Amen!" In other episodes, Christian holidays provide a rationale for conviviality and fellowship. While the rancher's life involves solitary work in an isolated location, the American ideal requires the existence of a small-scale local community to which one is responsible. Easter, for instance, is a reminder to Drummond that she needs to reconnect with members of her church community. In this episode she delivers "hot cross buns" to her friends and neighbors, and later prepares a spinach dip for another church potluck.[78] In other episodes, church is an occasion to invite friends and neighbors for a celebratory brunch.[79] As she puts it, "there's ranching and then church."[80] The program represents church as the foundation of American democratic sentiment and the center of frontier civic life. In short, Christianity is portrayed as the foundation of authentic American community life.

Second, the Drummond's frontier life is portrayed as the perfection of the conservative small government ideal. This is particularly salient in relation to how the show represents the education and socialization of children. In addition to representations of the home as the ideal site of economic production, the show celebrates the ways in which the family has taken on the functions of government. For instances, several episodes emphasize how the family has successfully homeschooled their children. While Ladd is in the field, Ree and her homeschool co-op bring a small group of community children into the Drummond kitchen to impart science lessons through the process of cooking strawberry preserves.[81] In addition to learning the ranching trade, the Drummond children and their fellow students are also enthusiastic about learning the fundamentals of a secondary school education. In this episode, aptly titled "Little Schoolhouse on the Prairie," the program draws from the mythology of the "little red schoolhouse," the early American ideal of the one-room community school at the crossroads of a rural community. As Ronald Lee and Karen Lee contend, the Little Red Schoolhouse is part of American frontier mythology that reflects the rural character of democracy, moral order, and family as the basis of community.[82] A teacher, typically female, would both give students the basics of arithmetic, reading, and history while also instilling in children a strong Protestant work ethic and patriotic sentiment. They explain that "in this tale, students became industrious, respectful, patriotic, and, most of all, truly American."[83] Likewise, throughout the program, the children are shown learning the value of hard work in the field and in the community classroom, the ranch a self-contained and sustainable source of valuable educational lessons.[84] In other words, there is no need for educational resources beyond the ranch. As an alternative to government-funded public education, a co-op of ranch mothers can better fulfill the needs of their community than a state bureaucracy. This is a fitting representation of how local communities know how to best address their own parochial needs.

Finally, the family's leisure activities signify their adherence to patriotic ideals. The program emphasizes the importance of football to the Drummond family, a sport that codes as quintessentially American. Episodes depict Drummond constructing recipes for her son's football practice,[85] football games,[86] football camp,[87] televised college football,[88] homecoming events,[89] and "man cave" renovations.[90] These episodes weave football and football food into the place-identity of Oklahoma. For instance, as Drummond prepares a large batch of chicken wings, she enthusiastically tells the audience, "Saturday, Oklahoma, it can only mean one thing: football."[91] She declares confidently, "there's not a football player alive that doesn't love wings." Again, Drummond connects frontier identity with the masculine practice of meat-eating, but more importantly she attests to the family's appreciation for a hyper-masculine gladiatorial sport, or America's game. Perhaps a more important signifier of the family's patriotic fervor is their extravagant Fourth of July party and firework display.[92] In season 3, the Drummonds hosted a celebration with "hundreds of guests in attendance, including friends, family, fellow ranchers, and eighty kids from their church's youth ministry."[93] The portrayal of this spectacular celebration punctuates the program's patriotic ethos. Moreover, the image of country life as structured around hard work, church, football, and patriotic celebrations confirms that rural America is, in Palin's words, "more pro-American." In short, the frontier family stands in as all-American family.

FRONTIER ICONOGRAPHY

Visually, the program romanticizes open spaces and rural iconography. The frontier landscape is depicted as open, fecund, and awaiting subjugation. Meanwhile, the iconography of country kitsch represents American pastoralism, recalling the ancestral memory of the frontier settlers who paved the way for settlement. The program's cinematography and mise-en-scene cultivate a sentimental pastoralism that transports the audience to time and place of the imagined frontier. First, the countryside is frequently depicted in a wide frame, capturing the frontier as a sublime landscape. In the opening credits, Drummond welcomes the audience to "her frontier" in a wide angled close-up with her in foreground and the sprawling prairie in the background. Earlier in the sequence, a long shot captures cattle and cowboy silhouettes riding into a wide shot-encompassing sunset. Views from the ranch are captured from the vantage point of the "lodge," a guesthouse perched on a high bluff where the wide shots can capture the immensity of the landscape and the horizon.[94] Sublime landscapes juxtaposed with close and medium shots of cattle and bails of hay provide visual proof that the land is productive and fertile. But of all the techniques for representing the landscapes, the program relies most heavily on the travel shots. Drummond's frequent journeys from the ranch to Pawhuska, Bartlesville, or Tulsa and back give the camera crews an opportunity to give specific features to the massive prairie. For instance, when Drummond goes to town to pick up groceries, she narrates her recipe from inside her truck as she drives.[95] Her narration is interspersed with a series of natural shots that catalogue sage brush, grasses, native trees, and local flora and fauna. While the close shots of Drummond inside the cab are constricted if not claustrophobic, the cuts to open fields communicate the openness of the prairie and relieve the audience of being confined. The seeming endlessness of the frontier signifies the inviting openness of America's vast interior. Drummond's travel is only restricted by the parameters of the winding country road that in the wide shot reveal her to be its sole traveler. While the frontier landscapes appear open, shots of fences, roads, and power lines confirm that nature has been domesticated and transformed into property through hard labor. And with no other houses or towns in view of the camera, the prairie is indeed her frontier.

Second, the mise-en-scene is composed of pastoral memory objects that reference America's frontier past. Drummond cooks almost all her meals with a heavy cast iron skillet, she makes all her salad dressings in Mason jars, and she cooks in front of an elaborately constructed set comprised of an antique kitchen scale, a painted antique grocer sign, and an old tool box. At the same time, such objects commingle with expensive modern appliances and kitchen fixtures. But the contrast of ancient and modern visually connects the modern frontier to its pastoral roots. The presence of outdated or old-fashioned kitchen devices reminds the audience that the modern rancher is tied to the legacy of previous generations of pioneers, to a reverent time in which work was more strenuous and less convenient. The set, however, is less a replica of a pioneer kitchen than the reproduction of authenticity through the deployment of rustic pioneer style. The program uses objects that trigger memories of America's pioneer past; memories that are more the byproduct of mythology than history. The role of pioneer style is perhaps best exemplified in an episode that details Ladd and Ree's project to refurbish and open the mercantile exchange in Pawhuska.[96] This episode features old photos of the historic downtown that used to center around a series of vital store fronts and trading posts. The episode details the long process of renovation and concludes with Drummond cooking a dinner to thank her business associates who have been finding items to stock the exchange. This episode captures the nostalgia for the old West, diffusing it into the selection of objects that both appear on screen and that will likely be in their store. Like the program's mise-en-scene, the lore of the mercantile exchange as the center of frontier life orients the audience to view the frontier as a site of national heritage. While the show recognizes that modern life has updated country life, it implies that our contemporary identities are tied to our ancestral roots. In *The Pioneer Woman*, the objects remain to tell the story.

CONCLUSION

The Pioneer Woman puts its audience at ease with traditional American identity, locating mythic sources of national heritage and pride in the legacy of frontier settlement. It is a vision of an innocent nation, unburdened by its imperialist legacies, its structural inequities, its histories of violence. If Deen reopened the wounds of America's racial past, Drummond sutures those wounds closed before citizens have had time to reflect on the ways in which the legacy of Southern racism is also America's legacy. Like portrayals of comfort food, the program's mythological conception of American frontier life consummates the fantasy of ancestral return, offering to renew an embattled national identity. A return to simple tastes reflects the program's larger fantasy structure, namely, the return to a simple life. This fantasy evacuates everyday life of modern complications: the corruption of politics, the contradictions of history, and the alienation of mass society. The program's representation of the Drummond ranch functions as a kind of shelter from the globalized world, where traditional American values can be celebrated without criticism or consequence. The cowboy mystique offers salvation. America can once again be animated by hard work, patriotism, religion, and family values. This vision is exclusive, however. The ideal American is implicitly white, economically mobile, and faithful to the myth of American exceptionalism. The frontier myth evades the perverse race consciousness that haunts Southern hospitality, making it possible to celebrate heritage and tradition without accusations of exclusion and white privilege.

In the context of contemporary racial politics, I suggest that this construction of American identity appeals primarily though not exclusively to white conservatives, particularly those who identify with the Tea Party movement. The cowboy is an unassailable white populist American hero who exemplifies hard-work, independence, and freedom. An embodiment of both the American Dream and national virility, the cowboy is an unapologetic icon of American nationalism and global power. Through cowboy narratives and iconography, Drummond's program romanticizes those traditional (white) American values that Tea Party conservatives suggest are perpetually under attack. Drummond's lifestyle brand implicitly resists what some conservatives call "the nanny state," what they believe to be an elitist, atheistic, and techno-scientific bureaucracy that wants to micromanage the health and welfare of the citizenry.[97] As public officials, celebrity chefs, and even the First Lady make pleas for healthy food and exercise to combat obesity, Drummond's version of comfort food is defiantly fattening. Although it is unlikely that Drummond is trying to make a political statement with her liberal use of butter, cream, and bacon, her indulgent country cuisine runs contrary to progressively coded food trends and public health policies that encourage portion and calorie control. Alongside depictions of the Drummonds as hard-working, patriotic, family-oriented Christians, comfort food is a synecdoche for a neoconservative vision of American history and citizenship, the frontier once again making America anew.

NOTES

1. "Document: Paula Deen's Testimony," *CNN*, May 17, 2013, http://www.cnn.com/interactive/2013/06/entertainment/deen-deposition/index.html.

2. Alan Blinder, "Racial Bias Claim Dismissed for Paula Deen," *The New York Times*, August 12, 2013, http://www.nytimes.com/2013/08/13/us/racial-bias-claim-dismissed-for-paula-deen.html; Rene Lynch, "Paula Deen Fired by Food Network over Use of Racial Epithet," *Los Angeles Times*, June 21, 2013, http://articles.latimes.com/2013/jun/21/news/la-dd-paula-deen-fired-by-food-network-over-use-of-the-nword-20130621; and Clare O'Connor, "Paula Deen Dumped by Home Depot and Diabetes Drug Company Novo Nordisk As Target, Sears, QVC Mull Next Move," *Forbes*, June 27, 2013, http://www.forbes.com/sites/clareoconnor/2013/06/27/paula-deen-dumped-by-home-depot-and-diabetes-drug-company-novo-nordisk-as-target-sears-qvc-mull-next-move/.

3. Anjali Vats, "Cooking Up Hashtag Activism: #PaulasBestDishes and Counternarratives of Southern Food," *Communication and Critical/Cultural Studies* 12, no. 2 (2015): 209–13.

4. See Carol M. Megehee and Deborah F. Spake, "Decoding Southern Culture and Hospitality," *International Journal of Culture, Tourism and Hospitality Research* 2, issue 2 (2008): 97–101.

5. Noteable examples include programs such as *Heartland Table* and *Farmhouse Rules*.

6. Keach Hagey, "Paula Deen's Other Problem: Stale Ratings," *Wall Street Journal*, June 25, 2013, www.wsj.com/articles/SB10001424127887323998604578567832751771860.

7. Anna Weaver and Heather Schwedel, "Who Will Grab the Butter Baton?," *Slate,* January 19, 2012, www.slate.com/blogs/browbeat/2012/01/19/paula_deen_has_ diabetes_who_s_going _to_help_us_cook_our_favorite_fatty_foods_now_.html. Other "New South" candidates included Trisha Yearwood (*Trish's Southern Kitchen*), Damaris Phillips (*Southern at Heart*), Patrick and Fina Neely (*Down Home with the Neelys*), Amy Thielen (*Heartland Table*), and Melissa d'Arabian (*Ten Dollar Dinners*).

8. The original title for the Typepad blog (pioneerwoman.typepad.com) was "Confessions of a Pioneer Woman." It was later hosted by Rackspace. The blog won Weblog of the Year in 2007–2009, and 2010. Lewis Wallace, "SXSW: Pioneer Woman Nabs Top Honors at 2009 Bloggies," *WIRED,* March 16, 2009, http://www.wired.com/2009/03/ bloggies-tk-tk/.

9. Ree Drummond, *Black Heels to Tractor Wheels: A Love Story* (New York, NY: William Morrow Paperbacks, 2007); *The Pioneer Woman Cooks: Recipes from an Accidental Country Girl,* Later Printing edition (New York, NY: William Morrow Cookbooks, 2009).

10. Julia Moskin, "Cookbooks as Edible Adventures," *The New York Times,* November 4, 2009, http://www.nytimes.com/2009/11/04/dining/04book.html.

11. This idyllic vision of the frontier occludes not only genocidal violence against American Indians but also the extent to which Western states, fearing the migration of free blacks and manumitted slaves, erected legal barriers to black citizenship. See Eugene H. Berwanger, *The Frontier against Slavery: Western Anti-Negro Prejudice and the Slavery Extension Controversy* (Champaign-Urbana: University of Illinois Press, 1967); David R. Roediger, *The Wages of Whiteness: Race and the Making of the American Working Class* (New York, NY: Verso, 1999); and Richard Slotkin, *The Gunfighter Nation: Myth of the Frontier in Twentieth-Century America* (Norman: University of Oklahoma Press, 1998).

12. See Paul F. Starrs, *Let the Cowboy Ride: Cattle Ranching in the American West* (Baltimore, MD: Johns Hopkins University Press, 2000).

13. See Greg Dickinson, Brian L. Ott, and Eric Aoki, "Memory and Myth at the Buffalo Bill Museum," *Western Journal of Communication* 69, no. 2 (April 2005): 85–108; Mary Stuckey, "The Donner Party and the Rhetoric of Western Expansion," *Rhetoric & Public Affairs* 14, no. 2 (2011): 229–60; Zoë Hess Carney and Mary E. Stuckey, "The World as the American Frontier: Racialized Presidential War Rhetoric," *Southern Communication Journal* 80, no. 3 (July 2015): 163–88; and Janice Hocker Rushing, "Evolution of 'the New Frontier' in Alien and Aliens: Patriarchal Co-Optation of the Feminine Archetype," *Quarterly Journal of Speech* 75, no. 1 (1989): 1–20.

14. See Frederick Jackson Turner, *The Significance of the Frontier in American History* (London: Penguin UK, 2008). Original work published in 1890.

15. Slotkin, *Gunfighter Nation*, 14.

16. Slotkin, *Gunfighter Nation*, 4.

17. Eduardo Bonilla-Silva, *Racism Without Racists: Color-Blind Racism and the Persistence of Racial Inequality in the United States* (Lanham, MD: Rowman & Littlefield, 2010); and David Theo Goldberg, *The Threat of Race: Reflections on Racial Neoliberalism* (New York, NY: John Wiley & Sons, 2011).

18. Richard Slotkin, *Regeneration through Violence: The Mythology of the American Frontier, 1600–1860* (Norman: University of Oklahoma Press, 2000); and *The Fatal Environment: The Myth of the Frontier in the Age of Industrialization, 1800-1890* (Norman: University of Oklahoma Press, 1998).

19. Kristen Hoerl, "Selective Amnesia and Racial Transcendence in News Coverage of President Obama's Inauguration," *Quarterly Journal of Speech* 98, no. 2 (May 1, 2012): 178–202.

20. Ellie Krieger, *Comfort Food Fix: Feel-Good Favorites Made Healthy* (New York, NY: Houghton Mifflin Harcourt, 2011), 1.

21. Ree Drummond, "Iron My Vegetables," *The Pioneer Woman,* July 26, 2010, http:// thepioneerwoman.com/confessions/iron-my-vegetables/.

22. Amanda Fortini, "O Pioneer Woman!," *The New Yorker*, May 9, 2011, http://www.newyorker.com/magazine/2011/05/09/o-pioneer-woman.

23. Scripps Network Interactive, "News Release: Food Network Drew Record Viewership in 2012," December 11, 2012, http://www.scrippsnetworksinteractive.com/newsroom/company-news/Food-Network-drew-record-viewership-in-2012/

24. Fortini, "O Pioneer Woman."

25. See Stephanie Coontz, *The Way We Never Were: American Families and the Nostalgia Trap* (New York, NY: Basic Books, 1993).

26. See Leroy G. Dorsey, *We Are All Americans, Pure and Simple: Theodore Roosevelt and the Myth of Americanism* (Tuscaloosa, AL: University of Alabama Press, 2013); James E. Combs, *The Reagan Range: The Nostalgic Myth in American Politics* (Bowling Green, OH: Bowling Green State University Press, 1993); and Mark West and Chris Carey, "(Re)Enacting Frontier Justice: The Bush Administration's Tactical Narration of the Old West Fantasy after September 11," *Quarterly Journal of Speech* 92, no. 4 (November 2006): 379–412.

27. Blake Allmendinger, *The Cowboy: Representations of Labor in an American Work Culture* (New York, NY: Oxford University Press, 1992); Mark Cronlund Anderson, *Cowboy Imperialism and Hollywood Film* (New York, NY: Peter Lang, 2007); John E. O'Connor and Peter Rollins, *Hollywood's West: The American Frontier in Film, Television, and History* (Lexington, KY: University Press of Kentucky, 2005); and William W. Savage, *The Cowboy Hero: His Image in American History & Culture* (Norman, OK: University of Oklahoma Press, 1979).

28. Will Wright, *The Wild West: The Mythical Cowboy and Social Theory* (Thousand Oaks, CA: SAGE, 2001), 6.

29. Beth E. Levy, *Frontier Figures: American Music and the Mythology of the American West* (Berkeley, CA: University of California Press, 2012), 2.

30. See Laura Sjoberg and Sandra Via, *Gender, War, and Militarism: Feminist Perspectives* (Santa Barbara, CA: ABC-CLIO, 2010); and Tom R. Sullivan, *Cowboys and Caudillos: Frontier Ideology of the Americas* (Bowling Green, OH: Bowling Green State University Press, 1990).

31. Richard W. Slatta, *Cowboys of the Americas* (New Haven, CT: Yale University Press, 1994), 191.

32. See Gail Bederman, *Manliness and Civilization: A Cultural History of Gender and Race in the United States, 1880-1917* (Chicago, IL: University of Chicago Press, 2008); Matthew Carter, *Myth of the Western: New Perspectives on Hollywood's Frontier Narrative* (Edinburgh, UK: Edinburgh University Press, 2015); R. W. Connell and Raewyn Connell, *Masculinities* (Berkeley, CA: University of California Press, 1995); Debra L. Donahue, *The Western Range Revisited: Removing Livestock from Public Lands to Conserve Native Biodiversity* (Norman, OK: University of Oklahoma Press, 1999); and Arnaldo Testi, "The Gender of Reform Politics: Theodore Roosevelt and the Culture of Masculinity," *The Journal of American History* 81, no. 4 (1995): 1509–33.

33. Starrs, *Let the Cowboy Ride*, 19.

34. Evelyn A. Schlatter, *Aryan Cowboys: White Supremacists and the Search for a New Frontier, 1970-2000* (Austin, TX: University of Texas Press, 2009), 55.

35. Schlatter, *Aryan Cowboy*, 56.

36. David Nibert, *Animal Oppression and Human Violence: Domesecration, Capitalism, and Global Conflict* (New York, NY: Columbia University Press, 2013).

37. Steven L. Danver, *Encyclopedia of Politics of the American West* (Thousand Oaks, CA: CQ Press, 2013); and Peter Iverson, *When Indians Became Cowboys: Native Peoples and Cattle Ranching in the American West* (Norman, OK: University of Oklahoma Press, 1997).

38. William Loren Katz, *The Black West: A Documentary and Pictorial History of the African American Role in the Westward Expansion of the United States* (New York, NY: Harlem Moon/Broadway Books, 1971); Quintard Taylor, *In Search of the Racial Frontier: African Americans in the American West 1528-1990* (New York, NY: W. W. Norton & Company, 1999).

39. See Meghan A. Burke, *Race, Gender, and Class in the Tea Party: What the Movement Reflects about Mainstream Ideologies* (Lanham, MD: Lexington Books, 2015); and Christopher S. Parker and Matt A. Barreto, *Change They Can't Believe In: The Tea Party and Reactionary Politics in America* (Princeton, NJ: Princeton University Press, 2014).

40. Aaron Blake, "Cliven Bundy: The Tea Party's Latest Anti-Hero," *Washington Post*, April 24, 2014, https://www.washingtonpost.com/news/the-fix/wp/2014/04/24/cliven-bundy-the-tea-partys-latest-anti-hero/

41. Evan Perez and Holly Yan, "Oregon: Ammon Bundy, Others Arrested; LaVoy Finicum Killed - CNN.com," January 1, 2016, http://www.cnn.com/2016/01/26/us/oregon-wildlife-refuge-siege-arrests/index.html; and David A. Graham, "The Decline of the Bundy Rebellion," *The Atlantic*, January 12, 2016, http://www.theatlantic.com/politics/archive/2016/01/the-decline-of-the-bundy-rebellion/423693/.

42. Pat Morrison, "How Not to Pick a Hero: The Cliven Bundy Story," *Los Angeles Times*, May 4, 2014, http://www.latimes.com/opinion/op-ed/la-oe-morrison-bundy-racism-tea-party-20140504-column.html.

43. Darrel Enck-Wanzer, "Barack Obama, the Tea Party, and the Threat of Race: On Racial Neoliberalism and Born Again Racism," *Communication, Culture & Critique* 4, no. 1 (2011): 23–30.

44. Enck-Wanzer, "Born Again Racism," 26.

45. See also Douglas Kellner, *Guys and Guns Amok: Domestic Terrorism and School Shootings from the Oklahoma City Bombing to the Virginia Tech Massacre* (New York, NY: Routledge, 2008).

46. Despite the movement's anti-government ethos, ranching is a struggling industry that depends on government support, including farm subsidies and inexpensive leases for grazing cattle on government property. The most significant threat to the independent rancher is not government regulations but instead corporate consolidation in the fast food industry. Many ranches have turned to tourism as their primary source of income largely in response to fast food chains such as McDonald's shifting to only a few large beef suppliers. What some critics term "ranch fundamentalism" or "ranch welfare" characterizes the irony that subsidization is required to keep afloat an industry that prides itself on independence from government. See Donahue, *The Western Range Revisited*; Schlosser, *Fast Food Nation*.

47. Michael Omi and Howard Winant, *Racial Formation in the United States* (London: Psychology Press, 1994).

48. Richard Dyer, *White: Essays on Race and Culture* (New York: Routledge, 1997), 28.

49. The pleasures of "opting out" is also a common postfeminist trope, employed as a legitimation of traditionalism (even anti-feminism) its own form of feminist empowerment. See Mary Douglas Vavrus, "Opting Out Moms in the News," *Feminist Media Studies* 7, no. 1 (2007): 47–63.

50. Brigitte Georgi-Findlay, *The Frontiers of Women's Writing: Women's Narratives and the Rhetoric of Westward Expansion* (Tucson, AZ: University of Arizona Press, 1996); and Elizabeth Jameson and Susan Hodge Armitage, *Writing the Range: Race, Class, and Culture in the Women's West* (Norman, OK: University of Oklahoma Press, 1997).

51. See Ree Drummond, *The Pioneer Woman Cooks: Food from My Frontier* (New York: William Morrow Cookbooks, 2012).

52. *Pioneer Woman*, "Home on the Ranch," The Food Network, August 27, 2011, written by Graham Sherringham and Ree Drummond.

53. *Pioneer Woman*, "Kitchen Confessionals: Chocolate," The Food Network, February 7, 2015, written by Olivia Grove and Ree Drummond.

54. *Pioneer Woman*, "Feeding 101," The Food Network, March 12, 2016, written by Ree Drummond.

55. *Pioneer Woman*, "Surprise Birthday," The Food Network, September 3, 2011, written by Graham Sherringham and Ree Drummond.

56. *Pioneer Woman*, "Home on the Ranch."

57. *Pioneer Woman*, "Outdoor Cookout, Indoor Grilling," The Food Network, August 30, 2014, written by Olivia Ball and Ree Drummond.

58. *Pioneer Woman*, "A Tale of Four Lunches," The Food Network, April 9, 2016, written by Ree Drummond.

59. *Pioneer Woman*, "Girl Time and Burger Time," The Food Network, September 8, 2012, written by Olivia Ball and Ree Drummond.

60. *Pioneer Woman*, "Girl Time and Burger Time."

61. *Pioneer Woman*, "Girl Time and Burger Time."

62. *Pioneer Woman*, "Anniversary," The Food Network, December 12, 2015, written by Olivia Ball.

63. *Pioneer Woman*, "Home on the Ranch."

64. See Carol J. Adams, *The Sexual Politics of Meat: A Feminist-Vegetarian Critical Theory, 20th Anniversary Edition* (New York: Bloomsbury Academic, 2010).

65. While the show adopts a working class ethos, the Drummonds are relatively wealthy. In addition to the millions of dollars in revenue from Ree Drummond's blog and books, the family is the seventeenth largest land owner in the United States. The family has also received nearly $1.2 million in farm subsidies since 1992. EWG's Farm Subsidy Database, "EWG's Farm Subsidy Database," n.d. http://farm.ewg.org/person-detail.php?custnumber=A09311209; and Paul Fairchild, "Historic Oklahoma Ranches," *Oklahoma Magazine*, February 2014, http://www.okmag.com/issue-archive/.

66. See Cloud, "Hegemony or Concordance?"; J. Emmett Winn, "Every Dream Has Its Price: Personal Failure and the American Dream in Wall Street and The Firm," *Southern Communication Journal* 68, no. 4 (Summer 2003): 307–18; Luke Winslow, "Comforting the Comfortable: Extreme Makeover Home Edition's Ideological Conquest," *Critical Studies in Media Communication* 27, no. 3 (August 2010): 267–90.

67. See *Pioneer Woman*, "Cowboy and Cowgirl Lunch," September 21, 2013, written by Olivia Ball; and "Tale of Four Lunches."

68. *Pioneer Woman*, "Tasty Treats to Go," The Food Network, October 25, 2014, written by Stuart Bateup; "Feeding 101"; "Kit and Caboodle," May 21, 2016, written by Ree Drummond.

69. *Pioneer Woman*, "All Work and Some Play," August 11, 2012, written by Olivia Ball and Ree Drummond.

70. *Pioneer Woman*, "Fence Work," October 4, 2014, written by Stuart Biteup and Stephen O'Leary.

71. *Pioneer Woman*, "Tasty Treats to Go."

72. *Pioneer Woman*, "Tasty Treats to Go."

73. *Pioneer Woman*, "Tale of Four Lunches."

74. Oklahoma State Department of Health, "Community Health Improvement Plan - Obesity (Fit Kids of Southwest Oklahoma)," 2016, https://www.ok.gov/health/County_Health_Departments/Comanche_County_Health_Department/Community/Obesity/index.html.

75. Susan Davis, "Palin Touts the 'Pro-America' Areas of the Country," *Wall Street Journal*, October 17, 2008, http://blogs.wsj.com/washwire/2008/10/17/palin-touts-the-pro-america-areas-of-the-country/.

76. See Robert O. Self, *All in the Family: The Realignment of American Democracy Since the 1960s*, Reprint edition (New York, NY: Hill and Wang, 2012).

77. *Pioneer Woman*, "Make Ahead Pot Luck," February 1, 2014, written by Olivia Ball.

78. *Pioneer Woman*, "Easter Weekend," March 28, 2015, written by Olivia Ball.

79. See *Pioneer Woman*, "Frontier Family" September 24, 2011, written by Graham Sherringham; and "Sunday Brunch," March 23, 2013, written by Olivia Ball.

80. *Pioneer Woman*, "Make Ahead Pot Luck."

81. *Pioneer Woman*, "Little Schoolhouse on the Prairie," February 4, 2012, written by Olivia Ball.

82. Ronald Lee and Karen King Lee, "Multicultural Education in the Little Red Schoolhouse: A Rhetorical Exploration of Ideological Justification and Mythic Repair," *Communication Studies* 49, no. 1 (Spring 1998): 1–17.

83. Lee and Lee, "Multicultural Education," 4.

84. *Pioneer Woman*, "School Day," March 30, 2013, written by Olivia Ball; and "Five Girls and a Baby," July 6, 2013, written by Olivia Ball.

85. *Pioneer Woman*, "Double Game Day," January 30, 2016, written by Olivia Ball.

86. *Pioneer Woman*, "Food and Football," March 9, 2013, written by Olivia Ball.

87. *Pioneer Woman*, "Football Camp," January 25, 2014, written by Olivia Ball.

88. *Pioneer Woman*, "The Big Game," January 28, 2012, written by Olivia Ball.

89. *Pioneer Woman*, "Football, Football, Football," January 24, 2015, written by Olivia Ball and Stephen O'Leary.

90. *Pioneer Woman*, "Man Cave," July 26, 2014, written by Olivia Ball.

91. *Pioneer Woman*, "Double Game Day."

92. The Drummonds have been criticized by equine welfare groups for putting on a loud fireworks display in such close proximity to a wild horse preserve. See "BLM Contractor Blasts Fireworks near Wild Horses, Again!," *The PPJ Gazette*, July 9, 2013, https://ppjg.me/2013/07/09/blm-contractor-blasts-fireworks-near-wild-horses-again/. The episode that took place during this event has been removed from the Food Network website.

93. *The Pioneer Woman*, "Fourth of July," October 10, 2012, written by Olivia Ball.

94. Drummond had the guest house remodeled into a kitchen studio for the program. This enabled the production crew to stay for extended periods of time filming episodes. See Fortini, "The Pioneer Woman Gets Lost on the Range."

95. *Pioneer Woman*, "Bulk Buys," January 18, 2014, written by Olivia Ball.

96. *Pioneer Woman*, "Market Meet Up," April 23, 2016, written by Ree Drummond.

97. R. S. Magnusson, "Case Studies in Nanny State Name-Calling: What Can We Learn?," *Public Health* 129, no. 8 (August 2015): 1074–82.

FOUR

America, the Abundant

Man v. Food *and* Diners, Drive-Ins and Dives

In the pilot episode of the Travel Channel's *Man v. Food*, host Adam Richman travels to Amarillo, Texas to take on "The Big Texan Challenge," in which he is allotted one hour to consume a four-and-a-half-pound steak, a large salad, and baked potato.[1] Alongside two other local competitors, Richman takes a make-shift stage at the center hearth of the Big Texas Steak Ranch. To the sounds of a cheering crowd, he and his fellow competitive gurgitators vigorously chew, strain, grunt, agonize, and perspire as they engage in a sporting spectacle of carnivorous over-consumption. As the other competitors begrudgingly admit defeat, Richman overrides his body's resistance to triumphantly conquer a meal that could feed a family of four. Upon victory he accepts his reward — a t-shirt and a picture on the restaurant's "wall of fame" — and declares "today in the battle of man versus food, man won!" His adoring fans erupt in applause. In *Man v. Food*, Richman travels the country to "find the nation's greatest pig out spots" and "take on the country's most legendary eating challenges." While each episode begins with visits to local diners and eateries whose fare exemplify regional comfort cuisines, they conclude with "the challenge" where Richman attempts a seemingly impossible promotional eating feat. The food is measured in pounds and inches: a seven-pound burrito, a ten-pound sandwich, five pounds of hot wings, a seven-and-a-half-pound burger, a seven-pound pizza, and a forty-inch bratwurst to name a few. The program's hook is novelty: the spectacular yet light-hearted overconsumption of foods technically considered "indulgences" for their excessively high quotients of fat, salt, and sugar. *Man v. Food* celebrates those aspects of American cuisine that signify abundance and valorize the ambitious if not unlimited pursuit of personal desires without contemplation or consequence.

While *Man v. Food* is perhaps the only food travel program to feature amateur competitive eating, joyful overindulgence is a common theme throughout the genre. If not in terms of large portions, abundance can also be experienced through encounters with culinary variety, choice, and consumer satisfaction. For instance, in the Food Network's *Diners, Drive-Ins and Dives* host Guy Fieri drives his vintage red Camaro across the country less in search of novelty-sized portions—though the portions are indeed supersized—than for the myriad of ways in which the classic American diner has evolved to satisfy the nation's voracious appetite for diverse combinations of salt, fat, and sugar. Each episode features three segments in three different cities loosely organized around a different aspect of diner culture, such as "blue plate specials," "classics," "BBQ," "house specials," "American cooking," and "totally fried," or iconic culinary sites such as "Route 66," "Seaside Eats," "The New Jersey Diner Tour," and "The Memphis BBQ Tour." The program is a nostalgic portrait of affordable decadence, featuring accessible and unrefined foods for the every-person: burgers, hot dogs, fries, hot wings, colas, barbeque, milk shakes, and an assortment of other fried and sugary concoctions. The show's valorization of relaxed, unpretentious, casual eating is accentuated by Fieri's oft-maligned anti-elitist visage: bowling shirts with tank tops, spikey dyed blond hair, tacky jewelry, tattoos, and sunglasses. Here, America's abundance is experienced, sometimes quite literally, as a melting pot of diverse cuisines adapted to the tastes of ordinary working-class people. For better or worse, *Diner's, Drive-Ins and Dives* democratizes "foodie" culture, making the love of decadent food accessible to the taste of the masses; the glutton is the new gourmand.[2] The small mom-and-pop business, satisfied customers with unlimited and affordable options, and the open-road all symbolize the American ideal of upward mobility.

These two popular programs exemplify how representations of American dining, (over)consumption, and mass consumer tastes are part of the rhetorical structure of the American Dream, a post-war social ideal of unbounded class mobility and affluence achieved through hard work and faith in democratic capitalism.[3] At its genesis, burgeoning prosperity for America's working-classes promised access to luxuries and mass produced consumer goods unavailable to previous generations, including suburban homes with state of the art appliances, televisions, automobiles, fashionable wears, and a plentiful variety of sumptuous food stuffs. The community life of the budding suburb was organized around mobility and convenience, surrounded on all sides by an increasingly standardized array of malls, diners, grocers, and other consumer comforts for an ascending middle-class. As Greg Dickinson observes, the suburban fantasy of "the good life" was and remains structured around, among other topoi, rhetorics of "abundance" and "choice."[4] When articulated as a part of American national identity, these discourses represent the unification of consumer ideology with the principles of democratic pluralism. These topoi, in short, are the marker of distinction in a mass consumer culture. As civic ideals, abundance and choice are the scaffolding of what Marita Sturken calls a consumer republic wherein "the highest values are equated with the promises of mass consumption, both in terms of material life and in relation to freedom, democracy, and equality; in other words, consumption is the route to social ideals."[5] Thus, the celebration of over-consumption and overindulgence—both in terms of portion size and calorie count—can be situated within a broader set of commercial discourses that conflate liberal notions of independence and liberty with the freedom, if not right, to consume. Moreover, when positioned against the "nanny state" foil, excess becomes a heroic act of resistance in defense of the American way of life.

Whereas *The Pioneer Woman* roots American identity in the food cultures of the mythic Western frontier, *Man v. Food* and *Diners, Drive-Ins and Dives* ground the national character in the more contemporary consumerist ideologies that took shape in post-war America and evolved into what is best described as the American Dream. At the nexus of work and leisure, diner culture remains an under-examined facet of the American Dream mythology. That is to say that changing tastes and dining practices signified new forms of class permeability and served as symbols for tenability of the "affluent society."[6] For those who had lived through the scarcity of the Great Depression and wartime rationing, the widespread availability of diverse high-calorie foods on demand was viewed as the spoils of the new peacetime economy. And, the new forms of class sociality that formed around the suburb—and, consequently, the diner—attested to civic benefits of an emerging consumer society.[7] In terms of work, the development of the come-as-you-are diner, where all classes commingled, both accommodated long commutes from the suburbs and engendered the consumerist spirit of quickness, convenience, and affordability. The demand for such food, in turn, provided newly arrived immigrants with the opportunity to make a living as entrepreneurs while assimilating into the melting pot.[8] In terms of leisure, the carhop, the drive-in, and roadside restaurant supported travelers and tourists on family vacations with the convenience and comforts of home. Indeed, auto-mobility and its support infrastructure were potent symbols of middle-class progress. In his history of the American diner, Andrew Hurley argues that diner culture was a counterpart to domestic peace and prosperity. Fashioned as a symbol of national identity, "in America, the diner was democracy."[9] In other words, diner culture connected new convenient eating practices with the larger transformations in the social and economic geography of America. It was a testament to the mythology that America was the land of the abundant.

This chapter explores how both programs draw from and update diner culture mythology to craft mass consumer tastes as a marker of cultural distinction. While both programs celebrate the American tradition of affordable indulgence, each emphasizes a different yet complementary conception of the national cuisine. *Man v. Food* is a carnivalesque panegyric to America's resource wealth and the nation's voracious appetite for more. If emblematic of American identity, the irreverent spectacle of overconsumption testifies to America's abundance and suggests the possibility of unending consumption without consequence; both in terms of body and nation. The program's frivolity constitutes what Helene Shugart calls "defiant decadence," the notion that excessive consumption is a defense of traditional American values.[10] In a slightly different vein, *Diner's, Drive-Ins and Dives* provides a nostalgic portrait of mass culture tastes and consumer kitsch. What some might deride as pedestrian tastes, Fieri's program champions affordable yet decadent American diner classics; a food culture of accessible luxuries that signifies the attainment of middle class respectability.[11] Here, mass consumer culture serves the needs of both business and customer alike: to make a decent living through hard work and to be rewarded with a piece of "the good life." Taken together, these shows advance the mythology of the "affluent society" in which an upwardly mobile middle class can attain its portion of America's unending prosperity. From the fragments of diner culture, these programs suture American food identities not to sustainability, or adjacent virtues, but to the freedom and the imperative to consume.

The significance of this mythology to the larger American Dream ideology is, at the very least, as important as the virtues of hard work. That is to say that predominant eating practices—be they fasting, dieting, or overindulgence—are condensation symbols of broader culture values. Shugart's recent inquiry into the cultural discourse of obesity suggests that the American diet is sutured at times to public conceptions of what constitutes individual character, and at others to "glorified nationalist tropes of independence and autonomy" that tie mass consumption to the vocabulary of classical liberalism.[12] As Frederick Kaufman writes in *A Short History of the American Stomach*, "the stomach lies at the center of this American idea. Our understanding of virtue and vice, success and failure, has long been expressed in the language of appetite, consumption, and digestion."[13] Thus, the valorization of overconsumption and indulgence as everyday American values elides more insidious inequalities that are either downplayed or obfuscated by American Dream discourse. Economically speaking, this includes an expanding gap between the rich and poor, downward pressure on wages, the outsourcing of union jobs, and dwindling opportunities for working class families, among others. Gastronomically speaking, this includes dependence on high-calorie low nutrition foods, the corporate takeover of the food industry, and skyrocketing rates of obesity. Choice and abundance structure adherence to a consumerist ideology, steeped in nostalgia for the post-War promise that a rising tide lifts all boats. Upward mobility and class permeability are, however, occluded by structural inequalities that cannot be overcome by faith and hard work alone. Yet, these programs imply that consumption and indulgence—synonymous with individualism and autonomy—signify success, progress, and the achievability of the American Dream. The program's culinary travels confirm that America is an exceptional, innocent nation characterized by abundance and unending prosperity.

SPECTACULAR (OVER)CONSUMPTION: *MAN V. FOOD*

The celebration of excessive food consumption represents the twentieth-century fusion of American liberalism with consumer capitalism; civic identity enacted through participation in a culture of mass consumption. This consumerist facet of the American Dream is engendered in how the food and dining industry promoted itself as a quintessential part of the American experience. In what could otherwise be read as a novelty, promotional gimmick, or low-brow subculture, early twentieth-century eating competitions emerged as a carnivalesque expression of American prosperity. On July 4, 1916, Nathan Handwerker (Nathan's Hotdogs) hosted the first hot dog eating contest on New York's Coney Island pier.[14] Tied to patriotic sentiments, the festive atmosphere of the eating competition lured spectators in with a fantasy of unrestrained satisfaction of bodily desire, authorized to temporarily abandon the virtues of self-restraint by the civic guarantee of individual liberty without resource constraints or the sacrifice of the social contract. Onlookers who themselves likely adhered to the virtues of thrift and self-denial were beseeched to revel in America's triumphant resource wealth. Frugal working-class spectators—many of whom were immigrants fleeing the scarcity of Eastern Europe and who would typically revile such waste—were dazzled with extraordinary displays of America's consumptive capacity.

While the hook for *Man v. Food* is also novelty, the program is an extension of a long-standing set of consumerist rituals designed to engender faith in the myth of unending prosperity and resource exploitation. The extreme eating challenges presented to Richman are expressions of the consumerist foundations of the American Dream, evincing the ways in which the food industry and diner culture helped tether American identity to ritualistic overconsumption.[15] Thus, the program borrows from the vaudevillian showmanship of the dining industry's performative enactment of American consumer identity. Historically, the eating contest was promoted as a popular and festive expression of patriotism. For instance, pie eating contests became popularized during World War

I—at both home and on the frontlines—as ways to boost morale and national pride.[16] Every Independence Day, the Nathan's Hotdog eating competition along with similar ones across the nation promoted excessive consumption as part of the ritualistic consummation of national unity. As with Mikhail Bakhtin's analysis of the medieval carnival as that "extrapolitical aspects of the world" where sacred and profane are allowed to commingle, where the line between performance and spectatorship is blurred, the eating contest was a licensed transgression from norms of thrift and self-denial.[17] But, as Adrienne Rose Johnson notes, "unlike the medieval carnival, however, competitive eating attends to very modern ideas of consumerism, assimilation, and American abundance."[18]

Eating competitions fostered a specific relationship with consumption wherein overeating transformed into an expression of American values. First, as eating transcended class, race, and language barriers, it formed the basis of an all-encompassing American mass consumer identity. As Johnson observes, competitive eating was an "empathetic and democratic endeavor," an accessible sport based on shared needs that "smuggle[d] serious ideas about nation-building and American identity in an approachable rhetoric of frivolity."[19] Contests inspired unity and fraternity among spectators. Eating served as a common touchstone that cultivated cross-cultural camaraderie amongst America's melting pot. Second, eating competitions enculturated newly arrived immigrant communities into an American consumerist identity. For immigrants, eating competitions were expressions of gratitude that celebrated America's vast natural resources, a stark contrast to the poverty, famine, and religious persecution many immigrants had left behind in search of a better life.[20] Third, eating competitions embodied the core tenets of class permeability. At these events, the universal practice of eating transformed into an individualistic expression of competition and strength. They represented a version of meritocracy where material limitations such as bodily fitness or class position were not impediments to personal success. Moreover, greedy consumption blossomed into the virtues of the private accumulation of wealth, something magically accessible to all who put in the work. Charges of vulgarity were offset by the fantasy bribe of universal ascension to the middle or upper classes.[21]

If its predecessors signified the triumph of a consumer society, the contemporary eating competition engenders the acceleration of hyperconsumption within neoliberal globalization and postindustrial capitalism. Consider that the first winner of Nathan's competition consumed ten hotdogs in twelve minutes. By contrast, at the one hundredth year anniversary celebration in 2016, competitive eater Joey "Jaws" Chestnut broke the world record by consuming seventy hotdogs in ten minutes.[22] In part due to Nathan's promotion, the Major League Eating (MLE; formerly the International Federation of Competitive Eating) hosts nearly

100 competitions per year, some of which are broadcast on ESPN.[23] The restaurant industry has followed suit by using eating challenges as methods of commercial promotion. Indeed, the transformation of competitive eating is symbolic of the current state of consumer capitalism. The aggressive promotion of overconsumption by the MLE and the restaurant industry writ large recasts the practice of overeating as a ritualistic consummation of American consumer identity. In other words, to be American is to painfully overextend oneself beyond their means to invest in lifestyles that are largely unattainable and unsustainable.[24] Overconsumption of food aligns with a globalized corporate narrative of consumer citizenship that offers luxuries to a waning middle class with the promise of credit to continue purchasing beyond all reasonable limits.[25] Consider that while savings dwindled, the amount of disposable income devoted to consumer spending rose from 62 percent in 1975 to 127.2 percent in 2005.[26] Through the creation of international megabrands, corporate conglomerates promote American-style hyperconsumerism as a model for global economic growth.[27] Overeating, then, aptly symbolizes the corporate philosophy of globalization: consume until it hurts.

Like eating competitions, *Man v. Food* plainly emphasizes those aspects of American consumer and dining culture that encourage gluttony and waste. But unlike the novelty of individual contests, the program's repetitive format establishes overeating as a ubiquitous and normalized pattern of consumption throughout the nation. City by city, American food identities are linked to immense portion sizes and the freedom to consume according to one's stated preference regardless of health, economic, or environmental concerns. Though powerful constitutive moments in their own right, disparate contests throughout the country (often only known to local residents) are presented at a local level, not as singular examples of a larger collective phenomenon but a recurring set of social rituals. And while overeating as an everyday practice is emblematic of the present state of American consumerism, *Man v. Food* sutures these individual subcultural spectacles and promotional gimmicks to broader narratives about American history and identity. Thus, the program does distinct cultural work by repackaging singular events, each emanating from particular subcultures of dining, as the common element (overconsumption) that unites the diversity of American cuisine. As the Travel Channel's highest rating debut program, I consider *Man v. Food* a highly visible and widely consumed text that links hyperconsumption, or "defiant decadence," with the ideological constructs of the American Dream: abundance and choice.[28]

In brief, each episode of *Man v. Food* is divided into three parts. First, Richman introduces the city's food culture which he will later experience through a series of escalating challenges, beginning with small samples of indulgent cuisine that culminate toward a final confrontation. This introduction is narrated over iconic shots of the city's landscapes interspersed with images of people tasting the local fare. Second, Richman visits two local restaurants that exemplify the city's best "pig out spots," places that boast large portions, extensive menus, and bargain prices. Richman briefly narrates the unique history of these iconic establishments, often over shots of vintage photographs of previous generations of owners and patrons. Finally, Richman takes on "the challenge": a dish of extraordinary size, or in some cases spice-level, that contestants are rarely able to consume. The challenge typically involves some kind of reward, such as a free t-shirt or induction into the restaurant's wall of fame. The challenge is accompanied by a stadium-like atmosphere of cheering and supportive fans. After the contest concludes, Richman declares either "food" or "man" the victor and holds a satirical press conference in which he answers frivolous questions about his experience. What distinguishes the program from carnival performances or broadcasts of competitive eating is that it narrativizes overconsumption, linking indulgent eating to the unique development of each city's consumer economy. In the process, overconsumption is articulated as an American tradition, a marker of taste and cultural capital.

In *Man v. Food*, abundance has less to do with the widespread availability of food than how the individual can maximize his or her share of available food resources. As such, the individual consumption of massive portions of food reflects not the egalitarian values of a resource economy that provides for the basic needs of all, but instead an economic system that privileges the private accumulation of wealth and zero-sum competition. In that case, the size of one's portion relative to others is vastly more important to the concept of "the good life" than other liberal virtues such as access and equality. The show embraces the virtues of private accumulation through a preoccupation with weights and measures; a repetitive chronicling of the staggering quantity of food to be consumed by one individual. As host, part of Richman's role is to not only marvel and express reverence for the large portions he encounters, but to help convey to audiences the extraordinary details of its immensity. The goal is to produce awe through perspective, to help the audience grasp the scope of unbelievable portions of food and, in turn, comprehend the physical agency of one person to consume as such.

For instance, in New Brunswick, New Jersey he brags about encountering a sandwich "weighing nearly ten pounds," a legend visually confirmed by the camera as it focuses on enormous portions of deli meat piled on to a kitchen scale. Incredulous, Richman comments "this is unbelievable."[29] At a restaurant in Boulder, Colorado he looks on with awe at an extra large pizza that weighs in at nearly fourteen pounds.[30] In Chicago he samples a pizza that "can weigh up to five pounds," while a more impressive pizza in Kennesaw, Georgia weighed in at "a whopping seven pounds," including "five pounds of meat."[31] In Austin, Texas he encounters a donut he calls a "sugary monster" measuring "fourteen inches in diameter and weigh[ing] over two pounds."[32] In Boston he is presented with a fifteen-pound lobster while he instructs the audience to "look at these portions" and observe the "heaping plates of seafood."[33] In New York City, he seeks an estimate on the amount of meat served weekly at an iconic deli and is subsequently delighted by the proprietor's confident estimate of "10,000 pounds."[34] In Minneapolis, Richman is allowed back into the kitchen to observe the preparation of his "three pound, 40-inch bratwurst plus two sides."[35] The list goes on. As evidenced by this recurring pattern of specific measurements, abundance is transformed from abstraction to quantification, from an idea of what it means to have needs and desires met to a set of discrete and calculable numbers that define the absolute limits of the human capacity for consumption. Staggering weights and measurements convey a sense of what it means to consume not for nourishment, or even taste for that matter, but instead as a form of private accumulation. Aggregating ingredients and dishes into pounds and inches constructs satiation in terms of testing the absolute and definable limits of the human body. The program conflates the pleasure of consumption with Richman's extraordinary capacity to consume.

Where abundance cannot be measured in exact weight or length, Richman employs emphatic language, comical metaphors, and humorous embellishment to valorize ritualized overeating. These framing choices comprise a light-hearted and irreverent frame that ostensibly celebrates extreme caloric intake. Richman humorously compares the massive dishes he encounters to bicycle cushions,[36] shoes,[37] mountains,[38] and small children.[39] Elsewhere he employs military metaphors to dramatize his challenges, taking on an "Armada of Oysters" in New Orleans, the "Bataan Death March of ice cream" in St. Louis, and a "beef battlefield" in Amarillo. In other cases, he compares his challenges to feats of athleticism. In Memphis, he reenacts the training montage from the film *Rocky* in preparation for eating a seven-pound burger. In Columbus, Ohio he simulates a football practice, complete with cheerleaders, before eating a sandwich consisting of twenty-one ounces of deli cold cuts along with a pound of French fries. Upon completing this challenge, he compares himself to Olympic swimmer Michael Phelps, declaring that he "taste[s] victory." The connection between food and athleticism is further accentuated by the appearance of competitive eater Joey "Jaws" Chestnut, who makes a cameo to eat a massive burrito in San Jose, California.[40] At other points he simply jokes about unhealthy ingredients and portion sizes. In Memphis, Richman calls the portions "huge, hairy ape monkey big,"[41] and in Atlanta he remarks that "the burgers are heart-stoppingly good" while calling in jest for a cardiologist.[42] At any rate, Richman finds a diversity of ways to maintain an irreverent attitude that treats excessive consumption as a spectator sport, or a cheerful celebration of American values.

Second only to large portion size is the program's preoccupation with limitless choices of high-calorie food. The program emphasizes that one of the signature features of American dining culture is that it affirms people's right to have their consumer desires met on demand. The audience is imagined as a market whose freedom and autonomy is derived from their power to consume. While this subject position is advanced with tongue-in-cheek, it nonetheless suggests that freedom and autonomy are enacted primarily through the act of consumption, as opposed to the kind of activities associated with civic identity. Thus, Richman's highest praise for the diners he visits is that they empower the consumer through choice and customizability. For instance, in Knoxville, Tennessee Richman talks with the customers of Ye Old Steakhouse who proudly proclaim that "you can get whatever you want" and "100% satisfaction [is] guaranteed." As the camera cuts to grilling steaks being basted in butter, Richman responds "its kind of power to the beefy people."[43] In a voice over, he tells the audience "I am going to exercise *my* freedom of choice by ordering one of the biggest cuts they offer. A 60 ounce New York Strip." In Chicago he boasts, "look at all the options you can get, like everything from eggs and bacon, to turkey, to ham, to Cajun chicken, plus you'll get the fries and the coleslaw."[44] In San Francisco, he marvels at the "meat fiesta" of burrito toppings, noting "all the magnificent options from juicy chicken, to succulent pork, to mouth-watering steak" with "up to 12 different spices." His only lament is that he cannot "pack all the meats into [his] super burrito."[45] In Denver, he is enamored by customization, "with 21 toppings at my disposal I can't wait to create my own Cricket Burger."[46] At a restaurant named the Buckhorn Exchange, Richman relays to the audience a fantasy of consuming any and all types of meat, including yak, ostrich, elk, buffalo, and even Rocky Mountain oysters (bull testicles). Surrounded by décor comprised of taxidermy animals and portraits of Wild Bill Hickok and Theodore Roosevelt, Richman explains, "nowhere else can you chow down on so many members of the animal kingdom."[47] This recurring pattern suggests that the consumer is king, their demand for culinary variety and large portions met like a petition for basic individual rights. Dining culture is the one area of public life that is responsive to our collective desire for empowerment and freedom. Though fleeting, it is the promise of the good life that remains unfulfilled as upward mobility wanes, something that can only be purchased at a discount in the form of customizable ingredients done to the consumer's specification.

Indeed, the fantasy enacted by such an eating experience is of every demand met regardless of novelty or size. Richman conveys a populist conception of taste in which everyone should be able to have access to the good life. Yet, this conception of the good life is extraordinarily narrow, reducing the privileges of an open society to the right to consume whatever, however possible. Thus, Richman routinely uses democratic language to describe the wide selection of cuisines available at his selected "pig out spots." Particularly illustrative, an episode in Richmond, Virginia uses the city's proximity to the nation's capital to frame choice and consumption in patriotic terms. To the tune of the national anthem, this episode begins with iconic shots of the city's Revolutionary War history, including monuments and colonial architecture. Richman narrates, "my cross country crusade has brought me to a colonial capital of historic Richmond, Virginia for some all American eats. A part of the original colonies and the site of Patrick Henry's war cry 'give me liberty or give me death!' Richmond played an integral role in the declaration of the country's independence and today they are still showing that independent spirit with their love of revolutionary barbeque."[48] Here, Richman inadvertently names the process by which the political vocabulary of classic liberalism has been translated by market capitalism into a consumer demand for more products. Diner culture is the one area of public life that can fulfill the American promise of abundance and nourish our collective fantasies of wealth, freedom, and independence.

Finally, in *Man v. Food* overconsumption moves from extreme spectacle to long-standing, mainstream American tradition. This message is conveyed through verbal and visual narratives that historicize the cities and restaurants chronicled in each episode. The show represents "pig out spots" as pillars of the community, businesses that catapulted the entrepreneurial working class, particularly immigrant families, into middle class respectability. In each episode, Richman provides voice over narration in which he briefly details the background of the establishments he visits. Narration is complemented with shots of old family photos from past generations of owners, workers, and patrons. In the scenes that follow, Richman takes a tour of the kitchen to meet with the current owners who are portrayed proudly carrying on the restaurant's long-standing tradition of serving indulgent, high-calorie meals. For example, in Austin, Texas Richman narrates the history of Round Rock Donuts as the camera displays images of the owner's Eastern European family being naturalized at Ellis Island. He notes, "because of a wave of immigrants from Eastern Europe in the nineteenth century, Texas has one of the richest donut traditions in the country."[49] In Columbus, Richman narrates the region's German immigrant heritage over top of shots of black and white photos of settlers building restaurants and store fronts, serving customers, and interacting with the community. Richman explains, "in the early 1800s many Germans settled here, bringing with them their culture, their customs, and most importantly, their food . . . they've opened a meat lover's fantasy, a sausage buffet, all you can eat, so big that they call it the autobahn . . . this place is pure tradition."[50] In New York City, the pattern is repeated at Katz's deli, where the segment begins with iconic shots of lower Manhattan interspersed with late nineteenth-century photographs from the restaurant's founding. Richman narrates that since 1888, the deli has been "supplying a true taste of home to Eastern Europeans and today that same smorgasbord is served just like it was a century ago, simple cafeteria style, where you can chow down on deli staples like matzo ball soup, and the knish."[51]

Of course, this pattern continues throughout each episode, but these particular examples are illustrative of how the program weaves contemporary diner culture into the fantasy structure of the American Dream. The diner is employed as a symbol of middle class respectability, a pathway for assimilation into America's melting pot, the civic lifeblood of the suburb or close-knit neighborhood community, and an institution historically dedicated to distributing the spoils of an abundant postwar economy. Although the program's displays of competitive eating provide a more extreme spectacle of abundance, its commemoration of diner culture normalizes overconsumption as fundamental to the modern conception of the good life. In short, overeating is part of American history and cultural identity.

WELCOME TO FLAVORTOWN, USA: DINERS, DRIVE-INS AND DIVES

Whereas *Man v. Food* constitutes a straightforward endorsement of gluttony, *Diners, Drive-Ins and Dives* reframes the glutton as the new gourmand. In stark contrast to high-end dining trends such as molecular gastronomy and popular health foods such as kale and gluten-free pastries, Fieri celebrates the diner cuisine of the everyday working class American, such as burgers, barbeque, hot dogs, hot wings, and French fries. As a restaurateur and food television personality, Fieri employs his culinary acumen to give what might be considered more pedestrian tastes the same level of attention and depth that rarified culinary magazines might provide for the newest trends in haute cuisine. The program's appeal is that it is relatable, with portraits of small family businesses, details about the construction of unpretentious meals, embrace of Americana and consumer kitsch, and visions of (auto)mobility all included. Fieri is an enthusiastic and plain-spoken host, always treating the people he meets, as well as his audience, as equals. Moreover, the program is steeped in nostalgia for the 1950s diner, an American institution imagined as a come-as-you-are third space where everyday Americans commingled and tasted their share of the good life. The program is an homage to a populist version of American cuisine, a valorization of an anti-elitist palate that is distrustful of expensive ingredients or anything that resembles fine dining. And whereas *Man v. Food* is concerned with large portions and limitless choices, *Diners, Drive-Ins and Dives* is concerned with cost and accessibility; or, more specifically, the kind of indulgences that are accessible for everyone in a mass consumer society. In short, everyone gets to be a foodie, and, more importantly, everyday Americans get access to a piece of the affluent society.

In part, the show derives its populist ethos from Fieri's infamous public persona. Fieri's food television career began in 2006 after winning season 2 of the reality television competition *Food Network Star* with overwhelming audience support. Previously, Fieri had been part-owner of two California restaurants (*Johnny Garlic's* and *Tex Wasabi*), places well-known to locals for their iconoclastic recipes, including unconventional fusion dishes such as barbeque sushi and Cajun pasta. As audiences learned throughout his television debut, Fieri fashions himself an everyman, with an expressed interest in classic American cars, rock-and-roll music, and diner-style comfort food. His personal appearance also engenders his irreverent attitude toward traditional haute cuisine: bowling shirts, frosted spiked hair, and visible tattoos. Of course, his identity and brand also generate visceral anti-fandom, including scathing reviews of his cuisine, satirical internet memes, and most recently, a viral video comprised of close-up shots of Fieri eating to the tune of Johnny Cash's version of "Hurt." Nonetheless, Fieri remains one of the most prominent faces of the Food Network. In addition to *Diners, Drive-Ins and Dives*, he hosts or has appeared on a variety of other food programming, including *Guy's Big Bite* (2006), *Guy's Off the Hook* (2008), *Ultimate Recipe Showdown* (2008–2011), *Minute to Win It* (NBC, 2010–2012) *Guy vs. Rachel Celebrity Cookoff* (2012–2013), and *Guy's Grocery Games* (2013–).[52] Since 2007, *Diners, Drive-Ins and Dives* remains his most successful and highly rated program (675,000 viewers per episode). Derived from the premise of his program, Fieri has also co-authored four books including two *New York Times* best sellers: *Diners, Drive-ins and Dives: An All-American Road Trip . . . with Recipes!* (2008), and *More Diners, Drive-Ins and Dives: Another Drop-Top Culinary Cruise through America's Finest and Funkiest* (2009).[53] Adding to the show's aura of authenticity, Fieri makes friendly visits to small independent establishments that resemble his own restaurant where he pleasantly interacts with owners, employees, and customers. His affable, working-class persona renders his exploration of everyday food culture a common point of identification with a mass audience.

As the title suggests, *Diners, Drive-Ins and Dives* grounds its concept of taste in kitsch, or the cheap consumables of mass culture that some might consider in *poor* taste. The program embraces establishments that dispense with high society manners, and whose menus reflect a mass culture simulacra of American cuisine (burgers, pie, and so on). Lest he embrace the chain fast food restaurant, Fieri is quick to emphasize that the uniform elements of national cuisine are always accompanied by innovative adaptations, or what he continually refers to as "funk." As he notes in one episode "On triple D I say it all the time: If it's funky I'll find it. What does funky mean? Funky is a good thing. Funky is different. Funky is unique. Funky is off the hook. It could be the people. It could be the place. It could be the story. Or in this case it's the menu."[54] In this sense, kitsch is what adds character and diversity to a uniform national cuisine. In this way, the program inverts the logics of elite food culture where gourmets and those with cultural capital shape the public conception of taste. Instead, the program advances a democratic or bottom-up perspective on American food in which the storied everyday diner, with its defiant decadence for all patrons, defines a new conception of gourmet. And though there is nothing inherently wrong with inexpensive conveniences, this portrait of diner culture is situated in the mythology of market capitalism wherein the triumph of consumer culture offers universal uplift for the working class. Returning to Sturken momentarily, this valorization and commemoration of kitsch affirms a version of American identity in which hyperconsumerism represents the newest iteration of democratic populism. The diner transforms into the engine of modern democratic pluralism where the consumer is king and a taste of the good life is accessible to all.

Thus, *Diners, Drive-Ins and Dives* makes its own distinct contribution to the consumerist framework of the American Dream. First, the program is a nostalgic recovery of an innocent version of 1950s life, organized around a series of consumer fetishes and lost objects that engender sentimental affects. Take for instance the object economy of the show's introduction. Fieri begins each episode by narrating his journey from the driver's seat of his red 1967 Camaro convertible while travelling on a generic country road or suburb thoroughfare. The vintage automobile, traveling from diner to diner, is reminiscent of the post-war fantasy of middle class mobility wherein the widespread availability of cars unlocked new potentials for both work and leisure.[55] The diner was a support mechanism for this fantasy as it nourished both commuting workers and weary travelers on family vacations. A soundtrack of generic 1950s rock-and-roll accompanies Fieri's narration, as the camera cuts to brief scenes of Fieri visiting three destinations across the country. Alongside the soundtrack, Fieri provides an enthusiastic preview of the forthcoming episode. The recurring credits are initiated and the music shifts from rock-and-rock to a 1950s sock-hop beat, reminiscent of the period's blending of rock-and-roll and ragtime swing. Next, comes a pastiche of diner icons: a cartoon cheeseburger positioned in the center of the screen with rows of stars arranged in the background. The burger tilts to the side and pushes back to make room for a metallic railroad car diner bathed in pink neon. The arrangement transitions to an image of an impatient waitress in full serving regalia behind a bright sign reading "drive-ins." She holds a serving platter in her right hand extended above her shoulder. The server is flanked by a red corvette, a giant cartoon hot dog, and a soda fountain style milkshake with a cherry on top. Next, "dives" appears with an arrangement of cheesesteak sandwiches. Fieri enters the shot, spins the show's logo, folds his arms, and smiles. This arrangement of objects invites the audience to relate to food through an idyllic past represented in fetishized consumer icons, products that mediate what Sturken characterizes as an innocent national identity. By innocent, I mean to reference a cultural fantasy zone of idyllic American life imagined by cultural conservatives to have existed before the political turmoil of the 1960s. The lost objects that introduce the show constitute a fantasy of return to an Edenic moment of American life where suburban communities were structured around small independent businesses and family-friendly establishments. Pleasures were innocent: milkshakes, car rides, and sockhops. The introduction softens Fieri's rock-and-roll persona, his irreverent take on cuisine itself simply a monument to post-war mass culture fused with the rebellious individuation of contemporary postmodern style.

The show delivers on this nostalgic fantasy by profiling restaurants that serve 1950s classics and that maintain the style and décor of the period. For instance, in the series' pilot, Fieri establishes the tone of the program by claiming to detail businesses that serve "American classics, doing great food their own way."[56] His tour begins in small town Texas, where he arrives in his convertible via a two lane black top against the backdrop of bucolic farm land. He remarks on the town's beautiful simplicity: "They've got a post office, a general store, and a roadside place called Mac & Ernie's Roadside Eatery."[57] His description of Tarpley, Texas closely aligns with the rural American ideal of a close-knit community of humble working families with simple needs and simple tastes. Later, he travels to Wichita, Kansas to visit a restaurant serving "old time diner classics." Marveling at the family-owned suburban diner that serves food its "own particular way," Fieri tells the owner "you've got the life going here."[58] Whereas Mac & Ernie's is used to symbolize the small town ideal of a restaurant that is the third space of community life, at Brint's Diner the camera captures the aesthetic dimensions of the model working-class suburban diner: a lunch counter with communal red leather seats on bright aluminum stools, a checkered linoleum floor, Coke signs on the walls, and a short-order cook working a large plancha-style grill. In both cases (and repeated throughout nearly every episode), Fieri remarks that these are "classics" because they serve food *their* own way. As such, the program praises their sentimental attachment to timeworn traditions, consumer styles, and food trends. Modern day kitsch serves as a memorial to the 1950s ideal and the persistence of diner culture into the twenty-first century becomes a defiant rebuke of new American cuisine and the values for which it stands.

And while *Man v. Food* most accurately encapsulated the politics of overconsumption, *Diners, Drive-Ins and Dives* enters the fray of the culture wars by honoring a restaurant subculture committed to fulfilling child-like consumer desire over nourishment. In other words, the "family-friendly" diner, routinely featured throughout the program, serves mostly high-calorie and often outdated foods that primarily appeal to small children who have yet to develop sophisticated palates or health concerns that might divert them from addictive combinations of salt, fat, and sugar. Diner nostalgia, then, is a different kind of defiance in which the consumer is encouraged to view healthy sustainable food alternatives as somehow in opposition to "family friendly" cuisine. For the consumer, high-calorie food becomes associated with the warm feelings of childhood memory—of "being a kid again" as it were—whereas health food represents the more unglamorous and austere trappings of adulthood. Of course, "family friendly" is not simply a designate for institutions that cater to parents with children, but is instead a cipher for the 1950s fantasy of a public culture organized around the fulfillment and protection of children.[59] An episode entitled "Blue Plate Special" is particularly illustrative of this point. In this episode, Fieri visits The Penguin in Charlotte, North Carolina, a place he proclaims has been "rockin' for 50 years" serving "huge burgers [and] hand-dipped corndogs."[60] After eating a decadent customized corndog that the owner calls "a heart attack waiting to happen," Fieri remarks that the charm of the diner is that it "caters to families and kids but still looks like a biker bar."[61] The jukebox soundtrack of ragtime and swing music contributes additional aural cues that help the program suture the diner diet to 1950s family values. Indeed, while diners may have a rough working class exterior, their menus provide the comforts and innocent pleasures of childhood. And, of course, children are particularly welcome.

At another restaurant in this episode, the program suggests that the diner's defiance of food trends and adherence to classics honors America's past. Again, the notion of ancestral return becomes important because the audience is invited to return to both childhood as well as a period in American history in which the nation itself was considered "innocent." Fieri visits The Frosted Mug, a Chicago-area carhop that features female servers in roller skates and cheerleader uniforms with a menu consisting of burgers, corndogs, and root beer floats. Fieri asks a customer to describe what it means to take a "trip back in time," and he responds, "we call it nostalgia but it is part of the fabric of America, right now you are in a little piece of America. We fancy it our own piece of American history."[62] The notion that restaurants are repositories of cultural memory illustrates how the mythology of the diner is a conduit to the fantasy of national innocence. Fieri notes the pleasures of recall himself when he consumes a root beer float on camera. Remarking once again that the dish is a "total step back in time" he tells the audience with excitement, "I haven't had this in a long time." Fieri, too, is portrayed as another willing participant in the fantasy of return. Here, diner food is woven into the fabric of American public memory of the 1950s and yet also fortified in the present against efforts to consign it to the past. As such, the program's notion that "family friendly" has not gone out of style provides a concrete example of how it remains possible to return home, as it were. Of course, home is that romanticized period in American history that spawned the American Dream and presently provides a touchstone for the possibility of its fulfillment despite its obvious structural limitations.

Though demonstrating reverence for family friendly classics, the program also conveys a rebellious and unconventional attitude toward food. That is to say, Fieri deliberately pushes the boundaries of decorum and what foodies might consider "good taste" in order to make food accessible to lay audiences. Yet, his rebellion manifests less as culinary populism than a belabored counterculture identity consummated through the consumption of products.[63] In other words, Fieri's persona typifies the cooptation and commodification of rebellion and authenticity in consumer culture. For a show that valorizes the 1950s, rebellion deflects criticisms of the decade's less virtuous attributes, such as conformity, conspicuous consumption, and vulgar materialism. As Thomas Frank explains in *The Conquest of Cool*, America's culture industry has a long history of transforming countercultural ideas such as dissent and rebellion into products and brands. He writes that transgressive ideas are often "translated into harmless consumer commodities, emptied of content, and sold to their very originators as substitutes for the real thing."[64] Likewise, Herbert Marcuse keenly observed that market capitalism facilitates the development of a control society by turning anti-authoritarian ideas into advertising slogans that deprive the populace of valuable linguistic resources to enact political critique.[65] All of this is to say that Fieri's irreverent style is a vector for consumer culture to commodify defiance and attach it to the mindless consumption of high-calorie foods. Indeed, we need not look further than Shugart's terminology to see consumer culture at work: *decadence* is a consumptive behavior that is presently one of the primary ways in which conservatives encourage consumers to direct their *defiance* toward the "nanny state." Fieri's rebellious on-screen persona makes low-brow mass consumption seem edgy, unconventional, and outside the mainstream. In a consumer society, rebellion promises to individuate alienated mass consumers. Or put simply, rebellion authorizes consumers to be different, just like everyone else.

Fieri, who boasts a love of rock-and-roll music, tattoos, and flashy jewelry, is a fitting ambassador of mass consumer culture. He embodies a kind of hollow, acceptable rebellion that can be characterized as more of a brand than a political orientation. The effect of this brand is to render mass consumption hip, unpretentious, and authentic. Indeed, the program has no shortage of celebrity guests who mirror his own iconoclastic aesthetic, including Matthew McConaughey, Kid Rock, Gene Simmons, Sammy Hagar, Steve Harwell of the band Smash Mouth, and Andrew Zimmern. But, it is in Fieri's less spectacular encounters that crass overconsumption is given a countercultural edge. One way in which Fieri conveys a rebellious attitude is by playfully disregarding norms of appropriateness. When Fieri is invited into restaurant kitchens, he violates rules of etiquette by dipping his fingers into ingredients, eating with his hands, squirting sauces directly into his mouth, and overstuffing and talking with his mouth full. In one episode, he garners laughs by dumping his face into a tub of ranch dressing after eating excessively spicy hot wings.[66] He then calls in his "culinary gangsters," his cast and crew, to finish the wings for him. In another, he chases a giant onion ring with a shot of ketchup.[67] In other episodes he crassly refers to mayonnaise and other condiments as "food lube," an edgy yet relatively safe sexual innuendo.[68] He makes crass jokes about "chug[ging] some of the buttermilk" and wishing he "could get toothpaste that tastes like [popovers]."[69]

Of course, Fieri makes visits to places that brand themselves against conventional taste, including Las Vegas's Road Kill Café where patrons eat mystery meats at picnic benches and Stillwater, Minnesota's Smalley's Barbeque, a pirate-themed Jamaican-fusion restaurant. Yet another way in which Fieri communicates hip irreverence is by using a series of marketable catchphrases such as "rocking out,"[70] "off the hook,"[71] and going to "flavortown."[72] His use of slang terms creates an atmosphere of informality in which food culture seems accessible and familiar. Though Fieri's transgressions may be admonished by some, for others his violations expose the constricting norms of elite tastes and behaviors. Rebellion makes his brand relatable to the average consumer who might be disinterested in high food culture. Moreover, crass overconsumption of decadent food becomes a modality of resistance to elitism. Yet, rebellion is the very mechanism by which consumer culture depoliticizes the public and supplants civic identities with consumer identities.

In sum, *Diners, Drive-Ins and Dives* hails Americans as mass consumers, for whom the good life constitutes access to cheap indulgences and the freedom to consume without consequence. The program constructs mass consumption and kitsch as symbols of empowerment, or signs of the American Dream fulfilled. The nation is innocent in this narrative, reborn is the infantile consumer pleasures of a simulacra of 1950s America. The carhop, the soda fountain, the working-class diner all remain steeped in the market mythology of the affluent society where the class system is permeable and greater purchasing power for the middle class ensures equal and unending prosperity. These iconic consumer institutions provided the infrastructure for work and leisure in the new economy. Fieri's program is emblematic of how a mass consumer ideology, wherein personal indulgence is a civic identity, draws strength from the celebration of diner culture. *Diners, Drive-Ins and Dives* imparts a food-place-identity that bespeaks the triumph of the consumer over the citizen, of the market over the demos.

CONCLUSION

Man v. Food and *Diners, Drive-Ins and Dives* represent two fundamental constructs of the American Dream: abundance and equality of opportunity in a democratic marketplace. Whereas Richman draws from those aspects of mass food culture that have historically celebrated overconsumption as an American virtue, Fieri imports with great reverence a post-war orientation toward mass consumption in which the availability of cheap luxuries confirmed the feasibility of the American Dream. In both cases, overindulgence in large portions of high-calorie dishes engenders what were at one time concepts associated with civic identities, such as freedom, equal opportunity, autonomy, liberty, and choice. In both programs, overconsumption can even be a populist expression of patriotism. These programs challenge elite conceptions of taste, exchanging foodie culture with a mass consumer simulacra of a national cuisine. Moreover, the changing taste of food television highlights the importance of abundance and choice in the construction of American consumer identity. In short, America's taste and voracious hunger reflect its abundance.

Why does overconsumption and indulgence engender such strong sentiments? Why is mass consumption so tightly sutured to the American Dream? In one sense, contemporary mass food culture is profoundly more alienating than the triumphant sentimental version presented on television. Ultimately, the diner served as the template for the modern fast food chain, an institution that standardized national convenience foods and then actively worked to replace independent restaurants and even the home-cooked meal. In their history of American fast food, John Jakle and Keith Sculle note the following:

> The American restaurant, especially what Americans today call fast-food restaurants, are to many people inherently alienating in a social sense. They attract customers through standardized physical formats, ply them with standardized food, and hurry them along so that others may take their place. Customers are not invited to linger. The restaurant experience is orchestrated almost solely to corporate profit-taking, the turnover of customers foremost. Only with difficulty are such places colonized by those who would linger to see and be seen. Only with some difficulty do customers assert a sense of possession.[73]

With the triumph of consumer culture, more and more independent establishments struggle to remain outside the process of standardization. And with convenience and accessibility, consumers are left alienated not only by their lack of control and the illusion of choice, but also the experience of having authenticity mass produced, branded, and sold back to them. The appeal of the programs analyzed in this chapter is that they present a counterfactual version of the American Dream in which mass consumption delivered on its promise of abundance, equality, and empowerment for all. The Dream did not become a nightmare in which wages stagnated, the social safety net evaporated, and consumers were left with but cheap imitations of the good life for purchase at the mega-supermarket or the fast food chain down the street. In these programs America remains an innocent nation where consumerism brought fulfillment and prosperity to the populace; abundance and choice are markers of the nation's exceptional combination of democracy and market capitalism. These programs appeal to a nostalgic vision of unending prosperity and nearly limitless resource wealth. The overflowing plate of quintessentially American cuisine represents that fantasy of consumption without prohibition or consequence. Like the competitive eater, the viewer is invited to consume until it hurts, and then consume some more.

NOTES

1. *Man v. Food*, "Amarillo," The Travel Channel, December 3, 2008, written by Dan Kornfeld and Adam Richman.

2. Carlnita Greene observes that in contemporary food discourse, an appreciation for overindulgence (gluttons) is often framed as a discerning interest in fine dining (gourmands). See *Gourmands & Gluttons: The Rhetoric of Food Excess* (New York, NY: Peter Lang, 2015).

3. While the phrase "American Dream" does not appear until 1931, the concept can be traced to early American discourses of meritocracy in contradistinction to European aristocracy. Indeed, there are also religious roots in American Protestantism, that hard work is a noble article of faith accorded with divine rewards. See Ernest G. Bormann, *The Force of Fantasy: Restoring the American Dream* (Carbondale, IL: Southern Illinois University Press, 2000); Jim Cullen, *The American Dream: A Short History of an Idea That Shaped a Nation* (London, UK: Oxford University Press, 2004); Cyril Ghosh, *The Politics of the American Dream: Democratic Inclusion in Contemporary American Political Culture* (New York: Palgrave Macmillan, 2012); Lawrence R. Samuel, *The American Dream: A Cultural History* (Syracuse, NY: Syracuse University Press, 2012).

4. Greg Dickinson, *Suburban Dreams: Imagining and Building the Good Life* (Tuscaloosa, AL: University of Alabama Press, 2015), 108.

5. Marita Sturken, *Tourists of History: Memory, Kitsch, and Consumerism from Oklahoma City to Ground Zero* (Durham, NC: Duke University Press, 2007), 39.

6. This phrase is borrowed from the barrage of post-war encomiums to free market capitalism by economists who embraced myths of unending prosperity, particularly in opposition to the work of John Maynard Keynes. See John Kenneth Galbraith, *The Affluent Society* (Boston: Mariner Books, 1998).

7. The most oft-cited testament to class permeability is the rages-to-riches story of nineteenth-century author Horatio Alger. His most famous novel, *Ragged Dick* (1867) chronicles a protagonist lifted out of poverty and into middle class respectability through hard work, thrift, and industriousness. The story has since been referenced by adherents to the American Dream mythology to exemplify meritocracy, or how class structures can be transcended through hard work and self-denial. Critics of the American Dream mythology, however, argue that the story and others like it are advanced to deflect criticism of the class system and cultivate active investments in work subjugation. See Cloud, "Hegemony or Concordance?"; Kristen Hoerl, "Monstrous Youth in Suburbia: Disruption and Recovery of the American Dream," *Southern Communication Journal* 67, no. 3 (September 1, 2002): 259–75; and Winn, "Every Dream Has Its Price."

8. See Michael Karl Witzel, *The American Diner* (Minneapolis, MN: MBI Publishing Company LLC, 2006).

9. Andrew Hurley, *Diners, Bowling Alleys, and Trailer Parks: Chasing the American Dream* (New York, NY: Basic Books, 2002), 69.

10. Helene A. Shugart, *Heavy: The Obesity Crisis in Cultural Context* (London: Oxford University Press, 2016), 108.

11. For instance, Pete Wells's scathing review of Fieri's Time Square restaurant and the countless detractors of his brand harshly criticize his valorization of high-calorie pedestrian fare. See Joshua David Stein, "The Crispy Crimes of Guy Fieri: Junk Food T.V. Star Takes Times Square," *Observer*, October 2, 2012, http://observer.com/2012/10/the-crispy-crimes-of-guy-fieri/; and Pete Wells, "Restaurant Review: Guy's American Kitchen & Bar in Times Square," *The New York Times*, November 13, 2012, http://www.nytimes.com/2012/11/14/dining/reviews/restaurant-review-guys-american-kitchen-bar-in-times-square.html.

12. Shugart, *Heavy*.

13. Frederick Kaufman, *A Short History of the American Stomach* (Orlando, FL: Houghton Mifflin Harcourt, 2009), xv.

14. Ken Albala, "Competitive Eating," in *The SAGE Encyclopedia of Food Issues*, ed. Ken Albala, pp. 273–277 (Thousand Oaks, CA: SAGE Publications, 2015).

15. See Peter Naccarato and Kathleen Lebesco, *Culinary Capital* (New York: Bloomsbury Publishing, 2013).

16. See Rachel C. Hawley, "Pie as Nostalgia: What One Food Symbolizes for Every Generation of Americans," in *Devouring Cultures: Perspectives on Food, Power, and Identity from the Zombie Apocalypse to Downton Abbey*, ed. Cammie M. Sublette and Jennifer Martin, pp. 145–164 (Fayetteville, AR: University of Arkansas Press, 2015); and Ryan Nerz, *Eat This Book: A Year of Gorging and Glory on the Competitive Eating Circuit* (New York, NY: Macmillan, 2006).

17. Mikhail Mikhaĭlovich Bakhtin, *Rabelais and His World* (Bloomington, IN: Indiana University Press, 1984), 6.

18. Adrienne Rose Johnson, "The Magic Metabolisms of Competitive Eating," in *Taking Food Public: Redefining Foodways in a Changing World*, ed. Psyche Williams Forson and Carole Counihan (New York, NY: Routledge, 2013), 281.

19. Johnson, "Magic Metabolisms," 282.

20. See Susan L. Holak, "From Brighton Beach to Blogs: Exploring Food-Related Nostalgia in the Russian Diaspora," *Consumption Markets & Culture* 17, no. 2 (2014): 185–207; and Nerz, *Eat This Book*.

21. See Fredric Jameson, "Reification and Utopia in Mass Culture," *Social Text*, no. 1 (1979): 130–48.

22. Lauren DelValle, "Joey Chestnut Back as Top Dog in July Fourth Eating Contest," *CNN*, July 5, 2016, http://www.cnn.com/2016/07/04/us/hot-dog-eating-contest-ny/index.html.

23. Claire Suddath, "A Brief History of Competitive Eating," *Time*, July 3, 2008, http://content.time.com/time/nation/article/0,8599,1820052,00.html.

24. Rachel Heiman, *Driving after Class: Anxious Times in an American Suburb* (Berkeley, CA: University of California Press, 2015).

25. See Ralph Brubaker and Robert M. Lawless, *A Debtor World: Interdisciplinary Perspectives on Debt* (London, UK: Oxford University Press, 2012).

26. Barry Smart, *Consumer Society: Critical Issues & Environmental Consequences* (Thousand Oaks, CA: Sage, 2010).

27. Peter Stearns, *Consumerism in World History: The Global Transformation of Desire*, 2nd ed. (New York, NY: Routledge, 2006).

28. Los Angeles Times, "'Chopped': Food Network Stirs the Pot with Entertainment Format," *Latimes.com*, January 14, 2009, www.latimes.com/style/la-fo-chopped14-2009jan14-story.html.

29. *Man v. Food*, "New Jersey," The Travel Channel, December 9, 2009, written by Dan Kornfeld and Adam Richman.

30. *Man v. Food*, "Boulder," The Travel Channel, June 16, 2010, written by Dan Kornfeld and Adam Richman.

31. *Man v. Food*, "Chicago," The Travel Channel, December 24, 2008, written by Dan Kornfeld and Adam Richman; "Atlanta," The Travel Channel, January 7, 2009, written by Dan Kornfeld and Adam Richman.

32. *Man v. Food*, "Austin," The Travel Channel, December 17, 2008, written by Dan Kornfeld and Adam Richman.

33. *Man v. Food*, "Boston," The Travel Channel, January 14, 2009, written by Dan Kornfeld and Adam Richman.

34. *Man v. Food*, "New York City," The Travel Channel, January 21, 2009, written by Dan Kornfeld and Adam Richman.

35. *Man v. Food*, "Minneapolis," The Travel Channel, March 25, 2009, written by Dan Kornfeld and Adam Richman.

36. *Man v. Food*, "Memphis," The Travel Channel, December 3, 2008, written by Dan Kornfeld and Adam Richman.

37. *Man v. Food*, "Pittsburgh," The Travel Channel, December 10, 2008, written by Dan Kornfeld and Adam Richman.

38. *Man v. Food*, "Boulder."

39. *Man v. Food*, "San Jose," The Travel Channel, March 4, 2009, written by Dan Kornfeld and Adam Richman.

40. *Man v. Food*, "San Jose."

41. *Man v. Food*, "Memphis."

42. *Man v. Food*, "Atlanta."

43. *Man v. Food*, "Knoxville," The Travel Channel, October 13, 2010, written by Dan Kornfeld and Adam Richman.

44. *Man v. Food*, "Chicago."

45. *Man v. Food*, "San Francisco," The Travel Channel, August 26, 2009, written by Dan Kornfeld and Adam Richman.

46. *Man v. Food*, "Denver," The Travel Channel, March 11, 2009, written by Dan Kornfeld and Adam Richman.

47. *Man v. Food*, "Denver."

48. *Man v. Food*, "Richmond," The Travel Channel, June 30, 2010, written by Dan Kornfeld and Adam Richman.

49. *Man v. Food*, "Austin."

50. *Man v. Food*, "Columbus," The Travel Channel, December 10, 2008, written by Dan Kornfeld and Adam Richman.

51. *Man v. Food*, "New York City."

52. See "Guy Fieri Talks 'Mastery' of TV Chefs Who Have 'The Goods' When It's Time to Cook," *The Hollywood Reporter*, June 18, 2016, www.hollywoodreporter.com/news/guy-fieri-talks-mastery-tv-902411.

53. Julia Moskin, "Guy Fieri: Chef, Dude and Fan Magnet," *The New York Times*, August 10, 2010, http://www.nytimes.com/2010/08/11/dining/11Fieri.html.

54. *Diners, Drive-Ins and Dives*, "Belly Up," The Food Network, June 25, 2012, written by Tyler Young.

55. See Witzel, *The American Drive-In*; and John A. Jakle and Keith A. Sculle, *Fast Food: Roadside Restaurants in the Automobile Age* (Baltimore, MD: Johns Hopkins University Press, 2002).

56. *Diners, Drive-Ins and Dives*, "Classics," The Food Network, April 23, 2007, written by Erin Halden and Christopher Roach.

57. *Diners, Drive-Ins and Dives*, "Classics."

58. *Diners, Drive-Ins and Dives*, "Classics."

59. See Lauren Berlant, *The Queen of America Goes to Washington City: Essays on Sex and Citizenship* (Durham, NC: Duke University Press Books, 1997); Coontz, *The Way We Never Were*.

60. *Diners, Drive-Ins and Dives*, "Blue Plate Special," The Food Network, May 7, 2007, written by Erin Halden and Christopher Roach.

61. *Diners, Drive-Ins and Dives*, "Blue Plate Special."

62. *Diners, Drive-Ins and Dives*, "Blue Plate Special."

63. Fieri has effectively merchandised his brand through his own line of kitchen products and celebrity endorsement deals. In addition to his own brand of marinades, salsas, seasoning mixtures, sauces, frozen foods, coffee pods, knives, pans, and other kitchen utensils sold at Target and Walmart, Fieri has also done paid endorsements for TGI Fridays and cross promotion with Carnival Cruises, MillerCoors, and Chevy. His current net worth is approximately $8 million. See Dorothy Pomerantz, "Gordon Ramsay Tops Our List of the Highest Earning Chefs," *Forbes*, July 18, 2012, http://www.forbes.com/sites/dorothypomerantz/2012/07/18/gordon-ramsay-tops-our-list-of-the-highest-earning-chefs/.

64. Thomas Frank, *The Conquest of Cool: Business Culture, Counterculture, and the Rise of Hip Consumerism* (Chicago: University of Chicago Press, 1998), 16.

65. See Herbert Marcuse, *One-Dimensional Man: Studies in the Ideology of Advanced Industrial Society, 2nd Edition* (Boston: Beacon Press, 1991).

66. *Diners, Drive-Ins and Dives*, "Unexpected Eats."

67. *Diners, Drive-Ins and Dives*, "That's Italian," The Food Network, April 30, 2007, written by Eric Halden.

68. *Diners, Drive-Ins and Dives*, "Unexpected Eats," March 7, 2012, written by Tyler Young; *Diners, Drive-Ins, and Dives*, "Belly Up"; and "Flavortown Medley," The Food Network, October 1, 2012, written by Tyler Young.

69. *Diners, Drive-Ins and Dives*, "Belly Up."

70. *Diners, Drive-Ins and Dives*, "Authentic Eats," The Food Network, December 10, 2012, written by Tyler Young.

71. *Diners, Drive-Ins and Dives*, "Authentic Eats."

72. *Diners, Drive-Ins and Dives*, "Flavortown"; "Unconventional Comforts," The Food Network, August 6, 2012, written by Tyler Young.

73. Jakle and Sculle, *Fast Food*, 4.

FIVE

Going Native

Anthony Bourdain and No Reservations

In his book *A Cook's Tour: In Search of the Perfect Meal* Anthony Bourdain, tongue-in-cheek, reflects on the roots of his divergent brand of food television:

> I wanted the perfect meal. I also wanted—to be absolutely frank—Col. Walter E. Kurtz, Lord Jim, Lawrence of Arabia, Kim Philby, the Consul, Fowler, Tony Po, B. Traven, Christopher Walken, . . . I wanted to find— no, I wanted to be—one of those debauched heroes and villains out of Graham Greene, Joseph Conrad, Francis Coppola, and Michael Cimino. I wanted to wander the world in a dirty seersucker suit, getting into trouble. I wanted adventures. I wanted to go up the Nung River to the heart of darkness in Cambodia.[1]

Countercultural, irreverent, intellectual, and urbane, Bourdain's persona stands in stark contrast to that of the typical food celebrities who populate the Food Network and the Travel Channel. Gravitas and masculine bravado aside, Bourdain's brand of food television is positioned against the mass-produced simulacra and tourist kitsch readily embraced by other programs examined in the previous chapter. Bourdain's irreverence and aura of authenticity are derived from his experience as a writer and his twenty-plus years of experience as a chef. For Bourdain, the food adventure can be a transgressive act, defying the well-worn paths of acceptable travel, violating standards of decorum, and deterritorializing the culinary map. As exemplified in his writing, the perfect meal is less an attainable object of desire than an impetus, a pretense, to travel as a kind of culinary outlaw who—through traversing from the metropole to the periphery—attempts to decenter and transform conventional mediated understandings of food, place, and identity. In short, Bourdain personifies culinary *mis*adventure, embracing the anxious displacement of travel and exploring cuisine by losing oneself in a culture, "going native" so to speak. His rarified film and literary references convey an admiration for the antiheroes of the adventure genre; those ambivalent cultural figures who, however problematic, disavowed their privilege, broke ranks, and identified with their Other.

Of course, the concept of "going native" is a source of discomfort for those who study the ethics of travel and tourism in a postcolonial world. The notion of what it means for a Westerner to renounce their privilege is quite often premised on a fixed and binary notion of culture, that behind the smokescreen of staged tourism is an authentic and knowable Other. Moreover, "going native" exempts the traveler from critiques of cultural commodification and globalization while the naive tourist remains duped by the façade and political economy of the multicultural spectacle. As Mary Mostafanezhad writes, "'going native' has similarly become a strategy for Westerners in the Third World—including anthropologists—to attempt to overcome their postcolonial guilt. Indeed, going native is a familiar Euro-American pastime."[2] While adopting the habits and perspectives of locals advances an alternative to travel and looks past the staged commodification of everyday life, the traveler remains comfortably individuated and enlightened, somehow outside of the spirit of Western cosmopolitanism that compels individuals to consume Otherness as a form of self-affirmation.

To be sure, Bourdain's writing and television programs express disdain for Eurocentricism, tourist kitsch, and mass consumerism. In his popular programs, including *A Cook's Tour* (2003–2005), *No Reservations* (2005–2012), *The Layover* (2011–2013), and *Parts Unknown* (2013–), Bourdain has admonished Western tourists, along with a host of celebrity chefs (Fieri and Richman included), for their lack of self-reflexivity, humility, creativity, and willingness to take risks. Like Andrew Zimmern, he pushed audience familiarity with the global culinary map by venturing to regions largely unexplored in mainstream food television, including Cambodia, Ghana, Lebanon, Mozambique, Uzbekistan, and Vietnam to name a few. Yet, his programs sharply diverge from Zimmern's. Bourdain's sense of "going native" is directed more at political contextualization than spectacular consumption, at conveying the partiality and contingency of viewers' cultural and culinary knowledge. In other words, travel reveals the limitations and inadequacies of Western knowledge production and mastery of the globe. While unfamiliar foods beseech each host, Bourdain attends to the historical and material conditions that account for cultural and culinary hybridity, food serving as an entry point into a broader inquiry into the relationship between identity, place, and power. The result is a program less interested in domesticating exotic foreign cuisines than interrogating the differences that make a difference. At his best, Bourdain contests and reframes the concept of taste that is articulated in programs that celebrate American mass consumerism. That is to say that he both defends an intellectual approach to global culinary practice and expands what Americans should consider comfort food. He invites his audience to reexamine foods and cultural experiences they may have considered exotic and Other as common and humanizing.

At the same time, this charitable read of Bourdain's brand is tempered by a growing awareness of the limitations of Western cosmopolitanism, many of which I set out at the beginning of this book. That is to say that postcolonial scholars have observed the tendency of concepts such as multiculturalism and, as of late, even hybridity to be coopted by proponents of Western globalization in ways that affirm the economic value of global diversity, the significance of trade and cross-culture exchange in integrating less developed countries into the global economy, and the obsolescence of borders, state sovereignty, and national identity. In particular, Marwan Kraidy[3] observes how hybridity—the notion that the identities of those living on the periphery are not totalized, fixed, or reducible to the differences articulated in Western colonial discourse—has grown to become less a sign of resistance than evidence that the periphery can both adapt Western globalization to their own ends and benefit from their pluralistic cultural identities. From this perspective, we might view Bourdain's distinction between tourists and travelers as simply a more ethical and self-reflexive form of globalization, able to more effectively locate and interface with people not yet fully integrated or mapped by global power networks. Although this critique is certainly applicable to much of food travel television, it is perhaps too totalizing and quick to dismiss the possibility that there might be an alternative ethic of travel and culinary adventurism. After all, Bourdain upended the traditional model of food travel television, which had largely consisted of advice and recommendations about where to stay and eating while abroad—something akin to Rick Steves's or *Lonely Planet* guide books adapted to television. Bourdain's programs routinely poke fun at the conventions of the television, breaking the fourth wall between audience and screen world to highlight the spectacular inauthenticity of food television. In fact, Bourdain notes that the Food Network's experiment with *A Cook's Tour* came to an abrupt end when incoming CEO Brooke Johnson introduced a new model of lucrative food television structured around, among other elements, celebrity chef brands and reality cooking competitions.[4] With global flows of people and capital unlikely to cease anytime soon, it is worth considering what kind of rhetorics of travel might transform television audience's conceptualization of place and identity as they navigate the globe.

The importance of criticism notwithstanding, arguing for representational purity also presumes that there is an unadulterated, authentic conception of the Other that is simply obscured by a system of hegemonic representation. No program will be perfect; no means of representation

will entirely escape the dominant ideology or produce a flawlessly progressive political agenda. The drawbacks of Bourdain's facile traveler/
tourist distinction must be weighed against the potential efficacy of his
indictments of Eurocentric attitudes and commitment to self-reflexivity.
Here, I am reminded of Said's somewhat controversial approach to Jo-
seph Conrad's *Heart of Darkness*, a novel that while critical of the inhumanity of colonialism has been ruthlessly critiqued for its dehumanizing
portrayals of African people as tragically subjugated and primitive.[5] Said
writes, "Conrad's realization is that if, like narrative, imperialism has
monopolized the entire system of representation . . . your self-conscious-
ness as an outsider can allow you actively to comprehend how the machine works, given that you and it are fundamentally not in perfect syn-
chrony or correspondence."[6] Bourdain, too, is at points an outsider,
someone asynchronous with the colonial ideologies that shape the culture, history, and present political circumstances of the places he visits.
Such a position affords him the ability to draw attention to how the food
traditions and people with whom he interfaces reflect the workings of
colonial machinery. At other points, he is complicit, an agent of the discourse of globalization or simply aligned too closely—as an American
traveler and former chef—with that which he critiques. His self-reflexivity and critical attention to ethics of culinary travel work within but
sometimes against the conceptions of self and Other that predominate in
contemporary food television.

In this chapter, I examine Bourdain's case for open and ethical culinary travel in light of the critique of globalization discourse I advance in
chapters 1 and 2 and the narratives of national innocence that unfold in
chapters 3 and 4. My purpose is not to merely apply the same insights of
these chapters to yet another case study, but rather, to bring this project
to a close by examining the potentials and challenges of food travel narratives that question that boundary between self and Other, criticize Eurocentric discourse, and indict the logics of mass consumption. Although
Bourdain's television career offers a wealth of texts for consideration, I
attend to the Travel Channel's *No Reservations*, a program that stood
against a line-up of broadcasts that by-and-large promoted commercial
tourism and exoticism. The program was an hour-long travel log, star-
ring and narrated by Bourdain, in which a camera crew followed his
visits to different country or region in each episode, 142 in total over eight
seasons.[7] The Travel Channel considered Bourdain an icon of the network, beloved for his mixture of erudite socio-political commentary and
sharp-tongued cynical wit.[8]

To be sure, Bourdain's other programs are certainly deserving of critical attention. For instance, across eight seasons Bourdain's current CNN
series *Parts Unknown* continues the project he developed in *No Reservations*. The move to a cable news network enabled Bourdain to travel to
some of the least accessible regions of the globe and to focus his attention

more specifically on issues of history and culture than food and travel. This chapter focuses on *No Reservations* because it is situated within and against the Scripps brand of food and travel television. Above all, I am interested in how Bourdain intervenes in those spaces where the ethics of travel are cultivated in food television. As such, I find *No Reservations* to be an invective against global tourist culture, a program structured like a long-form argument against closed-minded ethnocentric forms of food tourism. At the same time, the program exemplifies the friction between desires for an ethic of travel where individuals seek to experience a culture as it is lived and the problem of authenticity as a fiction always already constraining the traveler's sense of cultural difference. While this tension in many ways limits the possibility that travel might dissolve imperialist conceptions of self and Other, it might also transform cosmopolitanism as it is currently conceived by inviting audiences to reconsider their own desires for mastery and the limitations of their Eurocentric worldviews. The attempt to escape the conventional logics of tourism often prove illusive, but this should not preclude us from developing food television that directs us toward new ethics of global citizenship. Once made aware, how might travelers navigate the logics of globalization? What are the possibilities for new narratives in food television? This final chapter ties together the previous chapters' emphasis on food, taste, and travel to explore the possibilities of new ethical orientations toward global flows of people and capital that acknowledge hybridity as a fluid set of identity formations, the relationship between self and Other, and the challenges of authenticity in a global mass consumer culture.

TRAVEL NARRATIVES, HYBRIDITY, AND GLOBALIZATION REVISITED

One of the central assumptions behind this book is that travel and adventure narratives have long provided an ideological defense of imperialism. Travel writing, predominated by stories of adventure and discovery on the periphery, mapped the scope of empire and the wealth of places yet-to-be-conquered.[9] Stacy Burton writes that "they recounted explorations, reported discoveries, and documented unfamiliar cultures, languages, and landscapes. Travelers . . . wrote narratives and ethnographic studies that presented themselves as truthful accounts of first-hand experience and thus important sources of knowledge. Their work often played a formative role in imperial policy."[10] Until the formal end of colonialism in the twentieth century, travel narratives relied on geographical borders to serve as unequivocal and common-sense divisions between the civilized and primitive world. The travel narrative confirmed that geographic demarcations were real and concrete dividing lines that, once crossed, transported Westerners to an earlier time in human development.[11]

Though still shaped by many of the same assumptions, modern travel narratives lost their claim to authority and coherence following the decolonization of Asia, Africa, and Latin America and the near total destruction of the European continent. With the metropole ravaged by war and the emergence of newly liberated republics on the periphery, the old geographical distinctions failed to convey their former sense of stable meaning and national subjectivity. Old maps and their power lines were obsolete. There was no clear metropole from which the Western travel writer could speak, no position of authority from which to speak about the gifts of Enlightenment rationality for the exotic subjects of empire. The metanarrative of modernity's universal uplift was also in visible contradiction with the state of the globe in 1945. Whereas Nazi Germany had fashioned modern industrialism into a lethal and efficient system of mass murder, American physicists had weaponized scientific rationality by splitting the atom. Meanwhile, the great capital cities of Europe lay in ruin as new nations emerged in the postcolonial world. With Europe's role in the world in question, the travel narrative had lost its original purpose. In 1945 travel novelist Evelyn Waugh wrote, "my own traveling days are over and I do not expect to see many travel books in the near future. . . . There is no room for tourists in a world of 'displace persons.' Never again, I suppose, shall we land on foreign soil with letters of credit and passport . . . and feel the world wide open before us."[12] Waugh, who had traveled throughout the British empire, reflected with much melancholy that the golden era of a world open to the privileged Westerner had come to a close.[13]

Of course, Waugh's prediction that, like empire, travel writing was in its death throes proved premature. Rather than waning, postwar travel narratives transformed into a genre that was simply less sanguine about Europe and America's centrality to global progress and more critical of the traumatic legacy of Euro-American modernity. The genre grew to be more existential and reflexive, or as Burton explains, "the genre had to evolve, revise its claims to seriousness, apart to a postimperial world in which the place of the metropole was no longer secure—or fade into irrelevance."[14] Thus, travel narratives were forced to come to terms with the "shocking inhumanity of which advanced civilizations are capable and the cultural dispossession they can cause."[15] Ostensibly, travel narratives became delinked from imperialism and rearticulated to fit within the burgeoning paradigm of neoliberal globalization, cosmopolitanism, and global community. The emerging postwar economy's emphasis on interdependence and technological innovations made the exchange of goods and people across international borders more feasible and less cost prohibitive.[16] Emerging consumer markets in the developing world guided Westerners away from the old fantasies of plunder and conquest and instead toward how goods, resources, and experience could be appreciated, then monetized and consumed. Though not devoid of economic opportunism, new travel narratives decentered the metropole in favor of articulating the cultural experiences of those excluded from Western metanarratives.

Although many of the previous chapters have explored how travel narratives can reinscribe colonial hierarchies in the name of advancing a Western version of globalization, as a genre it need not uniformly serve such interests. The growth in travel writing and television certainly reflects how increased mobility, stronger infrastructure, and global flows of people and goods have generated interest in cultures and places that attest to the importance of global diversity.[17] One drawback I noted earlier in this book is the tendency of travel programs to celebrate difference without denoting the power inequities that account for Western hegemony. Consumption becomes a way of domesticating difference and imaging the globe as a playground for the cosmopolitan (culinary) traveler. But here I want to suggest that Bourdain's travel logs provide an important counterpoint to the unreflexive celebration of difference that is characteristic of travel narratives in an age of globalization. Indeed, there is something dissatisfying about globalization where the promise of leveling the economic playing field, breaking down barriers, and integrating outsiders into Western-dominated neoliberal institutions brings with it a homogenizing global monoculture. Of course, globalization can also produce the conditions for hybridity, but the prospect of homogenization portends a global cultural experience circumscribed by America's culture industries.

Bourdain's brand speaks to audiences who might be dissatisfied with the McDonaldization of global culture, a process whereby the exportation of Western mass consumer culture renders the world safe and familiar to travelers.[18] His focus on experiencing place by living and eating like locals also goes against the grain of the stage tourist spectacle where locals strategically perform what counts as authenticity to the uninformed visitor.[19] In their critical inquiries into contemporary tourist culture, Patrick Holland and Graham Huggan suggest that Western cosmopolitan audiences fear that globalization might standardize global culture and thus foreclose their opportunity to engage with cultures other than their own. Some audiences, they write, still want "evidence that the world is heterogeneous, unfathomable, bewildering; as proof that the spirit of adventure can hold off the threat of exhaustion."[20] Hence, a televised travel narrative that foregrounds the hybridity of global cultures offers Westerners an alternative engagement with the globe that questions both homogenization and exoticization. Hence, I read *No Reservations* as an engagement with the complacent beliefs and prevailing cultural stereotypes that pervade both travel narratives and food television. The question that remains is: to what degree is this engagement effective?

Does Bourdain offer a way through the comfort of homogeneity, on the one hand, and the spectacularization of cultural difference, on the other? Is there an effective critique to be leveled in the distinction between tourists and travelers?

HYBRIDITY RECONSIDERED

With the challenges of travel narratives in the foreground, *No Reservations* is a text concerned with how American food television represents the Other and the ethical responsibilities that accompany the power to represent cultures that are not one's own. First, it is important to consider the program's approach to representing the concept of cultural hybridity through the established tropes of the culinary adventure. And while hybridity characterizes how global cultures have been shaped by centuries of movement of people, goods, and cultural traditions across borders, food and travel television rarely reflects this dynamic fusion of subaltern and transnational identities. For instance, *Bizarre Foods* keeps cultural hybridity at arm's length when it evokes imperialist nostalgia, a romantic desire for a kind of pure and authentic cultural experience tragically destroyed by Western colonization. In other words, authenticity is sutured to the past, evacuated from a present that seems somehow diluted. Or, more simply, foods and cultural experiences that reflect hybridity are exoticized more than they are contextualized. At the same time, travel narratives might come to represent hybridity, or the degree to which the identity of the Other is not fixed in the position of colonial discourse. Instead, national identities and national cuisines can be acknowledged as the byproducts of historical transnational fusions, continually caught within the ongoing process of global flows of people, capital, and, tragically, armies crossing international borders. *No Reservations* contends with this ceaselessness of global flows by contextualizing global cuisine as byproducts not of a particular fixed place or national identity but instead as an amalgam of intercultural exchange, global diasporas, migration, colonialism, trade, and so on. In exploring the relationship between dynamic food traditions and everyday cultural practices, the program acknowledges that identities are complex and fluid, refusing to conflate culture with nationality.

As a travel writer, Bourdain uses voice over narration to provide social, political, and historical context to explain the culinary roots of the places he visits. While this approach distinguishes Bourdain from other food program hosts, it is his emphasis on the symbolism of food that distinguishes him from the travel genre. That is to say that Bourdain uses the compositional elements of different cuisine as a way of making sense of cultural identities that confound Western stereotypes of self/Other. His visit to the Azore Islands in the Atlantic—a place shaped by a combination of Arab, Spanish, Portuguese, African, and American influences—is a perfect case-in-point.[21] Here, he explains the strong connections between Azore residents and those populations who immigrated to New England, noting how each community's food traditions are reflected in one another. The episode includes short clips of immigrant families explaining where they are from and what kind of cuisine kept them connected to their community in the Azores. As Bourdain narrates, "The connection to the states remains strong, symbiotic, the subject of longing on both sides of the water." He notes that his experience with Azore cuisine was initially confounding because he could not easily place it as Mediterranean, Spanish, or Portuguese. His conversations with people on the islands illustrate how the cuisine reflects a fusion of national and regional influences shaped by centuries of traffic across the Atlantic and back. With his stereotypes debunked, Bourdain explains that "the Azores is a depository of influences from around the world" and "It's a hybrid. Its Atlantic but it feels vaguely Arab Mediterranean."[22] At the same time, he notes, "they've managed to keep their unique culture surprisingly intact." Bourdain is unable to fix Azore cuisine to a dominant national culinary tradition, resulting in a frame of acceptance toward liminality. The diverse mixture of ingredients that comprises Azore cuisine helps convey cultural dynamism of places shaped by a confluence of traditions.

Bourdain is careful to point out that hybridity is often the result of war and colonial conquest. At the same time, the program refuses to either adopt a tragic frame of imperialist nostalgia or glibly celebrate the unfortunate byproducts of colonial subjugation. In Vietnam, Bourdain narrates the nation's history of resilience in the face of colonial incursions from China, France, and the United States.[23] While he notes that the incursions of these foreign powers has strongly influenced its national and subnational cuisines, he observes how the Vietnamese have appropriated ingredients and assimilated them into their food culture. Vietnam is presented as a counterpoint to the homogenization thesis, a country portrayed as resistant to even violent impositions of foreign culture but also dynamic enough to adopt desirable elements of French, Chinese, and American culture. He narrates: "It's mysterious, it's beautiful, it's unknowable, it's one of my favorite places on earth, a crossroads where nearly every aspect of the culture, religion, government, and cuisine, have at some point in history been influenced by a foreign power. Yet, it remains something uniquely more than some of its parts. A place of few culinary inhibitions, endless hospitality, with a strong inner identity. But there's no other place like it."[24] Bourdain also explores the ways in which Vietnam has sought to capitalize on global tourism by staging its own attractive yet subversive forms of staged authenticity. He visits a state-run island resort "designed to lure tourists to be pampered in the world of the imperial past." Here, Bourdain is treated to performances of traditional Vietnamese dancing and a multi-course meal in an opulent resort-style setting. The program contrasts the complexity of everyday Vietnamese life with the strategic spectacle of authenticity Vietnam designed to appeal to Western mass consumers. The show illustrates how hybridization enables the Vietnamese to retain their traditional cultural practices while also taking advantage of the cosmopolitan turn in Western globalization.

In other cases, the program emphasizes how what are frequently constructed as singular national identities are, in fact, the unavoidable by-product of cultural hybridity, a nearly universal condition shaped by the ceaselessness of global movement. Hybridity not only characterizes the national politics of postcolonial societies but is also a natural condition in which identities are fused outside of colonial violence. In Malaysia, Bourdain describes the scene as "a land of natural fusion, a collusion of culture and cuisine that have blended together over the centuries. A place where indigenous peoples embrace the journey as a vital element of life. A place you can visit as a tourist, but best experienced as an enthusiasm. Just know whatever happens it's going to be good. . . . Much like New York, Malaysia is a melting pot of many cultures. And I've always said a place's food and more specifically its markets are the quickest, best way to gain entry into a culture and a people."[25] In this episode, Bourdain samples the intersection of South and Southeast Asian cuisines in the food markets of Kuala Lumpur. His use of food as entry point into culture invites the audience to think of the diverse array of cultural foodways available to Bourdain as a reflection of the unavoidable complexity of cultural identity. As Bourdain travels from the country's urban centers to its remote rural islands, the cuisine becomes more diverse. Malaysian identity becomes irreducible to one particular and knowable set of cultural rituals or geographic locations.

Similarly, while in Uzbekistan, Bourdain invites his audience to be comfortable with the lack of definitive labels.[26] A historic stop on the Silk Road trading route between Europe and Asia, the diverse religious and culture designations that characterize the nation today make it an ideal location to communicate how cultural identities are often overlapping, multiple, and fluid. As the camera cuts between shots of people, architecture, and street food, Bourdain explains, "Uzbekistan at various points in history has been conquered by, oh let's see, the Turks, the Mongols, the Russians, there've been Arabs through here, Persians, Indians, and you can kind of see that in the faces of the people around here. It's a little bit of everything and you see that in the food as well." Again, the fusion of ingredients becomes a common-sense metaphor for a way of thinking about identities as amalgams of diverse backgrounds and traditions. The conception of identity advanced in the program refuses fixed and static categories. Bourdain even allows his search for a definitive explanation of Uzbekistan to fail by asking: "Is it Asian? Is it Middle Eastern? Is it Russian? It's all of the above." The complexity of identity in both Malaysia and Uzbekistan presents a challenge to rigid and binary categories of difference, or where a singular national subjectivity supplants transnational and subnational cultural identifications. And in both cases, the complexity of food fusion provides audiences with a short-hand way of comprehending identities that are "both/and" rather than "either/or."

The program's interest in cultural hybridity works against homogenization—as both an effect of Western globalization as well as a pessimistic misperception about its universalizing tendencies. Moreover, the natural hybridity we attribute to culinary traditions helps Bourdain convey how hybridity manifests in fluid and overlapping identity categories that evade Western cultural stereotypes. As Homi Bhabha contends, the hybrid subject offers the possibility of resistance to the totalizing repression of colonialism and neocolonialism.[27] Identity can then be seen as a category of experience that is constructed through a negotiation with difference. To this end, *No Reservations* acknowledges the importance of the hybrid subject—shaped by a multiplicity of internal and external influences—as an alternative to the fixed one-dimensional portraits of singular national identities that conform to preconceived Western notions of foreign identity. On the program, borders no longer convey meaningful differences between cultures. Unlike colonial travel writing, identities cross borders and refuse to conform to the Western map. The program even selects locations where a geostrategic national border separates fused and interdependent food cultures, including places such as the US/Mexican border; Beirut, Lebanon; Rajasthan, India; and Kurdistan.[28] As such, *No Reservations* avoids replicating the fixed notions of identity that are replete throughout the travel genre. And though it is impossible for such a program to capture the depth and complexity of foreign cultural identities, the presumed complexity of international cuisines is superimposed over cultural identity in ways that transfer the principles of one onto the other. If people are as fluid and dynamic as cuisine, cultural identity becomes less static and, ultimately, less knowable in total. In this way, the show lives up to Holland and Huggan's view that travel narratives "have the potential to jolt its readers out of complacent beliefs and attitudes, and its challenge to prevailing stereotypes and cultural myths of place."[29]

WHOSE DEVELOPMENT?

After negotiating the complexities of cultural identity, *No Reservations* examines the relationship between food cultures and international economic development, particularly in episodes that feature developing nations. In some cases, the program notes the limitations of participation in a relatively more accessible global economy and, in other instances, lapses into a cosmopolitan entrepreneurialism in which unique national assets, including the nation's culinary culture, is a feasible way out of poverty and economic austerity. Thus, the program vacillates between structural pessimism concerning the opportunities for the developing nations and agental optimism that cultural and economic development will enable participation in the new global economy. Of course, Bourdain is not an economist; therefore, his insights are limited to anecdotal observations of everyday life and what he can divine from the state of the region's culinary culture. In much the same way that he translates culinary complexity into cultural hybridity, Bourdain uses local foodways to make sense of larger socio-economic and political forces. *No Reservations* negotiates developing nations' travails with globalization and the ambivalence that comes with Western-centered development paradigms that bring prosperity for some and austerity for others. The show invites guarded optimism about globalization, cultivating a sense that developing nations can adapt Western development toward their own end; yet, globalization might also bring displacement and inequality.

The program's faith and optimism in Western-style economic development is evident in its narrative context, where the story of developing nations moves from a dark period of fascism, communism, or colonialism to a proto-capitalist era in which market values create new opportunities for upward mobility. In Chile, Bourdain begins his uplift narrative with the history of the Nixon-backed Pinochet regime. He meets with a Chilean news columnist who lived through that period and explains the regime's brutal oppression of the Chilean people. After discussing disappearances and extrajudicial killings, the two travel to the famous La Fuente Alemana restaurant to discuss the nation's brighter future over iconic Chilean cuisine. B-roll of Pinochet's Chile transitions to shots of a brightly lit and lively café where patrons engage in animated conversations over beer and German fusion cuisine. Bourdain transitions from discussions of the country's dark fascist past to its sunnier capitalist future, explaining, "Chile's all about a country that wants to move forward. Over the past two decades this country has risen to the rank of economic powerhouse in South America. A prosperous country moving headlong into a new century, proud of the brighter aspects of its past, yet eager to move forward. Need proof check out this place."[30] Here, the vibrancy of the nation's food culture encapsulates the kind of equality of opportunity created by democratic capitalism, suggesting that a combination of civic freedoms and market values creates universal prosperity. The program suggests that innovations in Chilean cuisine, along with the excitement and enthusiasm of the nation's restaurant culture, symbolize the nation's successful entry into the global economy. As Bourdain bluntly concludes, "economic prosperity and civic freedoms allowed for a rebirth of Chilean culture."[31] Throughout the episode, the omnipresence of Chileans in cafés, bars, markets, bistros, and public squares, happily consuming and exercising their freedom cements the connection between globalization and democratic values. Chile is relatable because it ostensibly resembles a European metropolis.

For less successful developing nations, the program portrays the recent development of a culinary culture as an indication that peace and prosperity are likely to follow, or at the very least would seem to be the next progression in the country's integration into the global economy. In an episode featuring the Baja region of Mexico, Bourdain searches the region's culinary culture for signs of economic progress.[32] The episode begins with shots of Bourdain crossing the border on foot narrated by news reports of drug cartel violence and interspersed with b-roll of gang warfare in the streets of Tijuana. On his trip, however, Bourdain shares drinks with locals in a vibrant food and bar district, visits one of the most famous food carts in the world, and is treated to a five-star meal in the Baja wine country. In one sense, Bourdain helps dispel media myths that all of Mexico is enduring widespread civil unrest and open warfare in its streets. In another sense, the emergence of a more developed culinary culture is naturally followed by a more developed civil society. In other words, economic entrepreneurialism is represented as a civilizing force that likely brings peace and prosperity. Bourdain even expresses hope where he sees parallels between the food cultures of Baja and Europe. Again, whereas this episode begins with ominous overtones, it concludes with reserved optimism about a cultural renaissance through new patterns of consumption. He narrates, "Mexico is a country with some problems but they are our neighbor and, if you think about it, our relationship with Mexico, however reluctant, is in many ways a lot closer, a lot more intimate, and romantic even than we have with Canada. And I don't know if the determination of a few young chefs and musicians who've decided to make the best of a bad situation will, in the end, save the world. I don't know if incredible ingredients and an exciting emerging culinary scene will turn things around for Baja. But if there's any justice in the world, it should."[33] Though his optimism remains guarded, the pathway out of violence and poverty remains tied to individual self-determination and the capitalization of natural resources.

Indeed, this trope of dark past/bright future is repeated in episodes featuring the food cultures of nations that recently experienced collective trauma. In Cambodia, over a traditional meal, Bourdain speaks with a member of the opposition party who survived the reign of the Khmer Rouge.[34] The two discuss how the eradication of the intellectual and Chinese merchant class had profoundly inhibited the nation's economic and democratic development. Bourdain discusses the differences between his experience ten years earlier, noting that despite the nation's traumatic past, there is still a path toward modernity. Meanwhile, in the Czech Republic, Ukraine, and Uzbekistan, Bourdain observes how repressive Cold War-era communism held back and standardized what then became under market capitalism a burgeoning economy.[35] The existence of a thriving culinary culture indicates the success of free market and democratic principles at work. The industriousness that characterizes a successful culinary culture is portrayed as the same virtue that overcame the nations' past traumas. For instance, the program praises Ghana as a prime example of how postcolonial nations can harness their natural resources to compete and succeed in the global economy. Bourdain introduces the episode by narrating, "there are a lot of countries in West Central, Africa, and most have had a hard time making the transition from oppressed colony to modern independent state. Ghana is something special. The first of the sub-Saharan colonies to gain independence in 1957, Ghana became the living symbol of the idea of Africa for Africans. The nation once known as the Gold Coast is rich in gold and cocoa but burdened like some many African nations with an unbelievably tragic past. It was from here that so many departed for the New World packed into ships as slaves and dozens of slave forts still haunt the coast. Most are tourist sights now."[36] Note how unlike other African nations, Ghana's exceptional ability to capitalize on its natural resources and tourist attractions helps transcend a traumatic history of slavery and colonialism. As the camera shows images of the bustling Maloka Market in Akra, Ghana's industrious attitudes and behaviors bespeak the market-oriented values that enable success in the postcolonial world. And with those traits come the benefits of Western democracy. Bourdain continues, "modern day Ghana is an exciting place to see where hopefully much of Africa is headed. People here are proud of the fact that this is a land of democratic elections and rule of law. It has an economy that is struggling but relatively stable and growing. But it's the food, music, and natural beauty of Ghana that makes this first bite fascinating."[37] While Ghana's independence has certainly enabled the country to flourish relative to surrounding states in the region, there is the sense that market values are the same as civic values, even where the two might be in tension. Either way, globalization, free trade, and tourism are represented as salvation for independent postcolonial nations.

   While the logic of globalization is implicit, throughout the series Bourdain maintains a skeptical attitude toward the more formal and institutional elements of globalization. His travels to Mozambique are a perfect illustration of this point.[38] In this episode, Bourdain begins his travels by sharing a celebratory meal with a group of rural villagers that highlights the nation's extreme poverty after independence. He remarks on how many in the countryside "scrap[e] out a living under the scorching sun," and "like millions of others around the developing worlds, these guys are living on a diet of boiled cassava root. Animal protein, whether scrounged, hunted or bush meat, often a life giving luxury. Major source of protein around here day to day: rat."[39] Bourdain's conversations with his guide reveal that despite a general attitude of optimism in the country, a sixteen-year civil war along with a five-hundred-year history of slavery and colonialism have impinged the nation's economic and political development. Bourdain is quick to point out the hypocrisy that the nation is touted as a model for the developing world. He explains that "Mozambique, it should be point out, is a darling of the World Bank. It's seen as an African success story and the fact is things are good, very good here as compared to how things were in the past," yet it is a nation "with a devastated social fabric, economy, and only the memory of infrastructure." Bourdain's comments are less of an embrace of the nation's relative success than an indictment of what counts as success within international neoliberal institutions.[40] There is a profound disconnect between images of crumbling infrastructure, displaced people, and official pronouncements that the nation's economy is a model of international development. In this episode, Bourdain and his guide also register skepticism with the notion that tourism and attracting Western investors will help its poorest citizens. They agree that tourism will require the displacement of residents living in poverty to both attract and make room for foreign guests. Bourdain remarks, "if the tourists come where will all the people on the island, most in dire and decidedly untouristy conditions go? They'll have to be relocated, of course, seen as inconvenient to the common good." He goes on to engage in a conversation with two white Rhodesians who speak with reverence about the old city of Barra and its luxuries that catered to European foreign nationals. This conversation references a previous time in the nation's colonial history where importing European tourists and settlers was thought to result in the country's economic uplift. Walking through the ruins of the former colonial architecture, Bourdain points out that "for white Rhodesians it was a wonderland." Against the backdrop of luxury resort ruins, these conversations about the dire effects of attracting foreign investment, tourism, and settlement convey the darker side of globalization where the Western development paradigm introduced austerity, inequality, and displacement.

Though there are many episodes in which Western-style development is presumed to be a natural good, it is fair to say that Bourdain also acknowledges the more harmful and exclusionary aspects of neoliberal globalization. As a totality, it is hard to conceptualize, particularly within hegemonic cultural forms, an outside or alternative to globalization. For a program limited by the political economy of television, it is difficult for hosts, producers, and writers to illustrate what forces outside of the market might bring parity to the global economy. This might be simply asking too much of a program devoted primarily to the relationship between culture, location, and food. Yet, *No Reservations* illustrates the challenge of representing developing nations and the importance of contextualization. The program illustrates how globalization has uneven effects across the developing world. There are places where residents have been able to take advantage of the Western development paradigm for their own ends and others where globalization has promoted exploitation. For Bourdain, the state of the food culture reveals the travails of everyday life, the subtle resistances and survival strategies, ingenuity as well as failure. Either way, the developing world is shown to be neither agentless nor dependent; yet, also not perfectly poised to compete in a global economy dominated by Western interests.

GOING NATIVE: TRAVELERS AND TOURISTS

Though the standardization of American mass culture and its exportation overseas generates comfort and convenience for consumers, it also produces deep alienation over the prospect that objects and experiences we once considered autonomously produced are, in fact, mass-manufactured commodities. Horkheimer and Adorno registered this concern particularly as it pertains to leisure: as industrial labor had alienated the worker from the products of their labor, cultural commodification had transformed them into passive consumers of items devoid of authenticity and aesthetic worth.[41] The image of the "tourist trap" comes to mind, a place that lures in customers with cheap reproductions of popular items and prefabricated cultural experiences. Or, the theme-park resort (Disney World, Sandals Jamaica) that sells a pleasing simulacrum of authentic cultural life, its appeal residing in feelings of nostalgia for simulated realities that never existed but for in the world of the image.[42] Often, the simulacra capture the very alienation that they engender by claiming to be authentic and genuine; the tourist trap making claims to its own realism (i.e., "the original home of _____"). Where tourism and leisure are concerned, alienation generates the desire to escape, to seek out evidence that mass culture has not colonized the entirety of the life world. For Bourdain, inauthenticity is a primary concern. His frequent derision of "mass produced fun for middle America"[43] and food that resembles "TGI McFunsters" communicates deep antipathy toward the kind of kitsch embraced in the programs examined in the previous chapter. In *No Reservations*, Bourdain addresses the alienation of the mass consumer by 1) making a distinction between tourists and travelers and 2) encouraging them to "go native" and, as best they can, live like the locals. This approach to navigating the global spectacle of mass tourism is inviting as it enables the viewer or traveler to imagine themselves as existing outside of the process of cultural commodification. As an ethic of responsible travel there is little with which to argue, to the degree that travelers are encouraged to question the extent of their cultural knowledge and experience beyond what is convenient and comforting. At the same time, the show's ethic presumes the separate existence of a reality outside the spectacle, reality untouched by commodity culture and unspoiled by Western influence. This ethic elides the degree to which authenticity is itself a constructed, belabored reality.

No Reservations' commercial slogan is "be a traveler, not a tourist."[44] Ostensibly, Bourdain extorts his audience to seek out experiences, food in particular, that extend beyond that which caters to Westerners. Indeed, his choice of what some Americans might consider difficult locations— Kurdistan, Hong Kong, and Egypt—suggests that travel is more reward- ing when it is both more challenging and less familiar. Overall, a larger portion of the narration is devoted to reflecting on the personal transfor- mations that come with difficult travels. For instance, after spending time with a rural community in Borneo, Bourdain explains

> As you've probably noticed, I'm not an expert on the places I visit. I'm not an authority I'm a visitor, a traveler, an enthusiast. Travel isn't always pretty, its not always comfortable, sometimes it hurts, it even breaks your heart. But that's okay, the journey changes you, it should change you, it leaves marks on your memory, on your consciousness, on your heart, and on your body. It takes something with you, hopeful- ly you leave something good behind.[45]

This passage speaks to a relationship between travel and consciousness- raising, the possibility that behind the spectacle of mass tourism lies ca- tharsis and self-actualization. Whereas the tourist is a naïve and blissfully unaware mass consumer, the traveler is a savant who is privy to transcendent knowledge. To add further, in Peru he relays the signifi- cance of humility when he admits, "It seems that the more places I see and experience the bigger I realize the world to be. The more of it I become aware of the more I realize how relatively little I know of it, how many places I still have to go, how much more there is to learn, maybe that's enlightenment enough."[46] Though neither are experts, whereas the tourist feigns worldly knowledge, the traveler confesses their ignorance. In other episodes, he is quick to admit the experiences that make him uncomfortable or those which challenge his own cultural assumptions. Observing the evening Islamic call to prayer in Uzbekistan, Bourdain respectfully observes "this is about as far away from my own beliefs, my own inclinations, my own nature as anything can get."[47] Taken together, these statements construct a traveler archetype, the tourist its foil, who approaches travel as an opportunity to challenge their assumptions about the world, disavow their privilege, and experience personal growth.

Although this slogan captures the ethos of the program, for scholars the distinction between travelers and tourists is dubious at best. Of course, this distinction appeals to cosmopolitan audiences because it of- fers a fantasy of "self-exemption" whereby the more educated and worldly citizens among us may gain access to a seemingly pure and unmediated experience with a foreign culture.[48] Indeed, there are several problems in this distinction that are worth considering. First, this distinc- tion parses up the world into authentic and inauthentic culture. Hence, the more pastoral, innocent, underdeveloped, and primitive a culture appears the more it offers to travelers the possibility of escape from mass culture. This, however, belies the program's commitment to hybridity, where cultural identities are not fixed and exotic stereotypes not manipulated to make facile distinctions between self and Other. Moreover, culture, as a set of recurring rituals and everyday performances, is in one way or another always already staged.[49] It is difficult to distinguish, much less accord hierarchical value, to explicit performances designed to generate tourist revenue and implicit performances that inevitably occur in interactions between traveler/tourist and local residents. Second, this distinction exempts travelers from critiques of ethnocentrisms that are commonly leveled against tourists. The tourist makes for an easy scapegoat; their sense of entitlement, hubris, and poor etiquette. As Edward Bruner writes, "tourism is a mystifying subject because being a tourist is deprecated by almost everyone. Even tourists themselves belittle tourism as it connotes something commercial, tacky, and superficial."[50] The distinction serves to alleviate the guilt that accompanies an acute awareness of one's privilege and, among others, the potentially negative effects of tourism, including economic displacement and environmental degradation. The presumed superiority of the traveler belies the program's gestures toward self-reflexivity, those other moments in which Bourdain invites his audience to question their assumptions about travel. Finally, this distinction constitutes an unproblematic celebration of mobility and human freedom.[51] The superiority of the traveler is premised on rugged Western individualism, a masculine spirit of perseverance, strength, and self-reliance. The traveler is free from the constraints placed on the tourist who may not have the class, race, or gender privilege to freely navigate the globe without considering safety, affordability, and comfort. Though this is not universally the case, Bourdain has the luxury of traveling the world as white male—assisted by guides, experts, and producers—unaffected by structural barriers that might exclude some from escaping the inauthentic world of tourism.

Bourdain's other advice to would-be travelers is to live like the locals. In practice, this means avoiding tourist traps, eating at places that are preferred by local residents, observing the rituals of everyday life, and never offending one's host. Typically, he enacts this ethic by sharing meals with local guides in places frequented more so by local residents than foreign visitors. He never refuses a meal, whether it's fermented shark in Iceland or room temperature organ meat in Uzbekistan. But "going native" is more than avoiding tourist spots and commingling with local residents; instead, Bourdain suggests, it is something that requires a temporary disavowal of privilege. He frequently admonishes tourists for believing that they can purchase authenticity, what he considers an anemic form of multicultural celebration. For example, while observing indigenous village life on the banks of the Amazon River, he gests that "the Amazon, a favorite destination for eco-tourists, Sting fans, and well. . . .

Sting himself, who comes snapping photos and chanting their rallying cries of cultural appreciation. Wearing LL Bean, Gortex, and sleeping in $300 money bags, do they really get to know these people when they visit?"[52] As the argument goes, going native requires a certain amount of challenge and discomfort, a willingness to forgo typical travel luxuries and attempt to inhabit the subject position of the local. Thus, Bourdain decides to spend a day in the Amazon with a local guide named Rudolfo, who shows him how to harvest yucca and fish for piranhas. With shots of children playing in the river and families sharing meals, the experience is filmed with a romantic gaze toward traditional Amazonian life. Though the experience seems fundamentally more genuine than the foil of the bourgeois eco-tour, Bourdain retreats from sentiment, when he remarks, "what we are also talking about is poverty, I mean . . . that's back break-ing work. Isn't it kind of patronizing to say well, you know, they're happier, they live a simpler life closer to the soil maybe so. . . . The nagging feeling that I've got a long way to go in my own consciousness-raising endeavors."[53] To Bourdain's credit, he warns the audience against romanticizing some of the more difficult living conditions of the develop-ing world. And certainly his approach to living like the locals commits the traveler to a stance of open-mindedness and empathy over empty expressions of cultural appreciation. Yet, there remains the challenge of what constitutes authenticity. Between the tourist's romanticism and the traveler's realism, the local resident remains a conduit to a less alienated and more aesthetically valuable cultural experience. Appeals to self-reflexivity aside, going native is still premised on the traveler achieving self-actualization through encounters with people and experiences seem-ingly more "real" than what exists in mass consumer culture. At the same time, the notion that travel has the potential to destabilize cultural stereo-types and transform Eurocentric attitudes is, at least provisionally, a worthwhile endeavor even as the illusory search for authenticity yields little resistance to the culture industries that support global tourism.

DECENTERING THE METROPOLE

In contrast to many other food travel programs, *No Reservations* ap-proaches America with the same degree of curiosity and astonishment as any other nation featured. The program subjects American food and cul-tural traditions to the same set of quasi-anthropological inquiries as it does any other unfamiliar region of the world. Avoiding common tropes of American exceptionalism and the American Dream, *No Reservations* displaces America as a familiar home-like territory, a center by which all other cuisines and traditions are judged. First, the show treats everyday foods and behaviors in America as cultural traditions instead of the invis-ible norms from which all else in the world is marked with difference.

The effect is not self-exoticism, but instead an equality in global difference. Second, the program engages in a series of polemical arguments about what constitutes normal cultural foodways. In this way, Bourdain indicts American assumptions about what constitutes comfort food and attempts to normalize non-American foodways. Taken together, these discursive strategies constitute an invective against the ethnocentric conceptions of travel and food that pervade much of contemporary food television. Though, as I noted earlier, the program is in many ways constrained by its medium, Bourdain's arguments against ethnocentric ideals suggest that food television can destabilize conventional representations of food, place, and identity.

First, Bourdain invites a reciprocal attitude between foreign and domestic foodways. That is to say that he approaches both foreign and domestic travel with the same level of unfamiliarity and open-mindedness, privileging neither as more or less important or problematic. In Las Vegas, he allays his ennui toward American consumer culture by suggesting that "I have found that respecting that foreignness by simply cutting Americans as much slack as I would anyone else's indigenous culture has made things easier and a lot more enjoyable."[54] Thus, he treats the strange and the familiar as interchangeable as opposed to binary; America can be just as other-worldly as a foreign country can feel like home. For instance, Bourdain admits his lack of familiarity with his own city of New York, engendering feelings of displacement often associated with foreign travel. He laments, "my own city it appears, my home that I claim to be so proud of, its remains, if I'm gonna be perfectly honest, is a mystery. . . . I probably know Singapore better that the outer boroughs of my own city."[55] Similarly, in Charleston, South Carolina he remarks that "the South is as foreign a land to me as Singapore."[56] In these examples, audiences are asked to reconsider the chauvinism sutured to the concept of home, or the ways in which home escapes our critical attention because it is presumed to be the norm. Bourdain's uncanny admissions suggest that we might give the concept of home both the same level of scrutiny and generosity as any other place we might consider foreign.

At the same time, Bourdain suggests that places considered foreign can also engender the sentiments of home. For instance, in describing his feelings upon returning to Beirut, he notes "you hear Arabic, English, French interchangeably. Still, for whatever reason, even with all the problems and all the terrible things that have happened here over the years I step off the plane in Beirut and I feel strangely and inexplicably comfortable, at home."[57] *No Reservations* delinks home from nation, suggesting an alternative conception of emplacement more suited to the ethics of a wandering transnational subject. Any food or cultural tradition can provoke feelings of familiarity and/or strangeness; however, such feelings need not be tied to binaries of self/Other or domestic/foreign. While attuned to important differences between America and the rest of the globe, Bourdain suggests that travel might displace our nationalist conceptions of home, and decenter America from its near universal status as home*land*. Even when he visits his childhood home of New Jersey, he notes feeling an uncanny mixture of nostalgia and alienation. He visits a Howard Johnson's in Asbury Park along the New Jersey shoreline for a grilled sandwich. Shots of the diner reveal it to be in disrepair among the ruins of empty shoreline vendor stalls and closed businesses. Bourdain discusses childhood food memories with a mixture of nostalgia and criticism, the cuisine and places of the New Jersey shore no longer embodying a perfect sense of home. He reflects that his experience illustrates "the American Dream, both the good and the bad."[58]

Second, *No Reservations* defends the important contributions of foreign cuisines while asking American audiences to reconsider the limitations of their own. As it pertains to the former, the pilot episode provides a fitting example of the program's overall argumentative framework. In this episode titled "Why the French Don't Suck," Bourdain lays out his case against the wave of American Francophobia that followed France's decision to oppose America's 2003 military invasion of Iraq and Afghanistan. By defending the nation's worthwhile culinary traditions, Bourdain sets out to disabuse American's stereotypical, often disdainful, conceptions of France. He introduces the episode by declaring, "Some Americans are starting the think the French suck. But I think they are looking at them in the wrong way. And thus, not allowing ourselves to experience the world. . . . I'm here, an American in Paris to find supporting evidence for a deeply held conviction. To make a difficult argument in these unpleasantly Francophobic times. I call my thesis: why the French don't suck. France needs me I'm thinking now more than ever."[59] This opening narration frames the episode, and the series for that matter, as an ongoing debate with American misconceptions of the world. While the tone is polemical and at some times facetious, Bourdain adopts the role of provocateur by taking up positions that go against conventional wisdom. In this case, his central message is that American lives could be improved by learning from how the French relate to food. He observes that whereas Americans have an ambivalent and distant relationship with food, French culinary culture embraces sensuous pleasure and connectivity with one's food source. Stereotypically considered by some Americans as rarified and elitist, Bourdain finds French cuisine to be simpler, more accessible, and more honest about the source of its ingredients. In the famed *Les Halles* market, surrounded by vendors selling wild game birds, he observes "this is not factory farm food. Here food is not something to be shrink-wrapped into anonymous parcels. . . . Its something to be respected and celebrated for what it is."[60] At a Paris restaurant, he jokes, "you're not going to find this on the menu next to the jalapeno poppers at TGI McFunsters."[61] Frequently mocking the

American chain restaurant, Bourdain's polemics question the presumed normalcy, if not superiority, of American cuisine. He invites his audience to reconsider American commitments to standards such as abundance, convenience, and choice by presenting popularly dismissed foreign cultural ideals as an alternative way Americans might value food. He normalizes slow food, quality, and closeness with one's food source as opposed to the values currently embraced by America's corporate food culture and industrial agriculture. The program encourages audiences to reconsider both their relationship with food as well as their ethnocentric ideals that keep the world at arm's length.

CONCLUSION

In 2016, while filming *Parts Unknown* in Hanoi, Bourdain shared a meal of bun cha (Vietnamese pork and noodles) and beer with US President Barack Obama. Bourdain posted a photo via Twitter of the two talking over dinner, adding a note that the President's chop stick skills were "on point."[62] Since *No Reservations*, Bourdain has achieved iconoclastic status, continually pushing the boundaries between the personal and the political realms of food culture. His meal with President Obama in a small café in Vietnam is indicative of his particular mode of inquiry, a gesture at how food reveals the small intimate connections that unify all, both within and between cultures. Food and place provide common points of identification, reveal the lively dynamics of hybridity, and illustrate our collective values and commitments as a culture. Across all his platforms, Bourdain's project has been to jolt his viewers out of complacency, to engage in an ongoing polemic with American food and tourist culture directed against ethnocentrism and corporate food. Bourdain is positioned uneasily both within and against the contemporary food television, at once one of its most popular representatives and its staunchest critics. Who else in food television could pick President Obama's brain about food, share a jungle feast with former anti-communist headhunters in Malaysia, kill and eat a raw seal with Canadian Inuit, and host a holiday dinner with Marky Ramone. Its safe to say that Bourdain lived his countercultural fantasy of misadventure that he set out in *A Cook's Tour*, but for millions of viewers.

No Reservations provided a very different engagement with taste than the other programs examined in this book; however, the question remains as to whether his irreverent approach to food television cultivated a more ethical and open-minded encounter with the world. Indeed, this chapter is less sanguine than others about the program's connection to the operative concepts that structure this book: American exceptionalism, the American Dream, cosmopolitanism, exoticism, and mass consumer culture. Indeed, *No Reservations* is more difficult to categorize than other programs on the Food Network and the Travel Channel. Though on the one hand, *No Reservations* advances a cosmopolitan ethic, on the other, it acknowledges the significance of cultural hybridity through a deep engagement with diverse regions' food culture. While it adopts a Western development paradigm, it acknowledges the failure of international neoliberal institutions to bring global economic equality. Though it is haunted by the allusiveness of authenticity, it also presents an ethic of openness toward Others. And whereas the program assuages the liberal guilt associated with travel, it also decenters the chauvinism that structures concepts such as home, nation, self, and Other. Perhaps there is no perfect text, no one pure way in which food television can represent America and its place in the world. *No Reservations* is a text that confounds the theoretical underpinnings of this project. At the same time, it suggests that for food television to be a progressive force, it must aim for Bourdain's sense of self-reflexivity and ethics of travel, as flawed and as far from perfect as it may be.

NOTES

1. Anthony Bourdain, *A Cook's Tour: In Search of the Perfect Meal* (New York: Bloomsbury, 2010), 5.
2. Mary Mostafanezhad, *Volunteer Tourism: Popular Humanitarianism in Neoliberal Times* (New York: Routledge, 2016), 106.
3. Marwan M. Kraidy, *Hybridity: The Cultural Logic of Globalization* (Philadelphia, PA: Temple University Press, 2005).
4. See Anthony Bourdain, *Medium Raw: A Blood Valentine to the World of Food and the People Who Cook* (New York: Harper Collins, 2010).
5. See Chinua Achebe, *An Image of Africa: And, the Trouble with Nigeria* (New York: Penguin, 2010).
6. Edward W. Said, *Culture and Imperialism* (New York: Vintage Books, 1993), 25.
7. Bourdain decided to leave the Travel Channel for CNN in 2012 over a dispute over product placement. Producers inserted an endorsement for Cadillac in postproduction. Despite Bourdain's vocal resistance to the endorsement, the network continued to run the episode. See Patrick Kevin Day, "Anthony Bourdain Blasts Travel Channel on His Way Out," *Los Angeles Times*, November 13, 2012, http://articles.latimes.com/2012/nov/13/entertainment/la-et-st-anthony-bourdain-blasts-travel-channel-20121113.
8. Marisa Guthrie, "Anthony Bourdain Exits Travel Channel for CNN," *The Hollywood Reporter*, May 29, 2012, http://www.hollywoodreporter.com/news/anthony-bourdain-no-reservations-travel-channel-cnn-330350.
9. Michael C. Hall and Hazel Tucker, *Tourism and Postcolonialism: Contested Discourses, Identities and Representations* (New York: Routledge, 2004).
10. Stacy Burton, *Travel Narrative and the Ends of Modernity* (Cambridge: Cambridge University Press, 2013), 3.
11. For instance, Burton focuses her criticism on authors such as T.E. Lawrence, W.H. Auden, Rebecca West, Peter Fleming and H.V. Morton.
12. Evelyn Waugh, *When the Going Was Good* (New York: Penguin Books, 1951), 9.
13. See Mary Louise Pratt, *Imperial Eyes: Travel Writing and Transculturation* (London; New York: Routledge, 2007); and Stuart Ward, *British Culture and the End of Empire* (Manchester, UK: Manchester University Press, 2001).
14. Burton, *Travel Narrative*, 4.

15. Burton, *Travel Narrative*, 22.

16. Shelley Baranowski and Ellen Furlough, *Being Elsewhere: Tourism, Consumer Culture, and Identity in Modern Europe and North America* (Ann Arbor, MI: University of Michigan Press, 2001); and Arjun Kumar Bhatia, *The Business of Tourism: Concepts and Strategies* (New Delhi, India: Sterling Publishers Pvt. Ltd, 2006).

17. See Hall and Tucker, *Tourism and Postcolonialism*.

18. See George Ritzer, *The McDonaldization of Society* (Thousand Oaks, CA: Sage Publications, 2014).

19. See Edward M. Bruner, *Culture on Tour: Ethnographies of Travel* (Chicago, IL: University of Chicago Press, 2005); Jane Desmond, *Staging Tourism: Bodies on Display from Waikiki to Sea World* (Chicago, IL: University of Chicago Press, 1999).

20. Patrick Holland and Graham Huggan, *Tourists with Typewriters: Critical Reflections on Contemporary Travel Writing* (Ann Arbor, MI: University of Michigan Press, 2000), 2.

21. *No Reservations*, "Azores," Travel Channel, January 26, 2009, written by Anthony Bourdain.

22. *No Reservations*, "Azores."

23. *No Reservations*, "Vietnam: The Island of Mr. Sang," Travel Channel, August 15, 2005, written by Anthony Bourdain.

24. *No Reservations*, "Vietnam."

25. *No Reservations*, "Malaysia: Into the Jungle," Travel Channel, August 22, 2005, written by Anthony Bourdain.

26. *No Reservations*, "Uzbekistan," Travel Channel, October 24, 2005, written by Anthony Bourdain.

27. Homi K. Bhabha, *The Location of Culture* (New York: Routledge, 2004).

28. *No Reservations*, "US-Mexican Border." Travel Channel, May 22, 2006, written by Anthony Bourdain; "Beirut," Travel Channel, August, 21, 2006, written by Anthony Bourdain; "India: Rajasthan, May 29, 2009, written by Anthony Bourdain; and "Kurdistan," Travel Channel, August 22, 2011, written by Anthony Bourdain.

29. Holland and Huggan, *Tourists with Typewriters*, 3.

30. *No Reservations*, "Chile," Travel Channel, July 13, 2009, written by Anthony Bourdain.

31. *No Reservations*, "Chile."

32. *No Reservations*, "Baja," Travel Channel, May 28, 2012, written by Anthony Bourdain.

33. *No Reservations*, "Baja."

34. *No Reservations*, "Cambodia," Travel Channel, May 7, 2011, written by Anthony Bourdain.

35. *No Reservations*, "Prague," Travel Channel, February 1, 2010, written by Anthony Bourdain; "Ukraine," Travel Channel, August 15, 2011, written by Anthony Bourdain.

36. *No Reservations*, "Ghana," Travel Channel, January 8, 2001, written by Anthony Bourdain.

37. *No Reservations*, "Ghana."

38. *No Reservations*, "Mozambique," Travel Channel, April 9, 2012, written by Anthony Bourdain.

39. *No Reservations*, "Mozambique."

40. Four years after this episode aired, the World Bank suspended direct financial aid to the nation for its failure to disclose receiving loans from a Russian capital group. Mozambique is 180th out of 188 countries in the United Nations Human Development Index. See Julie Wernau and Matthieu Wirz, "World Bank Is Suspending Direct Financial Aid to Mozambique," *The Wall Street Journal*, April 27, 2016, http://www.wsj.com/articles/world-bank-is-suspending-direct-financial-aid-to-mozambique-1461775025.

41. Max Horkheimer and Theodor W. Adorno, *Dialectic of Enlightenment* (Palo Alto, CA: Stanford University Press, 1944).

42. Umberto Eco, *Travels in Hyper Reality: Essays* (New York: Houghton Mifflin Harcourt, 1986).

43. *No Reservations*, "Hawaii," Travel Channel, March 3, 2008, written by Anthony Bourdain.

44. Internet Movie Database, "No Reservations," last updated August, 5, 2016, http://www.imdb.com/title/tt0475900/?ref_=ttep_ep_tt.

45. *No Reservations*, "Malaysia."

46. *No Reservations*, "Peru," Travel Channel, April 10, 2006, written by Anthony Bourdain.

47. *No Reservations*, "Uzbekistan."

48. Holland and Huggan, *Tourists with Typewriters*, 3.

49. For the theory of everyday life performances see Erving Goffman, *The Presentation of Self in Everyday Life* (New York: Penguin Books, 1990).

50. Bruner, *Culture on Tour*, 7.

51. See John Urry, *The Tourist Gaze* (Thousand Oaks, CA: Sage, 2002); Stephen Wearing, Deborah Stevenson, and Tamara Young, *Tourist Cultures: Identity, Place and the Traveler* (Thousand Oaks, CA: Sage, 2009).

52. *No Reservations*, "Peru."

53. *No Reservations*, "Peru."

54. *No Reservations*, "Las Vegas," Travel Channel, October 17, 2005, written by Anthony Bourdain.

55. *No Reservations*, "New York City: Outer Burroughs," Travel Channel, September 7, 2009, written by Anthony Bourdain.

56. *No Reservations*, "South Carolina," Travel Channel, September 17, 2007, written by Anthony Bourdain.

57. *No Reservations*, "Back to Beruit," Travel Channel, August 23, 2010, written by Anthony Bourdain.

58. *No Reservations*, "New Jersey," Travel Channel, August 8, 2005, written by Anthony Bourdain.

59. *No Reservations*, "France: Why the French Don't Suck," Travel Channel, July 25, 2005, written by Anthony Bourdain.

60. *No Reservations*, "France."

61. *No Reservations*, "France."

62. *BBC News*, "Six Things about the $6 Bourdain-Obama Meal," May 24, 2016, http://www.bbc.com/news/world-asia-36365988.

Conclusion

Eric Wolf of the World Food Travel Association observes that merely a decade ago, culinary travel was merely a niche submarket of commercial tourism.[1] Observing near exponential growth, Wolf now estimates that food tourism is a $150 billion a year industry.[2] A recent industrial report on the market for culinary travel found that nearly three-quarters of American leisure travelers (131 million) can be categorized as culinary travelers, where encounters with food and cultural foodways is the primary motivation for travel.[3] Most within the restaurant and travel industries attribute the growth in culinary tourism to the advancement of food television and related food media, including food magazines, travel blogs, and social media sites such as Instagram.[4] As Erica Kritikides of Intrepid Food Adventures explains, "culinary travel-based TV shows, food magazines and food and travel blogs has generated a segment of travelers seeking a style of travel in which cuisine takes center stage."[5] Now, culinary programs not only mediate the globe for viewers in the comfort of their homes, but they also motivate audiences to emulate the adventures of the program's host. In many cases, a simple restaurant visit from Bourdain, Fieri, Richman, or Zimmern, or a product recommendation from Drummond inspires a wave of loyal fans to follow suit.[6] Food television has transformed American audiences' perception of culture, place, and global foodways; perceptions that now also structure how viewers navigate and consume the world. Food television intervenes into public conceptions of taste, giving preeminence to particular foodways and culinary experience. Presently, an active interest in food and food culture is a marker of distinction. For foodies, food television affirms their cosmopolitan values and serves as an additional source of food knowledge. For those who enjoy less adorned comforts and American mass culture, food television upholds core American values.

Although this book is not a methodological exercise in measuring audience perceptions and cause-and-effect relationships between media consumption and behavior, the documented effects of culinary media on American travelers' attitudes and consumer behaviors certainly demonstrates the stakes of this project. If culinary television inspires audience imitation, then it is vital that we consider what kinds of cultural assumptions about food, place, and difference circulate among viewers as they transform into participants. How are spectators prepared to interpret places, cuisines, and cultures other than their own? Though not without potential and optimism, this book demonstrates how much of popular food travel television continues to exoticize global food cultures, reinventing the old tropes and stereotypes invented to keep the West at the center of the world. Absent the Travel Channel and Food Network effect, culinary television also makes conjectures about American national identity, signified by what particular programs consider to be venerable about national and regional cuisines. Whereas the globe is a playground for the cosmopolitan explorer, cuisines of the American homeland testify to the nation's exceptionalism; its abundance the unique byproduct of democratic values and consumer economics. In food television, taste can be a marker of cultural distinction (*Bizarre Foods*), class status (*Bizarre Foods America*), traditional values (*The Pioneer Woman*), national identity (*Man v. Food* and *Diners, Drive-Ins and Dives*), open-mindedness (*No Reservations*), and of course much more. As competing conceptions of taste create commonsense distinctions between social groups according to our most intimate everyday rituals, it can form the basis of normative judgments of what appear on their surface to be innate distinctions between cultural groups. Hence, we should be concerned about how food television cultivates specific kinds of aesthetic judgments and the rhetorical implications of those judgments for how we make meaning of cultural difference.

My intent throughout this book has not been to attribute malicious intent to the hosts and producers of specific television programs, nor was it to blame food television personas for the ongoing mythology of American exceptionalism and the persistence of neocolonial ideologies. Rather, my purpose was to read food television as responsive to other cultural and economic anxieties for which food provides a common language to discuss by proxy. Though their immediate purpose is to educate audiences about the breadth and diversity of food culture—capitalizing on the public's increasing fascination with global cuisine—the programs examined in this book are responsive to much broader and often conflicting anxieties: the unclear status of Western cultural forms in a world that celebrates difference and the tenuousness of upward economic mobility under late capitalism—on the one hand—and the kind of ennui and anomie that accompanies mass consumption and cultural imperialism—on the other. But, what underlies both types of anxieties are a profound dissatisfaction with cultural inauthenticity, uncanny feelings of loss that demand a form of symbolic compensation. Food television is remarkably responsive to this postmodern malaise, assuring Western audiences that the world is still full of exotic quests of personal discovery and that America is still the land of abundance, wealth, and opportunity for all. For those still dissatisfied, food television can even locate an outside beyond the mass consumer spectacle, those places seemingly untouched by the homogenizing force of globalization. Either way, food television finds a variable common to all human existence to convey a concrete sense of place and identity in terms of both familiarity and strangeness. Whereas exotic food adventures create a knowable Other, comfort foods on the home front speak to the putative legibility of the self. This book has shown how representations of food become sutured to rhetorics of national identity and belonging; how, like tourism, discourse about food transforms into a "place-making technology."[7]

Although this book has been deeply critical, if not polemical at points, of contemporary food and travel television, I want to emphasize the caveat that no program should be beholden to standards of ideological and representational purity. In developing a progressive standard for representations of race, class, and gender in media texts, it is possible to make the perfect the enemy of the good. Edward Schiappa contends that critical media studies as a whole is inhibited by the demands of "representational correctness," or that media texts must be authentic or true in their representation of social groups and pure in liberatory possibilities to avoid the "distortion of stereotype."[8] He explains that "a good portion of popular media analysis is guided by the idea that *if* we can attain the goal of Representation Correctness *then* oppressed groups will be empowered or at least encouraged, and mainstream consumers and users of popular media will be motivated toward a more tolerant, open, and just society."[9] Representational correctness creates an untenable rhetorical exigency: omission of a group's experience creates the conditions for their invisibility while inclusion contributes to the distortion and/or commodification of the social group. Indeed, it is impossible for any one text to engage all progressive cultural struggles at once.

While Schiappa defends audience effects research as the solution to representational correctness, I contend that media criticism could be directed toward what Bhabha calls the "processes of subjectification made possible through stereotypical discourse."[10] Like Schiappa, Bhabha argues that to judge representations by a predetermined set of normative political assumptions only sanitizes or dismisses but does not displace stereotypical imagery. Purity and authenticity are illusory because there is no one true and real representation of reality. Instead, as Bhabha suggests, representation is a fluid process, open to reversals, which while always a work-in-progress can never encapsulate the truth of a social group's experience. Therefore, I conclude that we should conceive of representations of social groups as always-in-process provisional statements about political and social realities, often working within and sometimes against hegemonic conceptions of difference. This approach might take some pressure off media representations to be perfect or utopian reflections of progressive social realities. Instead, criticism would be forced to grapple with the complex rhetorical status of media texts as always by definition normative and stereotypical but not *necessarily* debilitating to a progressive politics of race, class, and gender.

What this concluding note on criticism means in the context of this project is that though food television has a long way to go in terms of introducing self-reflexivity, it retains the potential to challenge our hegemonic assumptions about taste and cultural identity. Food television, culinary travel in particular, is unlikely to go anywhere in the near future. Beyond an expanding lineup on the Travel Channel and the Food Network, BBC, PBS, and Voyage (France) have all developed their own travel programs to explore global foodways.[11] In some ways, new programs strive to deeply contextualize the food cultures they visit, with their hosts explicitly acknowledging the ineffability of certain cultural exchanges. Other programs express optimism about the possibility that food might engender cross-cultural understanding. For instance, the introductory credits to the BBC's *A Cook Abroad* expresses an explicit political mission to show "how the language of food transcends cultural differences." Of course, some are misguided. The Travel Channel's recent *Breaking Borders* (2015) takes the cross-cultural understanding motif so far that it suggests that historic political conflicts can be resolved through shared meals. In this program, former *Top Chef* winner Michael Voltaggio visits nations with deep histories of civil and political discord and tries to resolve animosities by cooking a meal for representatives from different factions or cultural groups. Perhaps well-intentioned, there are a host of problems with such a concept, including the individualization of structural conflicts such as apartheid, colonial occupation, and military violence. The program's therapeutic frame depoliticizes and oversimplifies the difficult process of reconciliation after extended periods of war and violence, reducing long-standing class and ethnic divisions to mere misunderstandings. At the same time, television producers are experimenting with new formats that acknowledge the important commonalities of food and attempt to convey the complex relationship between food, place, and identity, with varying degrees of self-reflexivity. In many ways, *No Reservations* and *Parts Unknown* have become a template for food travel television that can hopefully be pushed to new boundaries and can address some of the challenges of representation laid out in this book.

I want to conclude by turning attention to Michael Pollan's claim that eating and cooking are political acts.[12] What Pollan means by this statement is that we ostensibly vote with what we choose to eat, that we communicate to industry what kind of food and agricultural system we want to see. Of course, our agency is limited to the degree that we can afford to purchase fresh produce or find the luxury of time to spend cooking a meal at home. More broadly, we might consider how we choose to represent food as a kind of political frame that shapes and informs how viewers "vote" with their forks. Food television socializes audiences into culinary culture, encouraging particular kinds of relationships with food. In the case of *The Pioneer Woman, Man v. Food*, and

Diners, Drive-Ins and Dives, overindulgence signifies a political commitment to freedom, autonomy, and rugged individualism. In *Bizarre Foods* and *Bizarre Foods America*, consumption of risky and exotic foods aligns with a misguided politics of multicultural understanding and class diversity that elide broader structural analyses of globalization and poverty. *No Reservations* attempts to politicize food travel and critique ethnocentric attitudes. Whether explicit or implicit, all the programs examined in this book express some kind of political commitment through the common language of food. Pollan's statement can be expanded to include the notion that representing food and watching food television are political acts. Food television informs the ways in which audiences think politically about food, shaping public attitudes toward consumption, travel, national identity, and cultural difference. Food television will play an important role in shaping the kind of relationship with food we want for the future.

NOTES

1. Eric Wolf quoted in Michelle Baran, "Fueled by the Plate," *Travel Weekly*, April 9, 2013, http://www.travelweekly.com/Travel-News/Tour-Operators/Fueled-by-the-plate.
2. Baran, "Fueled by the Plate."
3. Mandala Research LLC, "The American Culinary Traveler Study," 2013, http://mandalaresearch.com/index.php/purchase-reports/view_document/75-the-american-culinary-traveler-study-.
4. Isabelle de Solier, *Food and the Self: Consumption, Production and Material Culture* (New York, NY: Bloomsbury Academic, 2013).
5. Erica Kritikides quoted in Parmjit Parmar, "How Culinary Tourism Is Becoming a Growing Trend in Travel," *The Huffington Post*, June 17, 2015, http://www.huffingtonpost.ca/parmjit-parmar/the-rise-of-culinary-tourism_b_7596704.html.
6. Leslie Balla, "Anthony Bourdain's CNN Show Inspires Rush of New Culinary Series," *The Hollywood Reporter*, accessed August 9, 2016, www.hollywoodreporter.com/news/anthony-bourdains-cnn-show-inspires-755515; John G. Ekizian, "The Fieri Effect," *New York Post*, May 21, 2012, nypost.com/2012/05/21/the-fieri-effect/; and David Roth, "Curry Heat Wave on East 6th Street," *Wall Street Journal*, July 22, 2010, www.wsj.com/articles/SB10001424052748703954804575381401688564796.
7. See Kristan Poirot and Shevaun E. Watson, "Memories of Freedom and White Resilience: Place, Tourism, and Urban Slavery," *RSQ: Rhetoric Society Quarterly* 45, no. 2 (March 2015): 91–116.
8. Edward Schiappa, *Beyond Representational Correctness: Rethinking Criticism of Popular Media* (Albany, NY: State University of New York Press, 2008), 9.
9. Schiappa, *Beyond*, 9.
10. Bhabha, *Location*, 25.
11. These programs include *A Cook Abroad* (BBC), *I'll Have What Phil is Having* (PBS), and *Street Foods of the World* (Voyage).
12. Michael Pollan, *In Defense of Food: An Eater's Manifesto* (New York, NY: Penguin, 2008).

Selected Bibliography

Adams, Carol J. 2010. *The Sexual Politics of Meat: A Feminist-Vegetarian Critical Theory, 20th Anniversary Edition*. New York, NY: Bloomsbury Academic.

Adorno, Theodor W. 2001. *The Culture Industry: Selected Essays on Mass Culture*. Edited by J. M. Bernstein. New York, NY: Routledge.

Albala, Ken. 2015. *The SAGE Encyclopedia of Food Issues*. Thousand Oaks, CA: Sage Publications.

Allmendinger, Blake. 1992. *The Cowboy: Representations of Labor in an American Work Culture*. New York, NY: Oxford University Press.

Anderson, Mark Cronlund. 2007. *Cowboy Imperialism and Hollywood Film*. New York, NY: Peter Lang.

Bakhtin, Mikhail Mikhaïlovich. 1984. *Rabelais and His World*. Bloomington, IN: Indiana University Press.

Baranowski, Shelley, and Ellen Furlough. 2001. *Being Elsewhere: Tourism, Consumer Culture, and Identity in Modern Europe and North America*. Ann Arbor, MI: University of Michigan Press.

Bederman, Gail. 2008. *Manliness and Civilization: A Cultural History of Gender and Race in the United States, 1880-1917*. Chicago, IL: University of Chicago Press.

Bhabha, Homi K. 2004. *The Location of Culture*. New York, NY: Routledge.

Bonilla-Silva, Eduardo. 2010. *Racism Without Racists: Color-Blind Racism and the Persistence of Racial Inequality in the United States*. Lanham, MD: Rowman & Littlefield.

Bormann, Ernest G. 2000. *The Force of Fantasy: Restoring the American Dream*. Carbondale, IL: Southern Illinois University Press.

Bruner, Edward M. 2005. *Culture on Tour: Ethnographies of Travel*. Chicago, IL: University of Chicago Press.

Burke, Meghan A. 2015. *Race, Gender, and Class in the Tea Party: What the Movement Reflects about Mainstream Ideologies*. Lanham, MD: Lexington Books.

Burton, Stacy. 2013. *Travel Narrative and the Ends of Modernity*. London, UK: Cambridge University Press.

Campbell, Mary B. 1991. *The Witness and the Other World: Exotic European Travel Writing, 400-1600*. Ithaca, NY: Cornell University Press.

Connell, R. W., and Raewyn Connell. 1995. *Masculinities*. Berkeley, CA: University of California Press.

Coontz, Stephanie. 1993. *The Way We Never Were: American Families and the Nostalgia Trap*. Reprint edition. New York, NY: Basic Books.

Cullen, Jim. 2004. *The American Dream: A Short History of an Idea That Shaped a Nation*. London, UK: Oxford University Press.

Debord, Guy. 2000. *Society of the Spectacle*. Detroit, MI: Black & Red.

Desmond, Jane. 1999. *Staging Tourism: Bodies on Display from Waikiki to Sea World*. Chicago, IL: University of Chicago Press.

Dickinson, Greg. 2015. *Suburban Dreams: Imagining and Building the Good Life*. Tuscaloosa, AL: University of Alabama Press.

Dyer, Richard. 1997. *White: Essays on Race and Culture*. New York, NY: Routledge.

Eco, Umberto. 1986. *Travels in Hyper Reality: Essays*. New York, NY: Houghton Mifflin Harcourt.

Frank, Thomas. 1998. *The Conquest of Cool: Business Culture, Counterculture, and the Rise of Hip Consumerism*. Chicago, IL: University of Chicago Press.

145

Galbraith, John Kenneth. 1998. *The Affluent Society.* 40 Anv Sub edition. Boston, MA: Mariner Books.

Goffman, Erving. 1990. *The Presentation of Self in Everyday Life.* New York, NY: Penguin Books.

Gray, Herman. 2004. *Watching Race: Television and the Struggle for Blackness.* Minneapolis, MN: University of Minnesota Press.

Greene, Carlnita P. 2015. *Gourmands & Gluttons: The Rhetoric of Food Excess.* New York, NY: Peter Lang.

Hall, Michael C., and Hazel Tucker. 2004. *Tourism and Postcolonialism: Contested Discourses, Identities and Representations.* New York, NY: Routledge.

Hall, Stuart, ed. 1997. *Representation: Cultural Representations and Signifying Practices.* Thousand Oaks, CA: Sage.

Heider, Karl G. 2009. *Ethnographic Film: Revised Edition.* Austin, TX: University of Texas Press.

Heiman, Rachel. 2015. *Driving after Class: Anxious Times in an American Suburb.* Berkeley, CA: University of California Press.

Heimann, Jim. 1996. *Car Hops and Curb Service: A History of American Drive-in Restaurants, 1920-1960.* San Francisco, CA: Chronicle Books.

Holland, Patrick, and Graham Huggan. 2000. *Tourists with Typewriters: Critical Reflections on Contemporary Travel Writing.* Ann Arbor, MI: University of Michigan Press.

hooks, bell. 1992. *Black Looks: Race and Representation.* 1st edition. Boston, MA: South End Press.

Horkheimer, Max and Theodor W. Adorno. 2002. *Dialectic of Enlightenment.* Palo Alto, CA: Stanford University Press.

Huggan, Graham. 2001. *The Postcolonial Exotic: Marketing the Margins.* New York, NY: Routledge.

Hurley, Andrew. 2002. *Diners, Bowling Alleys, and Trailer Parks: Chasing the American Dream in the Postwar Consumer Culture.* New York, NY: Basic Books.

Iverson, Peter. 1997. *When Indians Became Cowboys: Native Peoples and Cattle Ranching in the American West.* Norman, OK: University of Oklahoma Press.

Jakle, John A., and Keith A. Sculle. 2002. *Fast Food: Roadside Restaurants in the Automobile Age.* Baltimore, MD: Johns Hopkins University Press.

Kaufman, Frederick. 2009. *A Short History of the American Stomach.* Orlando, FL: Houghton Mifflin Harcourt.

Kraidy, Marwan M. 2005. *Hybridity: The Cultural Logic of Globalization.* 1st edition. Philadelphia, PA: Temple University Press.

Kurlansky, Mark. 2003. *Salt: A World History.* New York: Penguin Books.

———. 2010. *Cod: A Biography of the Fish That Changed the World.* 1st edition. New York, NY: Penguin Books.

Lawrance, Benjamin N., and Carolyn de la Peña. 2013. *Local Foods Meet Global Foodways: Tasting History.* New York, NY: Routledge.

Lisle, Debbie. 2006. *The Global Politics of Contemporary Travel Writing.* London, UK: Cambridge University Press.

Long, Lucy M. 2004. *Culinary Tourism.* Lexington, KY: University Press of Kentucky.

MacDougall, David. 2006. *The Corporeal Image: Film, Ethnography, and the Senses.* Princeton, NJ: Princeton University Press.

Mignolo, Walter D., and Arturo Escobar. 2013. *Globalization and the Decolonial Option.* New York, NY: Routledge.

Mostafanezhad, Mary. 2016. *Volunteer Tourism: Popular Humanitarianism in Neoliberal Times.* New York, NY: Routledge.

Naccarato, Peter, and Kathleen Lebesco. 2013. *Culinary Capital.* New York, NY: Bloomsbury Publishing.

Nerz, Ryan. 2006. *Eat This Book: A Year of Gorging and Glory on the Competitive Eating Circuit.* New York, NY: Macmillan.

Ono, Kent A. 2009. *Contemporary Media Culture and the Remnants of a Colonial Past.* New York, NY: Peter Lang.

Parker, Christopher S., and Matt A. Barreto. 2014. *Change They Can't Believe In: The Tea Party and Reactionary Politics in America.* Princeton, NJ: Princeton University Press.

Pezzullo, Phaedra Carmen. 2009. *Toxic Tourism: Rhetorics of Pollution, Travel, and Environmental Justice.* Tuscaloosa: University Alabama Press.

Pollan, Michael. 2007. *The Omnivore's Dilemma: A Natural History of Four Meals.* New York, NY: Penguin.

———. 2008. *In Defense of Food: An Eater's Manifesto.* New York, NY: Penguin.

Pratt, Mary Louise. 2007. *Imperial Eyes: Travel Writing and Transculturation.* New York, NY: Routledge.

Ritzer, George. 2014. *The McDonaldization of Society.* Thousand Oaks, CA: Sage.

Said, Edward W. 1979. *Orientalism.* New York, NY: Vintage Books.

———. 1993. *Culture and Imperialism.* New York, NY: Vintage Books.

Samuel, Lawrence R. 2012. *The American Dream: A Cultural History.* Syracuse, NY: Syracuse University Press.

Sartre, Jean-Paul, and Fredric Jameson. 2004. *Critique of Dialectical Reason, Volume One.* Edited by Jonathan Ree. Translated by Alan Sheridan-Smith. Revised edition. London; New York, NY: Verso.

Savage, William W. 1979. *The Cowboy Hero: His Image in American History & Culture.* Norman, OK: University of Oklahoma Press.

Schiappa, Edward. 2008. *Beyond Representational Correctness: Rethinking Criticism of Popular Media.* Albany, NY: State University of New York Press.

Schlatter, Evelyn A. 2009. *Aryan Cowboys: White Supremacists and the Search for a New Frontier, 1970–2000.* Austin, TX: University of Texas Press.

Schlosser, Eric. 2001. *Fast Food Nation: The Dark Side of the All-American Meal.* New York, NY: Houghton Mifflin Harcourt.

Schwartz-DuPre, Rae Lynn, ed. 2013. *Communicating Colonialism: Readings on Postcolonial Theory(s) and Communication.* New York: Peter Lang Publishing Inc.

Shaffer, Marjorie. 2014. *Pepper: A History of the World's Most Influential Spice.* Reprint edition. New York, NY: St. Martin's Griffin.

Shugart, Helene A. 2016. *Heavy: The Obesity Crisis in Cultural Context.* London: Oxford University Press.

Slotkin, Richard. 1992. *Gunfighter Nation: The Myth of the Frontier in Twentieth-Century America.* Norman, OK: University of Oklahoma Press.

Solier, Isabelle de. 2013. *Food and the Self: Consumption, Production and Material Culture.* New York, NY: Bloomsbury Academic.

Spurr, David. 1993. *The Rhetoric of Empire: Colonial Discourse in Journalism, Travel Writing, and Imperial Administration.* Durham, NC: Duke University Press.

Starrs, Paul F. 2000. *Let the Cowboy Ride: Cattle Ranching in the American West.* Baltimore, MD: Johns Hopkins University Press.

Sturken, Marita. 2007. *Tourists of History: Memory, Kitsch, and Consumerism from Oklahoma City to Ground Zero.* Durham, NC: Duke University Press.

Urry, John. 2002. *The Tourist Gaze.* Thousand Oaks, CA: Sage.

Index

A

abjection, 27, 31, 32, 33, 39, 44n43, 51
Adorno, Theodore, 7, 128
affluent society, 17, 91, 92, 100, 106
American dream, 57, 75, 76, 82, 90, 91, 92, 93, 95, 100, 102, 104, 106, 107, 108n3, 108n7, 132, 134
American exceptionalism, 5, 11, 12, 25, 67, 68, 72, 81, 93, 102, 103, 104, 106, 108, 116, 130, 131, 134, 140
anthropology, 6, 7, 12, 27, 42n21, 114, 131–132
appropriation (cultural), 9, 17, 23, 24, 25, 29, 59, 60

B

Bar Rescue, 1
Barefoot Contessa, 3
Bourdieu, Pierre, 7
Bakhatin, Mikhail, 93–94

C

capitalism, 18, 29, 47, 49, 51, 54, 60, 70, 90, 93, 94, 95, 98, 101, 105, 108, 108n6, 124, 126, 140
celebrity chefs, 1, 9, 48, 58–59, 114, 115
Chef's Table, 1
coloniality, 10, 13, 14
A Cook's Tour, 113, 114, 115, 134
comfort food, 4, 11, 16, 17, 65, 66, 67, 68, 73, 81, 82, 114, 131, 140
consumerism, 28, 51, 94, 95, 101, 108, 114
cosmopolitanism, 1, 10, 12, 13, 16, 18, 23, 24, 26, 27, 28, 30, 33, 38, 39, 40, 47, 48, 50, 60, 114, 115, 119, 121, 123, 129, 135, 139
cowboy mystique, 66, 67, 68–77
civic identity, 78, 91, 93, 98, 100, 106, 107, 124, 126
class, 3, 4, 6, 7, 11, 17, 18, 22n64, 24, 48, 49, 50, 51, 58, 59, 60, 67, 78, 90, 91, 92, 93, 94, 95, 99, 100, 101, 102, 103, 104, 105, 106, 108n7, 130, 141, 142, 143
The Chew, 1
culinary adventurism, 1, 4, 10, 11, 13, 16, 24, 27, 29, 33, 39, 40, 47, 58, 60, 113, 117, 119, 120, 134, 139, 140
culinary slumming, 17, 48, 50, 52, 56, 58, 60
culture industry, 9, 105, 130–131

D

Deen, Paula, 1, 3, 17, 65–68, 81
defiant decadence, 92, 95, 101–102, 103
Diamond, Jared, 6
diner culture, 8, 17, 91, 92, 93, 99, 100, 102, 103, 106
Douglas, Mary, 7
Dyer, Richard, 23, 72

E

eating competitions, 93, 94, 95
ethnocentrism, 18, 116, 129, 131, 133, 134
ethnotainment, 12, 13–14, 48, 52
exoticism, 9, 32, 36, 38, 48, 51, 56, 58, 59, 60, 73, 114, 116, 118, 119, 120, 131, 134, 135, 139, 140, 143

F

fast food, 7–8, 52, 85n46, 101, 107,
107–108
foodways, vii, 2, 3, 4, 16, 27, 31, 32, 48,
53, 60, 122, 123, 131, 132, 139, 142
foodies, 8, 12, 17, 57, 61, 100, 105, 107,
139
Food Network, 1, 2, 14, 16, 17, 65, 66,
67, 69, 73, 76, 90, 101, 115, 139, 142
Frank, Thomas, 105
The French Chef, 1
frontier myth, 2, 3, 11, 17, 36, 40, 51, 66,
67, 68, 69, 70, 72, 73, 74, 75, 76, 77,
78, 79, 80, 81, 82, 83n11, 91

G

gastronomy, 5, 6, 37, 65–66, 73–74, 100
globalization, 4, 6, 10, 11, 13, 16, 18, 23,
24, 26, 28, 94, 114, 115, 116, 118, 119,
121, 123, 125, 126, 127, 128, 143. *See
also* Neoliberalism
Gramsci, Antonio. *See* hegemony

H

habitus, 7
haute cuisine, 48, 53, 59, 74, 101
Heart of Darkness, 116
hegemony, 10, 11, 22n64, 23, 25, 26, 41,
43n37, 108n7, 119
Hell's Kitchen, 1
heritage, 38, 48, 50, 51, 53, 55, 56, 57, 58,
60, 67, 80, 81, 99
hooks, bell, 24, 47, 72
hunger, 40, 48–49
hybridity, 5, 16, 26, 36, 114, 115, 117,
119, 120, 121, 122, 123, 124, 130, 134,
135

I

imperialist nostalgia, 34, 120, 121

innocence. *See* American
Exceptionalism
individualism, 66, 68, 70, 72, 73, 75, 76,
92, 93, 94, 96, 98, 114, 130, 142, 143
inferential racism, 13, 71–72, 76
insect consumption, 8, 11, 25, 28, 32, 40,
47

J

Jim Crow, 52, 62n21, 66

K

kitsch, 1, 11, 17, 79–80, 92, 100, 101–102,
103, 106, 113, 114, 128

L

The Layover, 61n5, 114

M

Marcuse, Herbert, 105
multiculturalism, 10, 18, 23, 24, 27, 28,
29, 30, 38, 40, 41, 47, 50, 114, 115, 130

N

nanny state, 17, 71, 82, 90–91, 105
neocolonialism, 11, 13, 16, 27, 29, 30, 51,
123, 140
neoliberalism, 5, 10, 13, 24, 26, 28, 29,
30, 38, 40, 94, 118, 119, 126, 127, 135

O

obesity, 60, 76, 82, 92
Orientalism, 11, 24–25
overeating, 8, 17, 89, 91, 92, 93, 94, 95,
96, 97, 99, 100, 103, 105, 106, 107

P

Parts Unknown, 2, 52–53, 114, 116, 134, 142
place identities, 4, 9, 11, 12, 14, 16, 17, 18, 68, 75, 79, 106
Pollan, Michael, 1, 9, 142–143
popular culture, 2, 9, 13, 14, 15, 22n64, 26
postcolonialism, 14, 25, 29, 114, 115, 118, 122, 126
postracialism, 67, 68, 77
poverty, 17, 27, 36, 47, 48, 49, 50, 51, 52, 53, 54, 55, 56, 58, 60, 62n16, 94, 124, 125, 126, 127, 131

R

ranching, 2, 50, 66, 68–71, 73, 75–76, 78, 79, 79–81, 83n16
representations, 3, 4, 5, 7, 9, 11, 13, 14, 15, 16, 17, 24, 26, 28, 34, 40, 48, 50, 51, 54, 58, 67, 77, 78, 79, 81, 90, 115, 116, 132, 141, 142
rhetoric, 4, 7, 8, 13, 14, 15, 16, 17, 24, 25, 26, 27, 29, 43n37, 47, 51, 55, 71, 74, 90, 94, 115, 141
ritual, 3, 4, 5, 7–8, 10–11, 12, 13–14, 15–16, 24–25, 30, 31, 32–33, 35, 53, 56, 67–68, 93–94, 94–95, 97, 122, 129–130, 139–140

S

Scripps Networks, 1, 14, 30, 116–117
selective amnesia, 67
Semi-Homemade, 3

Slotkin, Richard, 66–67, 70, 83n11
soul food, 3, 36, 37, 61n4
Southern cuisine, 53, 55, 58, 59, 61, 65
spectacular consumption, 9, 10, 18, 93–100, 114, 119–120
suburbia, 3, 11, 48, 49–50, 90, 91, 100, 102–103, 108n7

T

taste, 1, 2, 3, 4, 5, 6, 7, 8, 9, 10, 11, 12, 15, 16, 24, 25, 26, 27, 28, 32, 33, 37, 40, 49, 53, 54, 58, 59, 60, 68, 69, 72, 73, 74, 81, 90, 91, 92, 96, 97, 98, 99, 100, 101, 102, 103, 105, 106, 107, 114, 117, 134, 139, 140, 142
Tea Party movement, 71, 71–72, 77, 82
tolerance, 23–24, 24–25, 26–27, 38–39, 47
Top Chef, 1
tourism, 4, 11, 15, 18, 30, 48, 50, 51, 59, 85n46, 114, 116, 117, 121, 126, 127, 128, 129, 130, 131, 139, 141
travel writing, 11, 27, 41n14, 117, 118, 119, 123
The Travel Channel, 1, 3, 14, 16, 17, 18, 25, 30, 31, 52, 89, 95, 113, 116, 135, 140, 142

W

whiteness, 4, 16, 23, 24, 25, 26, 27, 29, 30, 40

About the Author

Casey Ryan Kelly is associate professor of critical communication and media studies at Butler University in Indianapolis, IN. He is the author of *Abstinence Cinema: Virginity and the Rhetoric of Sexual Purity in Contemporary Film* (2016) and the recipient of the 2015 Outstanding New Investigator Award from the Critical/Cultural Division of the National Communication Association. His work has appeared in numerous journals including the *Quarterly Journal of Speech, Critical Studies in Media Communication, Text and Performance Quarterly,* and *Communication and Critical/Cultural Studies.*

Made in the USA
Monee, IL
22 January 2021